Managing Web-Enabled Technologies in Organizations: A Global Perspective

Mehdi Khosrowpour
Pennsylvania State University, USA

IDEA GROUP PUBLISHING
Hershey USA • London UK

Senior Editor: Mehdi Khosrowpour
Managing Editor: Jan Travers
Copy Editor: Brenda Zboray Klinger
Typesetter: Tamara Gillis
Cover Design: Connie Peltz
Printed at: BookCrafters

Published in the United States of America by
        Idea Group Publishing
        1331 E. Chocolate Avenue
        Hershey PA 17033-1117
        Tel: 717-533-8845
        Fax: 717-533-8661
        E-mail: jtravers@idea-group.com
        Website: http://www.idea-group.com

and in the United Kingdom by
        Idea Group Publishing
        3 Henrietta Street
        Covent Garden
        London WC2E 8LU
        Tel: +44 171-240 0856
        Fax: +44 171-379 0609
        http://www.eurospan.co.uk

Library of Congress Cataloging-in-Publication Data

Khosrowpour, Mehdi, 1951-
    Managing web-enabled technologies in organizations: a global perspective / Mehdi Khosrowpour.
        p. cm.
    Includes index.
    ISBN 1-878289-72-1 (paper)
        1. Information technology--Management. 2. Web sites--Management. 3. Organization.
I. Title

HD30.2 .K468 1999
658'.054678--dc21   99-048157

British Cataloguing in Publication Data
A Cataloguing in Publication record for this book is available from the British Library.

NEW from Idea Group Publishing

Managing Web-Enabled Technologies in Organizations: A Global Perspective

Table of Contents

Preface

During the past two decades, advances in computer technologies combined with telecommunication technologies have lead to the development of the Internet and its most popular application, the World Wide Web (WWW). During the past decade, many firms have benefited from the technologies of WWW better know as Web-Enabled Technologies. Through the use of Web-Enabled Technologies, organizations have managed to reach customers and suppliers throughout the world in ways that in the past would have been impossible. Web-Enabled technologies have allowed firms of all sizes and types to find new strategic opportunities or to improve their strategic posture through the use of these new technologies. At the same time, organizations have begun utilizing Web-Enabled technologies in support internal organizational functions, particularly in the area of communications and information dissemination related activities.

Like many other new technologies, Web-Enabled technologies have offered organizations many opportunities and trends as well as controversies and challenges. The primary focus of this book is to provide up-to-date research and practical findings related to Web-enabled technologies and their applications and managerial issues in modern organizations. The contributed chapters by many international researchers and managers in this book include coverage of many timely and important issues related to the overall management of Web-Enabled technologies in organizations. The coverage provided in this book ranges from development issues of Web-Enabled technology applications to the issue of training and viability of these technologies. The following paragraphs provide a chronology of the chapters of this book and their coverage of issues and applications.

Chapter One entitled "Web-Enabled Technologies Assessment and Management: Critical Issues, Challenges and Trends" by Mehdi Khosrowpour and Nancy Herman of the Pennsylvania State University (USA), provides an overall discussion of the Internet and WWW evolution and contemporary critical issues of the Web-Enabled technologies. The chapter reports on the findings of a study conducted by the authors of this chapter in determining the critical issues of the Web-Enabled technologies in modern organizations. Finally, the chapter reports a list of 20 critical issues ranked by many expert researchers and industry leaders, the issues of "Bandwidth and Latency" being ranked the number one critical issue and "Hype" being ranked as one of the least critical issues.

Chapter Two entitled "Developing Applications for the Web: Exploring Differences Between Traditional and World Wide Web Application Development" by Nancy L. Russo of the Northern Illinois University (USA), examines the nature of Web-Enabled Technology application development processes and its evolution in organizations during the past decade. The chapter discusses the issues of opportunity as well as risks associated with Web-based applications and how poorly designed and/or poorly implemented and maintained Web sites can tarnish an organization's reputation. The chapter also discusses the fact that although many people have the ability to put up a Web site, they my not have the skill, knowledge or training to ensure that the site is of the necessary level of quality in terms of aesthetics, functionality, or security. The chapters also examines the nature of Web application development in particular, the issue of the who and the how of Web development and discuss the role of methodologies in the Web development process.

Chapter Three entitled "Planning for Effective Web-Based Commerce Application Development" by Ming-te Lu, and W.L. Yeung, both of Lingnan University, Hong Kong (Hong Kong), provides the important issues of careful planing and preparation that are needed for organizations to achieve their intended goals and objectives for their utilization of Web-Enabled technology applications. The chapter proposes a framework for planning effective Web-based commerce application development based on prior research in hypermedia and human-computer interfaces and recent research on Web-based commerce. The framework regards Web application development as a type of software development project. At the onset, the project's social acceptability is investigated. Next, system feasibility is carried out. If the proposed project is viable, its Web-page interface is examined both from the functionality, contents, and navigability points of view. The use of the framework will contribute to more effective Web-based commerce application development.

Chapter Four entitled "Managing Web Technologies Acquisition, Utilization and Organization Change: Understanding Sociocognitive Processual Dynamics" by Mathew J. Klempa, an Information Systems Consultant (USA), presents a new perspective on web technologies acquisition, utilization, organization change and transformation. A contextualist analysis is processually based, emergent, situational, and holistic, marrying both theory and practice. This chapter's paradigm affords a substantive analytical tool to the practitioner for understanding and managing not only web-based IT acquisition, utilization and organization change, but all IT-based recursive, organization changes and transformations. The chapter also discusses the use of the IT acquisition and utilization paradigm for organization diagnosis, as well as customization of organization change interventions. The chapter suggests further typologically based research venues

Chapter Five entitled "The Five Stages of Customizing Web-Based Mass Information Systems" by Arno Scharl, University of Economics and Business Administration (Austria), discusses the issue of Web-enabled standard software for electronic commerce, incorporating adaptive components which can reduce the barriers between productive data processing and dispositive data processing like market analysis, Web-tracking, or data warehouses. This chapter presents a conceptual research framework for analyzing the evolution of electronic markets as well as their business ecosystem represents the foundation of a document-oriented modeling technique for analyzing and designing (adaptive) Web-based Mass Information Systems. A Java prototype based on this meta-model is presented which supports cooperative efforts of academic research, IS departments, top-level management, and functional units to map and classify individual and aggregated customer behavior.

Chapter Six entitled "Viability Through Web-Enabled Technologies" by Dirk Vriens, University of Nijmegen (The Netherlands) and Paul Hendriks, University of Nijmegen, (The Netherlands) discusses the role of the Internet and associated technologies in paving the way for new types of businesses, new types of consumer behavior and new types of services in organizations. This chapter examines the issue of "viability of organizations" and importance of Web-enabled technologies by questioning the true role of these technologies on the viability of the organization, and the strategies that maintain this viability. The chapter also provides extensive discussion of how organizations can systematically approach the assessment of their viability through Web-Enabled technologies through a "systematic approach" that consists of three elements. First, it involves an elaboration of the notion of viability as far as organizations are concerned. Secondly, it includes a description of the specific features of Web-Enabled technologies. Thirdly, it presents a framework that ties viability to the specific features of Web-Enabled technologies so that an individual organization can use it to assess the impact of the technology. This may be called a "generic framework.

Chapter Seven entitled "World Wide Wait" by Fui Hoon Nah and Kihyun Kim both of the University of Nebraska-Lincoln (USA), discusses the issue of communications delay and problems associated with communications speed and connections. The chapter claims that in light of the current communication limitations and difficulties, users sometimes equate the "WWW" acronym with "World Wide Wait"! Although information technology for supporting the infrastructure of WWW is continually being updated and improved, it is still not able to satisfy industry requirements and demand. The chapter also provides an extensive study usage pattern of WWW as well as topics related to speed of Internet access such as bandwidth, Internet connection alternatives, and technology to speed up WWW access. In addition, the chapter reports on experimental research that measured and analyzed users' "tolerable" waiting time in accessing the WWW. Based on the results of the study, the chapter suggests guidelines for web designers regarding page size restrictions in web development.

Chapter Eight entitled "A Matter of Necessity: Implementing Web-Based Subject Administration" by Paul Darbyshire, Victoria University of Technology and Andrew Wenn both of Victoria University of Technology (Australia), describes the design and development of a Web Based Learning Administration (WBLA) system that initially the authors of the chapter developed to complement work they began on Web Based Learning. The project was based on WBLA systems that were designed for a multi-campus of the Victoria University of Technology. The chapter discusses a development framework and a model for designing WBLA applications and the details of the architecture of the WBLA. Finally, the chapter provides the summary of some responses to a trial of the system and suggestions for future enhancements.

Chapter Nine entitled "Web-Based Competency and Training Management Systems for Distance Learning" by Tammy Whalen and David Wright both of the University of Ottawa (Canada), examines the major impact of Web-Enabled technologies on how corporate training departments manage employee training. Through the use of competency and training management systems such as the SIGAL system used by Bell Canada, organizational training plans can be efficiently communicated throughout the organization, training needs can be linked to the performance evaluations of individual employees, and on-line training materials can be conveniently delivered to employees at their desktops. The chapter predicts that training management systems will evolve to incorporate analytic tools that can calculate the return on training investment, evaluate the impact of training on job performance, and determine the impact of training on corporate profits. Finally, the chapter discusses the value to companies of using a Web-based system for competency and training management, using the case of Bell Canada as an example of how companies are implementing these tools today.

Chapter Ten entitled "Electronic Commerce in Egypt" by Sherif Kamel, American University in Cairo (Egypt) reports that as the world converges into a global village where supply and demand interacts across nations and continents, electronic commerce represents an opportunity for many countries around the world. Egypt, one of the rapidly growing economies among the developing world, has thoroughly invested in transforming its society to deal with the information-based global market economy of the coming century. This chapter demonstrates Egypt's vision with regard to electronic commerce and its possible utilization in its developmental and planning processes. Moreover, the chapter discusses the role of the government, the public and the private sector facing the challenges and opportunities enabled by electronic commerce, and how Egypt places the new enabled information and communication technologies as tools that can help in the nation's development process.

Chapter Eleven entitled "Managing the Business of Web-Enabled Education and Training: A Framework and Case Studies for Replacing Blackboards with Browsers for Distance Learning" by Mahesh S. Raisinghani, University of Dallas (USA) and David Baker, Digital Think, Inc. (USA), discusses the role of interactive learning applications in a multi-sensory learning environment that maximizes the way people retain information. This accelerates learning and permits novices to perform like experts while they learn new skills. Powerful authoring systems enable vast amounts of information to be compiled quickly and presented in compelling and meaningful ways. In addition, these applications are easy and inexpensive to update. With interactive multimedia, everyone sees the same information and is exposed to identical learning environments. The reliability of instruction, quality of information and presentation of material is consistent from user to user and from session to session. This chapter provides a framework for distance learning and distributed learning and two case studies of a web-based synchronous learning environment in two organizations with different corporate cultures.

I hope the diverse coverage of issues provided in the book will contribute to the existing literature and knowledge of Web-Enabled technologies management in organizations. The coverage provided in this book should be useful to both information technology managers and researchers in obtaining a greater understanding of the issues surrounding these technologies. It is my expectation that this book and its coverage will assist organizations in managing these technologies more effectively and leading them to discover innovative ways of utilization and management of Web-Enabled technologies in modern organizations.

Acknowledgments

Putting together a book of this magnitude requires a tremendous cooperation and assistance by everyone involved in the project. The first phase of an editing a quality book includes the process of identifying quality contributions and good reviewers. Each chapter of this book was carefully selected after each author(s) provided a proposal for their intended chapter. All submitted chapters were subjected to the rigorous blind review process, and based on the reviews and recommendation of the reviewers, the included chapters in this book were accepted. Authors of the accepted chapters were asked to revise their chapters based on the requirements of the reviewers. In some instances, chapters were revised 3-4 times before the chapter was finally accepted. Personally, I would like to express many thanks to my contributing authors for their excellent contributions to this book and also for assisting me in the review process. The second phase involves the constant interaction with production and copy editors associated with all productions activities of the book. In this area, I would like to express many thanks to my managing editor of Idea Group Publishing, Ms. Jan Travers for all her hard work, dedication and patience. I would also like to thank our assistant managing editor at Idea Group Publishing, Ms. Amanda Stauffer for her excellent contribution to the review process. Many thanks also go to my copy editor, Ms. Brenda Zboray Klinger, our cover design artist, Connie Pletz and our typesetter, Ms. Tamara Gillis. My warmest thanks are due to my wife Beth Peiffer for her support, wisdom, encouragement, understanding and patience. Finally, much gratitude goes to all my students who have taught me a lot during the past 20 years!

Chapter 1

Web-Enabled Technologies Assessment and Management: Critical Issues

Mehdi Khosrowpour
Pennsylvania State University at Harrisburg, USA

Nancy Herman
Pennsylvania State University at Harrisburg, USA

Abstract

During the past two decades, advances in computer technologies combined with telecommunication technologies have lead to the development of the Internet and its most popular application, the World Wide Web. Like many other technologies, the WWW has not been free of problems and challenges. A Delphi technique was utilized to assess a list of issues identified in the existing literature. In addition to this list, the panel of experts who participated in the Delphi study identified other critical issues and eventually ranked them in their order of priority and importance. The critical issue identified in this study provides closer insights into issues affecting the overall utilization and management of Web-enabled technologies and offers many implications and challenges for businesses, governments, and the user community.

Internet Technology Evolution

During the past two decades, the world has witnessed a technological evolution that has provided a totally new medium of communications entirely new to mankind. Through the use of networks, information in all forms has been disseminated throughout the world. What is known today as the World Wide Web (WWW) grew out of a project that began with a different intent (ARPANET). The ARPANET was designed and developed in 1969 by Bolt, Beranek and Newman under a contract for the Advanced Research Project Agency (ARPA) of the U.S. Department of Defense. The purpose of the Network was to study how researchers could share data, and how communications could be maintained in the event of a nuclear attack (Gilster, 1993). The ARPANET Project was eventually turned over to the National Science Foundation (NSF) and ultimately became known as "Internet" which the NSF allowed access to businesses, universities, and individuals (Mosley-Matchett, 1997). In the beginning, many resources such as electronic mail, news, telnet, FTP, and Gopher were offered through the Internet to its users (Misic, 1994).

One of the early applications of the Internet was its most popular application, the World Wide Web (WWW) or sometime known as "the Web". The WWW is one of the software tools that through the use of hypertext allows computers to link information in new ways different from a sequential reading approach, to make it easy to retrieve and add information from different computer sources through the use of communication links (Berners-Lee, 1992). In the short time since its inception, the Internet has indeed revolutionized business, in that it redefines the methods used in traditional business practices and offers another important channel for mass communication (Foo, et al., 1997).

During the early days of the Internet, the technology was primarily utilized as a medium for communication (e.g. e-mail) purposes. Soon after many organizations from both public and private sectors began to discover that in addition to use of the Internet and its popular WWW, they could utilize this technology in support of marketing and information dissemination purposes. This resulted in companies realizing that the greatest payback in investing in the technologies of WWW would be in sharing information about the firm's products and services to the firms' stakeholders (Gardner, 1997). As a result, successful organizations of all sizes and types have been

Table 1: A List of Reasons for Utilizing the Web for Marketing

• To establish a presence	• To stay in contact with salespeople
• To network	• To open international markets
• To make business information available	• To create 24-hour service
• To serve customers	• To make changing information available quickly
• To heighten public interest	
• To release time-sensitive data	• To allow feedback from customers
• To sell products and services	• To test market new services and products
• To reach a highly desirable demographic market	
	• To reach the media
• To answer frequently asked questions	• To reach a specialized market

Table 2: A Summary of Web-Enabled Applications/Technologies

- Mail Technologies
- Electronic Interchange
- Electronic Data Interchange (EDI)
- Electronic Commerce (EC)
- Network Management
- Organizational Intranets/Extranets
- On-Line Analytical Processing (OLAP)
- Teleconferencing

adopting different applications/technologies of WWW in discovering emerging ways of doing business that even a decade ago could not be imagined (Prawitt and Romney, 1997). In recent years, the WWW has become the glittering palace of information and electronic trading that some visionary pundits promised it would become (Jacobs, 1998). The Web has provided many improvements in the marketing business sector particularly in areas such as "identification of sales prospects", "immediate access to information (i.e. product/ service specifications and pricing) and allowing customers to obtain goods regardless of their geographical locations around the world (Hacker, 1996 & Presti, 1996).

According to Bird (1996), the main reasons why businesses are utilizing the Web are primarily marketing related. Table 1 lists these reasons.

The above data illustrates the changing foundation of marketing based on the emergence of the Web. Although the financial marketing advantages are not yet proven, the Web remains a fairly inexpensive form of communicating with potential customers (Bird, 1996).

In addition to using the Web for communication and marketing purposes, during the past two decades there have been many other emerging Web-enabled technologies. Table 2 summarizes some of these applications.

Critical Issues of Web-Enabled Technologies

Despite all its promises and glories, the Web-enabled technologies are not free of associated risks and controversies. Like many other emerging technologies, this technology has its share of associated problems and limitations. In order to clearly understand the total potentials of these technologies, one must also assess the limitations, stipulations, and provisions of these technologies in modern organizations. Among many issues, problems and limitations of the Web-enabled technologies are:

Bandwidth Restrictions and Latency

A large percentage of the Web users run low-speed modems 56K which in reality cause considerable delays in obtaining Web-based materials when the corresponding downloads incorporate images animation and audio (Berghel, 1996; Pitkow, 1996). A recent study by a popular server revealed that about 1 in 5 users were connecting with graphics turned off to eliminate the annoying latency of loading web pages (Fox, 1996). Latency issues are also being experienced with some of the more popular Web documents. In this case, the slowness relates to the number of requests an individual Web server can handle at once (Roush, 1995). Since the Web has evolved into a multimedia intensive tool, gridlock has become an even bigger problem than it is for the other part of the Internet.

Cyberloafing

Surfing the Internet, wasting time and accessing inappropriate materials are the primary concerns, which have been labeled as cyberloafing (Prawitt et al., 1997). Studies show that once users become more familiar with the Web, the cyberloafing practice becomes a common phenomenon (Hills, 1996; Frook, 1997). Cyberloafing can also take place in a different form where users receive unsolicited messages about all kinds of decent and indecent offers. In this case the user is not searching sites to explore; however, in the act of reading the unsolicited e-mail message he or she can be tempted to explore inappropriate materials. In the latter case when the cyberloafing takes place at work by an employee of an organization, beside the productivity lost, there is also the liability concern associated with cyberloafing if the act involves the downloading of indecent materials. These actions can create a company liability that potentially involves allegations of "harassment", "free speech", "privacy", "jurisdiction", and even "copyright infringement" (Sampson, 1997).

Equity

Some argue that the Web will bring forth a better democracy within the United States by returning the power to the people (Meeks, 1997). This may not come to pass if the issues of equity and demographic trends are poorly addressed. According to Pitkow (1996), of the users joining the Web, their estimated median income ($64,700 annually) is well above the national median of 36,950 as estimated by the 1993 U.S. Census and they are predominantly male (70%). Whether the explanations for the lack of utilization by some groups lie in the issue of availability, affordability, or usability remains a topic for additional research. However, all statistics clearly indicate that this technology is not equally utilized by all classes of the society in the U.S. as well as other countries.

Exposure Points

As more companies utilizing Web-enabled technologies incorporate the ability for remote access to their computer systems by their employees, there is a higher risk of information exposure (Prawitt et al., 1996). In other words, these emerging exposure points are inroads which can lead to sloppy data entry into the systems, as well as savvy hackers breaking into the system where inadequate control measures might not be applied at every exposure point.

Flooding of the Web with content for content's sake.

With the ease of access to the Internet and the availability to use web development tools, there is an abundance of slick and costly Web Pages on the Internet. Many of these WebPages include information that is not helpful to their viewers. They are merely on the Internet so the individuals or company that owns the site can claim that they have a website. In recent years, many companies are beginning to view content for content's sake as a wasteful exercise and instead are beginning to understand that the role of the website is to facilitate business processes (Gardner, 1997).

Inadequate search facilities on the WWW

One of the important issues of the Internet is that of inadequate search facilities with the lack of a high level query language for locating, filtering, and presenting WWW information (Foo et al., 1997). Some search engines search the document headers, some look for the document themselves, while others look for indices or directories. As a result, one can conclude that much of the information on the Web is presented in dynamic and a somewhat chaotic fashion. In a recent survey of Web users, 34.5% of the participants were not able to locate a site which was known to exist, and 23.7% were not able to figure out how to return to a site that they had previously visited (Pitkow, 1996).

Maintaining and integrity of data

The task of keeping up with commercial WebPages by maintaining the latest information is considered to be a costly issue facing many organizations. As a company's website becomes more elaborate and complex, the task of maintaining and validating information included in their websites becomes much more costly and complex too. Ultimately, it will reach a point where maintaining and ensuring the accuracy of information becomes difficult (Foo et al., 1997). Inaccurate and out-of-date information included in the website can contribute, in part, to decisions being made by the user of the information that is based on data that is either inaccurate or outdated which can harm the organization's business processes.

Security

The issue of Web security is considered being among the most important challenges of many organizations. Many security experts believe that the existing layers of security are considered to be inadequate and in some cases fragile (Hodges, 1997). It is important to note that security is a broad term. In some instances the term security is related to privacy, while in other contexts the term refers to the integrity of data (Grimshaw, 1997). Security issues can be better understood by examining the concrete examples of security threats and risks.

• E-mail risks

Berghel (1997) and Prawitt & Romney (1997) identify several unique risks related to e-mail including volume levels that overload systems, junk mail, mail bombs, "flaming" or flooding a user with messages, interception and unauthorized reading of electronic mail, and improper representations by employees.

• False store fronts

A false store front risk is presented when a hacker sets up a Web page that looks legitimate for business but uses the site to gather credit card numbers, account numbers or other confidential information from unsuspecting consumers (Bhimani, 1996; Prawitt et al., 1997). After which, the "business" disappears and the information obtained is utilized for unauthorized transactions.

• Industrial espionage

There is a growing concern that the Web requires additional methods to secure the confidential data accessible on the Web against interception and decryption by unauthorized users (Roush, 1995). "Sensitive about anything that touches their legacy applications and custom-built accounting and inventory tools that run the business side of the corporation, most companies have tiptoed carefully into so-called Webification" (Higgins, 1997). Most of the attacks launched at industry systems take advantage of simple holes largely attributed to misconfigured systems, poorly written software, mismanaged systems, or user neglect (Bhimani, 1996).

• Information vandalism

Vandalism in this context is the unauthorized modification of data that is available on the Web. Often this takes the form of "graffiti" placed in the text of a home page which is unauthorized, often embarrassing and potentially harmful (Prawitt et al., 1997). Another form is described by Bhimani (1996), whereby the contents of certain transactions are modified such as the payee of an electronic check or the amount of a bank account transfer.

• ISP linkage alterations
Internet Service Providers (ISP) provide access to the Internet via the maintenance of a domain name server, which provides a direct translation of a WWW address into an Internet address. If a link established within a WebPage is altered, then the user may be erroneously linked to an inappropriate, potentially embarrassing location within the Web (Prawitt et al., 1997).

• Viruses
With the increasing number of networked computers, the ability of a developer to place a virus within any number of programs and have that virus become widespread to all who download, open or execute the program or file is great (Prawitt et al., 1997).

• Webware
Many systems allow software developers to attach programs which are executed upon access to a WebPage (Felton, 1997). This software is termed Webware. "Simply visiting a WebPage may cause you to unknowingly download and run a program written by someone you don't know or don't trust" (Felton, 1997).

With the advent of Electronic Commerce (EC) and the overwhelming interest in utilization of this technology for modern commerce, there are many challenges presented by the security issues and risks. Although there are perceived issues with security, especially related to EC, there is still substantial interest in utilizing the Web technology for EC (Liu et al., 1997).

System incompatibilities
The issue of system incompatibilities has been a major issue during the past several years. In many cases, cross-platform compatibility is not always available in all of the emerging technologies being developed which can result in difficulty when trying to make them function in unison (Prawitt et al., 1997).

Unauthorized use of computer resources
Today's emerging interconnectivity technologies have presented opportunities for computer misuse which were not previously possible (Prawitt et al., 1997). The Boeing corporation recently has begun reviewing the issue of

URL filtering of objectionable material (Frook, 1997). According to the Computer Fraud and Abuse Act, computer usage in excess of one's level of authorization can result in personal liabilities for any harm caused (Sampson, 1997). Many companies are debating the best solution to this issue. In response, Boeing has decided that "restricting site access is a cumbersome management process, but unrestricted access to public Web sites could open the company up to legal issues" (Frook, 1997).

User ignorance and perceptions

The lack of adequate understanding of the Internet and its usage and risks has been a contributing factor in maintaining secure systems. Modern information systems are comprised of many different components of distributed hardware, software, and data maintained on different locations by different systems. According to Prawitt and Romney (1997), while it is becoming increasingly critical for users to exercise sound control practices, most are not adequately trained to do so".

Web Performance Tracking

With the explosive growth of Web applications, services, traffic volumes and contents, a management void has been created. If the performance and availability of the Web services are not managed and information cannot be accessed quickly, it is likely the user will jump to a competitor's site which results in the loss of business (McConnell, 1997). "To achieve peak performance, the IT department must harmonize many critical elements, including the transport network and its Featured Sites service levels, if any, Web server hardware and software and information content" (McConnell, 1997).

Study

To learn more about the critical issues related to the utilization and management of Web-enabled technologies modern organizations, a study was conducted. The Delphi method was utilized to assess the validation of the existing critical issues identified in the review of literature and to identify other critical issues.

The first task of the study was to select a group of experts on the subject of this research who could participate in the study. The main criterion for selecting experts was the research credentials with regard to their publications in the area of Web-enabled technologies. Initially a group of 57 experts was identified for possible participation in this Delphi study. Upon generating the list of experts, an invitation was sent to each requesting their commitment to participate in the study. The invitation also included a brief description of the research objective, the Delphi technique, and anticipated

Table 3: A Summary of Critical Issues of Web Technologies According to Existing Literature

Issue	Brief Explanation
Bandwidth Restrictions and Latency	Low-speed data transition caused by slow communication device such as a modem.
CyberLoafing	Surfing the Internet, wating time and accessing inappropriate materials.
Equity	Not equally utilized by all classes of society.
Exposure Points	Sloppy data entry as well as breaking into the system due to lack of adequate control measures applied at every remote control..
Flooding of the Web with Content for Content's Sake	Web sites that do not offer effective and useful information.
Inadequate Search Facilities on the WWW	Inadequate search facilities with lack of a high level query language for locating filtering, and presenting WWW information.
Maintenance and Integrity of Data	Keeping up with the task of maintaining and validating information included in Web sites.
Security	Treats risks and misuse of the system (e.g., e-mail risks, false store fronts, industrial espoinage, information vandalism, ISP linkage alterations, viruses and Webware).
System Incompatibilities	Lack of available crossplatform compatible communication networks.
Unauthorized Use of Computer Resources	Use of the Internet resources for personal use.
User Ignorance and Perception	Lack of user understanding of security risks and control.
Web Performance Tracking	Keeping track of systems performance and effectiveness.

time requirements of the study for their planning purposes. Seventeen individuals (30%) out of 57 experts responded to the invitation and agreed to participate in the study.

The next phase of the study was the data/opinion collection process from the group of the experts who agreed to participate. The process consisted of three (3) rounds of questionnaires sent to the participants. The initial round provided each expert in the group the alphabetical list of issues affecting the utilization of the emerging Web-enabled technologies as it was developed from the initial review of literature. Table 4 lists the issues included in the initial questionnaire. Each expert was asked to rank the issues listed in the questionnaire using the nine-point Likert scale (0 = unimportant, 9 = very important). The experts were also asked to include any additional issues that

Table 4: A List of Issues Included in the Initial Questionnaire

- Bandwidth restrictions and latency (estimated delay)
- Equity (equal access to technology within society)
- Exposure points (each point of remote access represents a risk)
- Flooding of the Web with content for content's sake
- Inadequate comprehensive search facilities on the WWW
- Security and control
- System incompatibilities (cross-platform)
- Unauthorized use of computer resources (unproductive WWW usage)
- User ignorance and perceptions (lack of adequate training)
- Web performance tracking

they believe warrant inclusion in the list of critical issues of this study.

Upon receipt of all the responses, their rankings were reviewed to eliminate any overlaps and then grouped. The weights assigned by each expert served as the study inputs. From these inputs, the issues were ranked in the order of the one with highest mean through the one with the lowest mean of ranking. Table 5 summarizes the ranking of the first round of the study.

As stated earlier, the expert panel for this study was asked to list any other issues that in their opinion should be included among the list of critical issue of Web-enabled technologies. Table 6 lists a summary of the additional issues identified by the participants.

A brief history and description of the Delphi Method

In the early 1960s, RAND researchers Helmer, Dalkey, and their colleagues introduced the Delphi technique designed to improve the use of expert opinion through polling based on three conditions: Anonymity, Statistical display, and Feedback of reasoning (Bright 1972). The Delphi technique is an elegant intuitive method of developing a consensus. The technique is used in forecasting; however, it should not be considered a forecasting technique as it combines the perceived wants or needs of the participants in an attempt to predict what will be (Cetron, 1969). The method employs polling of participants for the systematic solicitation of expert opinion. The method is executed via a carefully designed program of sequential individual interrogations, typically by questionnaire, interspersed with information and opinion feedback (Cetron, 1969). The method rests on the "assumption that a prediction upon which the majority of a category of people questioned can agree has greater credibility than the surmise of an individual" (Blohm and Steinbuch, 1972). The feedback of the input forms is the sole means of internal group communications in the Delphi process (Linstone and Turoff, 1975). This concept eliminates the committee activity due to the lack of open discussion, thus reducing "the influence of certain psychological factors, such as specious persuasion, unwillingness to abandon publicly expressed opinions, and the bandwagon effect of majority opinion" (Certon, 1969). The Delphi methodology incorporates the polling of experts and from the ensuing data develops a consensus which can be used for planning purposes (Certon, 1969). When the predications sought are directed toward technical development, the subjective opinions of experts predominate (Blohm and Steinbuch, 1972).

Table 5: A Summary of Rankings of the Critical Issues During the 1st Round of the Delphi Study

Ranking	Critical Issues	Mean
1	Bandwidth restrictions	7.41
2	Security	
3	Maintainability and integrity of data	7.07
4	Inadequate comprehensive search facilities	6.35
5	System incompatibilities	5.88
6	Web performance tracking	5.59
7	Equity	5.47
7	User ignorance and perceptions	5.47
8	Exposure points	4.29
9	Flooding of the Web with content	4.29
10	Unauthorized use of computer resources	4.06

Table 6: A Summary of Additional Issues Identified by the Experts During the First Round of the Study

- Hype
- Privacy and confidentiality agreements
- Low overhead e-payment facilities, "micropayments," so that advertising is no longer needed to cover costs of running servers and the content providers can sell information
- Use of metadata
- Global laws to deal with net crimes
- Required labelling of sites (not censoring, just labelling) which comes after having global laws in place for dealing with net crimes
- Failure of primary companies and their products to adhere to the standards that do exist (i.e., HTML and JavaScript)
- Expressability of HTML (ability to create documents that contain complex layouts)
- System utilization (what functionality of information sharing is best served on the Web)
- Access appliances that avoid computer software
- Unsolicited e-mail or spamming
- Lack of a standardized vector based graphic format for the Web

Upon completion of round one of this study, the list of issues with all their rankings and the list of the new issues identified during the first round were sent to the panel of experts for the second round of ranking. Again the experts were requested to review the list, make any additions necessary and rate each issue in light of the new ones added to the list. Note: Any participant whose round one scores on any issue were significantly distance from the panel's mean value was asked to write a brief explanation for the reasons for their position. Table 7 summarizes the results of the rankings of the issues forwarded to the panel of experts upon completion of the second round of the study.

Table 7: A Summary of Rankings of the Critical Issues During the 2nd Round of the Delphi Study

Ranking	Critical Issues	Mean
1	Bandwidth Restrictions and Latency	7.70
2	Low O/H E-payment Facilities	7.00
3	Inadequate Search Facilities	6.70
3	Maintainability and Integrity of Web Data	6.70
3	Security	6.70
4	Unsolicited E-mail (spamming)	6.20
5	Failure to Adhere to Standards	6.10
6	Use of Metadata	6.00
7	Privacy and Confidentiality	5.80
8	Systems Incompatibilities (cross-platform)	5.70
9	User Ignorance and Perceptions	5.40
9	Equity (Equal Access)	5.40
10	Global Laws for Net Crimes	5.10
11	Required Labelling of Sites	5.00
12	Web Performance Tracking	4.80
13	System Utilization	4.60
14	Expressability of HTML	4.50
15	Exposure Points	4.20
16	Unauthorized Use of Resources	3.80
16	Flooding the Web with Content	3.80
17	Lack of Standardized Vector Graphics	3.50
18	Access Appliances That Void Software	3.33
19	Hype	3.30

The following additional issue was added to the list of critical issues during round two of the Delphi study:

"Ensure the continued existence of a global body for consensus standardization, non-proprietary."

The feedback provided to the panel in round three was similar to the previous rounds with the addition of the issue that was added to the list of issues at the end of round two. Upon receipt of the round three ratings, the data was analyzed and summarized. Table 8 lists a summary of the results of the ranking of issues by the panel of experts during round three.

The study yielded a list of 24 issues (Table 8), which have an impact on

Table 8: A Summary of Rankings of the Critical Issues During the 3rd Round of the Delphi Study

Ranking	Critical Issues	Mean
1	Bandwidth Restrictions and Latency	7.70
2	Low O/H E-payment Facilities	7.33
3	Security	6.78
4	Inadequate Search Facilities	6.67
5	Maintainability and Integrity of Data	6.56
6	Failure to Adhere to Standards	6.11
6	Unsolicited E-mail (spamming)	6.11
7	Use of Metadata	6.00
8	Ensure a Continued Global Body	5.83
9	Privacy and Confidentiality	5.78
10	Equity (Equal Access)	5.67
10	Systems Incompatibilities (cross-platform)	5.67
11	User Ignorance and Perceptions	5.44
12	Global Laws for Net Crimes	4.89
11	Required Labelling of Sites	4.67
13	Web Performance Tracking	4.67
14	System Utilization	4.44
15	Expressability of HTML	4.33
16	Exposure Points	3.88
17	Unauthorized Use of Resources	3.56
18	Flooding the Web with Content	3.44
18	Lack of Standardized Vector Graphics	3.44
19	Hype	3.22
20	Access Appliances That Void Software	2.75

the emerging Web-enabled technologies. The final list was expanded from the original list of 11 critical issues, based on the additions offered by the expert panel members over the course of the study. The nature of the original issues was discussed in detail in the early part of this chapter. The following sections will discuss other issues pointed out by the panel of expert of the study.

Low Overhead E-Payment Facilities

Low overhead e-payment facilities, micropayments, are needed as a service on the WWW so that advertising is no longer necessary to cover the costs of running serves, and so that the content providers can sell information in the same fashion as the purchase of newspapers or a single song (Machlis, 1998). The process typically works, whereby, an account is opened with a micropayment system, and the software required is downloaded to work with the user's browser. Digital Equipment Corporation has developed a system that "will eliminate minimum purchase requirements of 10 to 25 cents now imposed by other electronic payment methods, allowing users to buy and sell information profitability down to fractions of a cent" (Digital, 1997).

Failure to Adhere to Standards

Failure of primary companies and their products to adhere to the standards that exist (e.g. HTML and JavaScript) is an issue that was ranked highly by the expert panel of the study. The primary importance of this issue is due to the fact that many companies, which have monopolistic power, such as Microsoft, do not abide by those standards that exist in the industry. Their lack of following the industry standards can be viewed as an attempt in creating a new "standard" with their products.

Unsolicited E-mail (spamming)

Spamming occurs when an endless stream of mail is received which can overflow the user's mailbox and can even choke the user's system (Highland, 1996). In recent years, with the easy to obtain free e-mail addresses from many different sources such as "Hotmail", "Juno", and "Netscape", the act of forwarding unsolicited e-mail messages has reached the crisis level for many users everyday. Users all around the world receive unsolicited e-mail messages for promoting products or services.

Use of Metadata

The World Wide Web currently has a huge amount of data with practically no classification information and this makes it extremely difficult to handle data/information effectively (Marchiori, 1998). Many systems can support knowledge management by establishing a metadata— information about information—standard so that users of data can obtain the raw materials that enables them to capture, store, and share knowledge that is gathered from different sources (Phillips, 1995). This task can be accomplished by adding to the Web objects a metadata classification which will assist search engines and Web-based digital libraries to properly classify and structure the information on the WWW (Bare, 1996 and Marchiori, 1998).

Ensure a Continued Global Body

Many users of the WWW are concerned that the body of knowledge created on the Internet consists of some kind of global understanding that users from all over the world can relate to. This task has been assigned to W3C to accomplish. The World Wide Web Consortium (W3C) is a global body that was founded to lead the WWW to its full potential by developing common protocols that promote its evolution and ensure its interoperability. The primary services offered by W3C to users and developers consist of (1) acting as a depository of information about the World Wide Web, (2) providing reference code implementations to embody and promote standards, and (3) providing various prototype and sample applications to demonstrate use of new technology.

Privacy & Confidentiality Agreements

The privacy and confidentiality agreements issue entails an aspect of the security issue in that it's a violation of users' privacy. This issue addresses the dilemma of how individual right to privacy and the sharing of confidential information about people in the society. With technology advances of the past two decades, many users believe that more information about their lives is now shared with others through the use of the Internet. Despite many existing laws in regard to the "right to privacy" of users of the Internet, everyday there are many cases of the violation of users' privacy and confidentiality where information that should not be shared by others is passed throughout the webs of this modern technology.

Global Laws for Net Crimes

Despite the fact that there is a global perception that crimes and criminals should be punished, there is considerable confusion regarding what is a criminal act on one society in comparison to another. The issue of global laws for net crimes is considered to be a complex issue that is anticipated to remain unsolved for a long time based on the current dilemma of establishing national laws regarding Internet activities (Rose, 1996; Weston, 1996; Charlesworth, 1997).

Required Labeling Sites

With millions of websites in existence and millions added constantly, there is a concern about how to differentiate Websites from each other regarding their contents. This particular issue can be considered an offset of two other critical issues discussed in this chapter, "inadequate search facilities" and "global laws". Supporters of this issue claim that by labeling sites, search engines can provide more effective and efficient search processes, and also labeling will assist the enforcement of any global laws related to net crimes. This issue becomes valid after having global laws in place to deal with net crimes.

System Utilization

The issue of system utilization deals with the overall question of what functionality or information sharing is best served on the World Wide Web. During the past decade, many users have seen the transformation of this technology into a business tool where businesses all over the world can conduct their commerce through this medium. The question of many users is what should be the overall functionality of the Internet in the future as this medium becomes more acceptable as a common medium for communication purposes.

Expressability of HTML

The expressability of HTML issue is primarily concerned with the ability of the user to create documents that contain complex layouts. This is very important to the functionality of the Web because of its usefulness in presenting information with all its characteristics and potentials. As more users rely on the use of this technology to share information with other users, the role of HTML or other tools will become more recognized. These tools should allow users at all levels to create documents that consist of the full picture and one not limited due to the limitation of the tool that they used.

Lack of Standardized Vector Graphics

This issue deals with the lack of incorporation of vector graphics in web designs. The adoption of vector graphics in web design would enable programmers to present better user interfaces to web applications, "Vector graphics scale easier, download faster and print better than their bit-mapped graphics counterparts GIF and JPEG" (Walsh, 1998). Standardization in this facet of the Web is at an early stage; whereby, a couple of proposals have been laced before the W3C for consideration (Walsh, 1998).

Hype

Web sites are effective if used imaginatively and intelligently. Many firms boast their web sites to be showcases for the firm's goods and services. Few, however, are very effective at serving the purpose for the firm's betterment. Despite this reality, there is a considerable degree of hype among organizations and their web designers that their websites should consist of more whistles and bells in order to compete with their competition, as well as to attract more customers.

Access Appliances that Avoid Computer Software Management

This particular issue was added by one of the expert panel members to the list of critical issues of this study during round one. (Other panel members questioned the real meaning of this issue, but, regrettably, the expert who suggested the issue did not provide any clarification or further responses after the first round. At the time of this writing, there is no clear explanation concerning this issue.

Consensus Measurement

As discussed earlier, the primary purpose of this study was to provide statistical conclusions based on the consensus of the expert opinions related to critical issues of Web-enabled technologies. The measurement of consensus can take various forms. According to Linstone and Turoff (1975), in most Delphi studies, "consensus is assumed to have been achieved when a certain percentage of the votes fall within a prescribed range— for example, when the interquartile range is no longer than two units on the ten-unit scale". This type of measurement, however, does not present the information available from the distribution characteristics of the results. "For example, a bimodal distribution may occur which will not be registered as a consensus, but indicates an important and apparently insoluble cleft opinion" (Linstone, et. al., 1975).

An alternate approach is to analyze the opinion stability of the expert panel as a method of consensus measurement. This approach allows the analysis to focus on the opinion of the group rather than on the amount of change in an individual's response from one round to the next (Linstone, et. al., 1975). Table 9 presents the results of a columnwise subtraction between the first and second, and the second and third round. The absolute values of the differences between each of the histograms form a total of the units of change. However, "since any one participant's change of opinion is reflected in the histogram differences by two units of change, net person-changes must be computed by dividing the total units of change by two" (Linstone, et. al., 1975). Finally, the final percentage change is calculated by dividing the net change by the number of participants, or experts, utilized in the study.

For the purposes of this study, a 15% change level was used to present a state of equilibrium. Based on this criterion, each of the issues presented in table 9 includes an analysis of the stability level achieved. In summary, all of the issues reached a stable opinion level with the exception of five of the issues. These five issues, marked by an unstable analysis status, did not achieve the group consensus measurement that the study was attempting to achieve. Since 79% of the issues did reach a stable opinion measurement, the study is thought to be successful in the identification and consensus classification of the critical issues associated with the emerging Web-enabled technologies.

Table 9: Summary of Stable and Unstable Issues

Issue		Rounds 1-2		Round 2-3	
#	Description	% Change	Analysis	% Change	Analysis
1	Bandwidth Restrictions	35%	Unstable	6%	Stable
2	Low O/H E-payment Facilities	N/A		17%	Unstable
3	Security	50%	Unstable	6%	Stable
4	Inadequate Search Facilities	45%	Unstable	6%	Stable
5	Maintainability and Integrity of Web Data	55%	Unstable	6%	Stable
6	Failure to Adhere to Standards	N/A		6%	Stable
7	Unsolicited E-mail (spamming)	N/A		6%	Stable
8	Use of Metadata	N/A		6%	Stable
9	Ensure Continued Global Body	N/A		42%	Unstable
10	Privacy and Confidentiality	N/A		6%	Stable
11	Equity (Equal Access)	45%	Unstable	17%	Unstable
12	Systems Incompatibilities (cross-platform)	30%	Unstable	6%	Stable
13	User Ignorance and Perceptions	55%	Unstable	6%	Stable
14	Global Laws for Net Crimes	N/A		6%	Stable
15	Web Performance Tracking	55%	Unstable	6%	Stable
16	Required Labelling of Sites	50%	Unstable	6%	Stable
17	System Utilization	N/A		6%	Stable
18	Expressability of HTML	N/A		6%	Stable
19	Exposure Points	55%	Unstable	6%	Stable
20	Unauthorized Use of Resources	45%	Unstable	6%	Stable
21	Lack of Standardized Vector Graphics	N/A		6%	Stable
22	Flooding the Web with Content	40%	Unstable	6%	Stable
23	Hype	N/A		17%	Unstable
24	Access Appliances That Void Software	N/A		19%	Unstable

Implications and Recommendations

Implications

This study defines and prioritizes the primary critical issues that are impeding the further growth of Web-enabled technologies. Although the issue rankings were somewhat diverse in terms of a range of values, the stability of expert opinion lends credence to the validity of study data. The study yielded four primary implications.

The initial implication derived from the study results points to the fact that the most prominent critical issues are those which impact Electronic Commerce (EC). The evidence in support of this implication is seen in the top three stable issues ranked. Namely, bandwidth restrictions, security, and inadequate search facilities. Of the issues compiled in the list, these three are the primary ones impacting the further development, acceptance and utilization of electronic commerce capabilities. This phenomenon is logical from the perspective of the industry trend toward electronic commerce.

The study also revealed an implication about the lack of concern over individuals misusing the Web capabilities. The primary issues that support this implication are unauthorized use of resources and flooding the Web with content's sake. By virtue of the fact that the issues were included in the list implies that they have some merit, however, these issues were ranked very low in terms of significance. The ranking of these issues can be interpreted by the fact that many experts view the overwhelming services provided on the Internet as far exceeding its down side, and these kind of misuses always will be part of the system utilization and management.

A third implication of the study results is that the critical issues regarding Web-enabled technologies are business effective oriented. Those issues pertaining to consumer concerns such as censorship of information available through the use of Web-enabled technologies did not appear as areas of concern in this study. This phenomenon is partly being driven by the compilation of business and academia oriented experts who participated in this study. However, the implication makes sense from the perspective of the strength and resources required by the business community to advance the Web technologies.

The final implication determined from this study deals with the results stability that were achieved utilizing the Delphi technique. The panel of experts were able to freely express their opinions and review those opinions presented by their colleagues in a manner that allowed them to provide consistency in their projections.

Recommendations

In order to address the issues brought to the forefront as a part of this study, various Web-enabled technologies user groups need to participate in the development of solution.

Recommendation for Businesses

Businesses need to understand the implications of the top critical issues and work with formal bodies such as the World Wide Web Consortium (W3C) to develop remedies and solutions to these critical issues. Workable solutions especially in the realm of electronic commerce (EC) can be only developed with the active participation of the business community. Business can also speed the process by expressing their business desire and need to improve the capability of the technology prior to incorporation. On the other hand, businesses should also pay close attention to many of the issues that concern users of their web sites such as users' unhappiness with excessive delays in graphic presentation loading experiences on some Web pages.

Perhaps by simplifying their websites, they can contribute to solving the issue of bandwidth (latency) until such time that much faster and efficient bandwidth channels are in existence.

Recommendations for Government

The recommendation most appropriate for government is to monitor closely, however, don't act hastily. The issues raised by the panel of experts in the study related to laws and governmental issues were "global laws for net crimes" and "required labeling sites". The ranking position of these issues, as well as the complexity of a potential solution, sends the warning to governments not to act in haste. The solution to these issues must be developed by a global body that can accomplish a consensus as to the definition of what actions are considered acceptable, and what actions are not acceptable or should be considered as crimes. Furthermore, such a global body can also determine what authoritative action is enforceable in this realm.

Recommendation for Web-enabled Technology Users

The users of the Web-enabled technologies need to actively participate in the development of a body of solutions in dealing with issues of this technology. From the business point of view, the thrust behind the technology is not centered on the protection of the individual users' rights, privileges, or privacy. On the contrary, these technologies are being developed primarily for the increased effectiveness of industry today and of course, for monetary gain. Businesses are in search of ways to execute their business transactions with fewer errors (reduce costs of doing business) and fewer personnel (increase employee productivity) to stay competitive. Therefore, users can provide many recommendations that will address these issues while allowing them to express other concerns that should be examined by business, governments, and other groups involved in the overall utilization and management of the Internet.

Conclusion

The World Wide Web is a vast collection of linked documents that reside on computer systems around the world. It is an exciting technological time where new emerging capabilities are being brought forth to utilize the Web. In order for the Web to expand and grow, the critical issues, causing the current roadblocks, must be identified and prioritized.

The objective of this study was to assess critical issues and trends related to the utilization and management of Web-enabled technologies. The initial review of literature identified a set of 11 critical issues. Through the use of

Delphi technique, these issues along with others identified by the panel of experts, were carefully assessed and evaluated in terms of their importance. The expert opinions shared with the panel members led to the identification of more than 24 critical issues for this study. Out of the 24, five issues were later identified as "Unstable", and the remaining issues were considered to be "Stable" ones.

The critical issues identified in this study offer many implications and challenges for businesses, governments, and the user community alike. With greater emphasis being placed on the WWW's capability, these issues must be dealt with continuously without delay. As the Web continues to expand, newer issues will arise that will present new challenges to the user and development communities to address.

References

Baer, Tony. (1996). I want my metadata. *Software Magazine*, 16(8), 53-60.

Berghel, Hal. (1996). The client's side of the World Wide Web. *Communications of the ACM*, 39(1), 30-40.

Berghel, Hal. (1997). Email - the good, the bad, and the ugly. *Communications of the ACM*, 40(4), 11-15.

Berners-Lee, T. J., Cailliau & Groff, J.F. (1992). The World Wide Web. *Computer Networks & ISDN Systems*, 25(4), 454-459.

Bhimani, Anish. (1996). Securing the commercial Internet. *Communications of the ACM*, 39(6), 29-31.

Bird, Jane. (1996). Untangling the web. *Management Today*, 68-70.

Blohm, Hans and Steinbuch, Karl. (1973). *Technological Forecasting in Practice*. Saxon House/Lexington Books.

Bright, James R. (1972). *A Brief Introduction to Technology Forecasting Concepts and Exercises*. The Parnaquid Press.

Cetron, Marvin J. (1969). *Technological Forecasting A Practical Approach*. Gordon and Breach Science Publishers.

Charlesworth, Andrew. (1997). Internet Law and Regulation/Law and the Information Superhighway. *International Review of Law, Computers & Technology*, 11(1), 175-179.

Felton, Edward W. (1997). Webware security. *Communications of the ACM*, 40(4), 130-131.

Foo, Schubert and Lim, Ee-Peng. (1997). A Hypermedia database to manage World-Wide-Web documents. *Information and Management*. 31(5), 235-249.

Fox, Armando & Eric A. Brewar. (1996). Reducing WWW latency and bandwidth requirements by real-time distillation. *Computer Networks & ISDN Systems*, 28(7-11), 1445-1456.

Frook, John Evan. (1997). Helping Employees Get Hip to the Web. *InternetWeek*, 647, 1-4.

Gardner, Dana. (1997). Top of the News: Web culture clash. *InfoWorld*.

Grimshaw, Andrew S. (1997). The Legion vision of the worldwide virtual computer.

Communications of the ACM, 40(1), 39-45.

Hacker, Robert C. (1996). The real value of the World Wide Web. *Target Marketing*, 19(2), 30-32.

Higgins, Kelly Jackson. (1997). Dare to Webify your Back Office. *InternetWeek*, 679, 1-5.

Hill, Richard. (1997). Electronic Commerce, The World Wide Web, Minitel, and EDI. *Information Society*, 13(1), 33-41.

Hodges, Mark. (1997). Building a bond of trust. *MIT's Technology Review*, 100(6), 26-27.

Jacobs, Ian G. (1998). Companies Get Wired For the Web - Internet VARs are leading their customers down a more viable business path. *VARBusiness*, 1401, 1-4.

Linstone, Harold A. and Turoff, Murray. (1975). *The Delphi Method Techniques and Applications*. Addison-Wesley Publishing Company, Inc.

Liu, Chang, Arnett, Kirk P., Capella, Louis M., and Beatty, Robert C. (1997). Web sites of the Fortune 500 companies: Facing customers through home pages. *Information and Management*, 31(6), 335-345.

Machlis, Sharon. (1998). Micropayments aren't just chump change. *Computerworld*, 32(9), 37-39.

Marchiori, Massimo. (1998). The limits of Web metadata, and beyond. *Computer Networks & ISDN Systems*, 30(1-7), 1-9.

McConnell, John. (1997). The Next Frontier: Web Performance Tracking. *InternetWeek*, 693, 1-3.

Meeks, Brock N. (1997). Better democracy through technology. *Communications of the ACM*, 40(2), 75-78.

Misic, M. (1994). Keys to success with the Internet. *Journal of Systems Management*. 45(11), 6-10.

Phillips, John T Jr. (1995). Metadata - Information about electronic records. *Records Management Quarterly*, 29(4), 52-55.

Pitkow, James E. (1996). Emerging trends in the WWW user population. *Communications of the ACM*, 39(6),106-108.

Prawitt, Douglas F. Romney & Marshal B. (1997). Emerging Business Technologies (list of new technologies and risks related to them). *Internal Audit*, 54(1), 24-32.

Presti, Ken. (1996). Corporate Intranet Growth Puts New Spin On World Wide Web. *Computer Reseller News*.

Rose, Lewis. (1996). Before you advertise on the 'Net - check the international marketing laws. *Bank Marketing*, 28(5), 40-42.

Roush, Wade. (1995). Spinning a better Web. *Technology Review*, 98(3), 11-13.

Sampson, Sandy. (1997). Wild Wild Web: Legal exposure on the Internet. *Software Magazine*, 17(13), 75-78.

Walsh, Jeff. (1998). Vector graphics gets major vendor boost. InfoWorld, 20(16), 59-60.

Weston, Randy. (1996). It's taxing to untangle Web commerce laws. *Computerworld*, 30(43), 28.

Chapter 2

Developing Applications for the Web: Exploring Differences Between Traditional and World Wide Web Application Development

Nancy L. Russo
Northern Illinois University, USA

Introduction

The use of the Internet, and the World Wide Web in particular, has grown at a phenomenal rate. The Internet, the world's largest computer network, grew from approximately 25,000 connected networks with over 6.6 million computers worldwide in 1996 (Neubarth, 1996) to more than 50,000 networks and 16 million computers today (Conger & Mason, 1998). The fastest growing resource on the Internet is the World Wide Web (hereafter called the Web). Between 1994 and 1996, the Web grew from 100 sites to 100,000 sites housing more than a million Web pages (Neubarth, 1996), and as of January, 1999, an electronic survey of web hosts found over 43 million sites (Network Wizards, 1999). Over 80% of America's Fortune 500 companies have some type of Web presence (*The Economist*, 1997).

The types of applications or sites found on the Web range from something as simple as an individual's personal home page listing favorite teams and movies to sophisticated full-blown organizational information systems such as on-line courses, electronic shopping, and sophisticated database-oriented applications. It is the development of these organizational systems

– whether business, educational, or non-profit – that are of particular interest here. When an organization creates a Web site, that site becomes a major point of contact with a vast number of potential customers. Thus a Web site offers great opportunity, as well as great risk. It is possible for a Web site to expose an organization to a huge new base of potential customers. However, a poorly designed and/or poorly implemented and maintained Web site can tarnish an organization's reputation with that same vast audience.

The ease of developing these sites belies their potential critical nature. Although many people have the ability to put up a Web site, they may not have the skills or knowledge or training to ensure that the site is of the necessary level of quality – in terms of aesthetics, functionality, or security. As was seen with end-user development, organizations should be aware of the need to monitor and control Web development activities to ensure that the organization is not put at risk due to poor decisions made by non-professional developers.

This chapter will examine the nature of Web application development as it is occurring in organizations today. In particular, it will address the *who* and the *how* of Web development and discuss the role of methodologies in the Web development process.

Background

The proliferation and high visibility of Web applications have raised concerns in many organizations. Because a Web site may be the initial contact a potential customer has with the organization, it is important that the information presented be accurate, timely, and reflect the objectives of the organization. However, most Web applications are developed with little or no control and without formalized processes.

The solution to the lack of structure and control in traditional system development environments has been the implementation of formalized system development methodologies. The use of an appropriate development methodology has been considered essential when designing and building computerized information systems. Some specific benefits of following a methodology include the ability to plan and monitor project progress based on the activities specified by the methodology, and the ability to ensure that sequential tasks are completed in the proper order, so that later tasks can build on earlier ones (Bakke, 1998). Another important outcome of method-ology use is documentation. Documentation formalizes understandings and agreements regarding the scope and functionality of the system; serves as a communication tool between those involved in the project; and provides a lasting repository of information about the project, which can be particularly valuable in the dynamic nature of the information systems workforce (Bakke, 1998). The failure to follow an appropriate methodology has been linked to poor quality systems, low levels of user acceptance, and high development costs.

However, we must question the appropriateness of applying existing methodologies to the Web application development environment. Do similarities exist between the tasks and activities involved in the development of applications for the Web and those used in the development of more traditional information systems? Or are the two environments so vastly different in nature and scope that the tools and techniques of the past are useless in this new environment?

There are differences between Web applications and traditional information system applications that may inhibit the use of existing methodologies in the Web environment. Web applications differ from traditional information systems in a variety of ways. One difference is in terms of the purpose and audience for which they are developed. Many Web applications are created initially simply to have a presence on the Web, rather than to replace any existing traditional information systems or to provide new functionality. The users of Web applications are likely to be outside of the organization and often cannot be identified in advance. This makes it much more difficult, if not impossible, to solicit the views of users when determining the information requirements for the Web application. Often the Web designer has to consider methods of promoting and drawing users to the site. The issue of "user-friendliness" is taken to extremes – sites must be not only accurate and complete, but also entertaining. Designers' creativity and graphic design skills are considered by some to be as important as their technical skills in this environment. Other differences are the communications technology (the Internet, which is the primary focus here, but also intranets and extranets), the requirement for multi-platform accessibility, and the non-sequential nature of the site content due to a reliance on hypertext links to other Web documents. Yet another difference has to do with who is developing Web applications. Research, some of which is discussed in the next section, indicates that many Web applications are initiated and developed outside of the information systems function (Russo and Misic, 1998).

Although there are many differences between Web application development and traditional information systems development, this is not to say that there is a totally different process at work. Whereas the ability to instantly publish a Web application appears to "trivialize" the need for planning and design (Balasubramanian and Bashian, 1998), experience has shown that insofar as Web applications are computer-based information systems, general systems development principles apply (Dennis, 1998). Although the means for completing the tasks might differ, both Web application development and traditional information system development require many of the same types of activities. In both environments, there is a need to define information and processing requirements, to design the interface, and to build, test, and maintain the system.

We will accept that some aspects of the Web application development process are sufficiently similar to those of the traditional development process so as to allow the application of information systems methodologies to Web development. The next task is then to examine existing information system development methodologies to determine whether they are satisfactory. Numerous studies have looked at the methodologies, tools, and techniques used in traditional systems development, and many have found that existing methodologies, where used at all, are typically modified and adapted to fit particular development contexts (e.g., Fitzgerald, 1994; Hardy, et al., 1995; Russo et al., 1995 & 1996). Based on such evidence, it would appear that existing methodologies and their related tools and techniques may not be adequate – in their current state – to support today's development projects, particularly those relating to Web applications.

Before we can come to any concrete conclusions regarding the applicability of system development methodologies to the Web development environment, it is important that we understand the nature of the Web development context. We need to understand who is developing these applications, and how they are doing it before we can make relevant comments regarding what we believe should be done. The remainder of this chapter examines Web application development to explore the development context and the role that methodologies can play in that context.

Web Application Development

A two-pronged approach is taken to examine the area of Web application development. One strategy is to directly question Web developers about how they are going about the process of developing Web applications. By going to the Web developers themselves, we can learn more about their background and the environment in which they are working.

A second strategy is to look for sources of Web development methodologies. Several methodologies are described and compared with each other and with traditional life cycle methodology.

Survey of Web Application Developers

To investigate current practice in Web application design and development, an electronic survey of Web developers was conducted. Five hundred

Web sites were randomly selected from the 1997 *Internet & Web Yellow Pages*. An electronic questionnaire was e-mailed to the developers of each of these Web sites. This questionnaire examined the *who* and *how* of Web application development. It specifically addressed the background, experience, and knowledge of Web developers and the methods they used for developing their Web applications. (A copy of the questionnaire is available from the author. For further information, see Russo and Misic, 1998.)

The results reported below came from fifty-seven responses. Approximately 45% of the Web applications described were devoted to advertising and selling a product. Over 50% of the applications were primarily information providing sites for various organizations. The remainder of the sites offered a particular service, such as calculating an insurance quotation or providing an application form for a permit to work with hazardous substances. Because of the vast size of the Internet, and its unstructured, dynamic, and unmanaged nature, it is impossible to define with any accuracy the exact population addressed by any Internet study. Therefore, the Web applications examined in this study should be viewed as examples, rather than as a representative sample of all Web applications.

Web Developers: Who Are They? Fewer than one third of the Web developers studied were employed in an information systems department. Their job titles included manager, programmer, president, Web coordinator, costume designer and many others. All of the respondents had some formal education. All had some type of university education, although not necessarily a degree, and approximately one third had master's degrees. Most did not come from traditional computer science/IS backgrounds; although a few had some prior programming knowledge (not necessarily work experience). The programming languages which were most commonly known by the responding Web developers were, in order of familiarity, BASIC, C, Visual Basic and COBOL. Less than 15% of the respondents received formal training in using hypertext markup language or other Web development tools/languages. Half of the Web developers had developed computerized information systems in the past (non-Web applications). Of this group, only a few indicated that they had used any type of systems development methodology while developing previous computerized information systems.

General Information on Web Development. The primary reason given for the initiation of most Web development efforts was simply to have a presence on the Web. Other reasons for creating a Web application were, in order of importance: for the purpose of creating a totally new type of application, to replace existing computerized systems, and to replace existing manual systems. (Respondents could indicate more than one reason.)

Most Web development projects were initiated by the developer rather than by a manager or customer. The number of Web applications developed by respondents ranged from one to thirty, and the amount of time it took to develop the applications ranged from a few days to over one year. An average of seven Web applications were developed in the last six months by the respondents, and their most recent Web application took an average of one month to complete (although most agreed that development was never completely finished due to the need to keep pages current).

System Development Methods. Slightly less than one third (29%) of the developers worked as part of a formal development team in developing their Web applications, 32% worked informally with users, and the remainder (39%) worked alone. Well over half (68%) of the respondents indicated that their organizations have no standards or guidelines for Web development. Some organizations are in the process of developing standards, and many developers indicated that they have their own informal guidelines or "rules of thumb" that they follow. None of the developers used a formal system development methodology. However, a small number of the developers did report using traditional development tools and techniques, such as entity-relationship diagramming, prototyping, decision tables, and flowcharting.

From the survey results, we can see that Web development is taking place in quite a different environment when compared to traditional information systems development. The initial motivation for the development projects differs. The locus of the project initiation and the development itself is most likely to be outside of the information systems function. Web development in most organizations is decentralized, and because it is often not the responsibility of any one group, it is very difficult to monitor and control. The individuals developing Web applications have neither training nor experience with formal development processes.

In the next section the applicability of development methods in this environment will be explored.

Web Development Methodology

As with traditional systems development, there are arguments both for and against the use of formal development methodologies in the Web environment. Those in favor of methodology use point to the ability of methodologies to provide structure for a process, to provide guidelines for activities to follow and documentation to produce. Particularly for the development of "mission critical" systems, those at the core of an organization's business, and the development of Web applications which must be integrated with these corporate information systems, the formalization provided

by a methodology is beneficial, if not essential. By mandating that developers follow a methodology, an organization can ensure that particular
aspects of the development process are taken into account (such as organizational standards) and that attention is paid to important issues such as
testing.

On the other side of the methodology issue are those who point to the
creative nature of Web application development. There are those who
believe that methodologies not only aren't needed, but can be detrimental
to the creative process. Because Web development is very much an iterative
process, sometimes with no new code written at all, it is viewed as more of
an informal design and prototyping process rather than a true development
project.

In actuality, there are truths in both positions. Some Web application
development processes can benefit from the use of formal development
methods, while others might not. Some Web applications are truly fully-
functioning information systems which are accessed via a Web browser.
These types of applications need the same amount of attention – if not more
– paid to the management of the development process as do traditional
information systems. Other applications, which are simply a series of linked
pages, may not require any type of formal structure. Their development is
more a process of converting paper documents to on-line documents and
linking them together. A traditional methodology might not be particularly
useful for these types of applications, but there may be a role for some type
of methodology for document design and a method for formalizing and
documenting the structure of the site.

In general, a traditional information systems methodology provides the
steps, or phases, to follow in developing a system and the tools and
techniques used to perform the activities which are contained in these steps.
A typical generic lifecycle methodology would include planning, analysis,
design, implementation (which includes coding and testing), and maintenance. These same general steps could be applied to Web development.

An action research project was conducted to examine the applicability
of a traditional structured development methodology to Web development.
A small development team created a Web-based database application for a
manufacturing organization. During the development process, the team
recorded and analyzed the activities they performed. They were specifically
asked to reflect on the usefulness of existing structured development
methodology tools. Based on this analysis, a Web application development
methodology was suggested. (For more details, see Russo and Graham,
1998). The development team felt that while the general steps applied, there

were modifications that needed to be made to acknowledge the differences in the Web environment. The steps of the recommended methodology could be grouped according to the five primary steps identified earlier of planning, analysis, design, implementation, and maintenance., albeit in some cases different names were used. Each of these will be discussed below.

Initiation. The initiation for most Web applications comes from outside the information systems function. Many of these applications are not the outcome of a formal strategic planning process, nor are they responses to specific problems. In fact, a large number of Web applications are developed primarily because the initiator saw a need to have a presence on the Web. Very frequently these applications are not considered part of the corporate information systems architecture at all. This, coupled with the fact that some Web applications can be so easily put together, might appear to minimize the need to evaluate the resources requirements of these systems. However, these issues should not be ignored. The costs, benefits, and overall feasibility of any development project should be considered. Of particular concern in the Web environment is the availability of hardware and software to support the desired functionality (both on the development side and on the user side) and the availability of personnel with the appropriate technical and graphic design skills.

Analysis. Whereas in a traditional information systems development project, analysis often focuses on the processes or functions that must be performed by the new system, in the world of Web applications, the focus is more likely to be on the information content and the aesthetic design of the site. A number of survey respondents described their analysis process as looking at company brochures and at other Web sites. In traditional IS development, developers expect to be able to obtain some information directly from users regarding what the users want and need in the new system. However, when a Web application is developed, the developers typically do not know exactly who the users will be. Therefore, much more responsibility is placed on the developer to decide not only who the users will be, but also what their needs and expectations will be.

Design of the application. In this phase of the Web application development process, the layout and content of the application is designed. Databases and processing functions would also be designed at this stage. Two additional activities were suggested by the design team for this phase. These were resource gathering and design review. The purpose of resource gathering is to ensure that the necessary resources, including hardware, software, communications links, and personnel skills, are available. Because there are many languages and packages and code libraries available to use in the development of Web applications, and several may be needed, integration issues must be part of the resource selection process. A specific design review step was considered necessary to reconcile the chosen design with the resources available. If these are incompatible, then the two previous steps are revisited. This may take several iterations as design ideas and technology change.

Implementation. In this phase, the application is built, tested, and put into operation. Once the final design review is complete, the application itself is created. The pages are developed and linked. Databases are built, and any necessary code (Java, CGI, etc.) is acquired or written. It is a very common and acceptable practice in Web development to "borrow" bits of code from other applications or from on-line libraries of code (Java applets, etc.). Testing in some ways is even more difficult in the Web environment than with traditional IS development. When a traditional information system is developed, it is typically for a known group of users and a known hardware/software/network environment. Web applications, however, many times are developed for an almost infinite group of users, working in vastly different environments. An important aspect of the testing, therefore, is to ensure that the site works as intended from all the types of users. In addition, many Web applications are hyperlinked to other applications, both internal and external. Not only must all of these links be tested before implementation, but they must also continuously be tested to ensure viability of the links. The actual installation of the Web application may be as simple as loading it onto a server. With traditional applications software, we would expect there to be a group of users waiting to use the system. This may not be the case with a Web application. Therefore, an important component of implementation for many Web sites is making the site known to the target audience. Some type of advertising or promotion of the site might be required.

Maintenance. Maintenance is particularly critical to the success of a Web application. Maintenance of a Web application goes well beyond the typical correction of errors and addition of new functions throughout the life of the application. Because Web applications are developed to serve as important sources of information for current and/or potential customers, it is essential that the information provided be up to date. Content and links must be monitored continuously to ensure that they remain current. To assist in this effort, many Web sites provide a format for feedback concerning the site, via e-mail, questionnaires, or other forms. This constant, interactive form of post-implementation evaluation allows Web sites to evolve to meet current needs and expectations.

In Table 1, this suggested Web development methodology is compared with a number of other existing Web development methodologies. Two of the methodologies are commercial methodologies, created and promoted by

Table 1. *Comparison of Web Development Methodologies*

Traditional Systems Development Methodology	Web Development Methodology	Bakke (1998)	Conger and Mason (1998)	December (1996)	Digital Focus (1998)
Problem Identification	Initiation	Web Site Study	Preparation - Idea	Planning	Value Identification
Analysis	Analysis	Customer Requirements	generation - Information analysis - Structuration	Analysis	Workshop
Design	Design - Resource gathering - Design review	System Design System Architecture	Design - Information - Links - Multimedia - Testing	Design	Solution Design and Planning
Implementation	Implementation - Coding - Testing - Installation	Iterative Development System Testing Implementation Planning Procedures & User Doc. Training	Implementation	Implementation Promotion	Construction Deployment
Maintenance	Maintenance Post-Implementation Review	90-Day Evaluation Review	Maintenance and Continuous Improvement	Innovation	

software development organizations (Bakke, 1998; Digital Focus, 1998). One is from a textbook on Web design (Conger and Mason, 1998) and fourth has been made available on the Web by an individual (December, 1996). This of course is by no means an exhaustive list of existing Web development methodologies. Instead, it is meant to be a representation of several of the types that are available.

Each of these methodologies contains somewhat different activities. However, for comparison purposes, in the table an attempt has been made to group the activities in relation to the steps in the traditional life cycle model. This comparison shows that all these Web development methodologies cover nearly the same general activities. One significant difference is the promotion step included in December's (1996) methodology. Promotion is described as announcing the Web site to general and focused subject and keyword outlets. This is a real difference between many public (versus Intranet) Web-based applications and traditional information systems. Web applications typically are not built at the request of a specific audience; therefore, the application must be marketed or advertised if the goal is to get potential customers to visit the site (Vidgen, 1998).

It seems clear that there is a role for methodologies in Web development. The nature of that role, however, will continue to evolve as the technology and the uses of that technology evolve over time.

The Future of Web Development

There are no signs indicating a slowing in the proliferation of Web applications. As the importance of Web-based information systems grows, organizations will increasingly seek to formalize and improve the development of these applications. In particular, the growing complexity of Web applications addressing database connectivity, transaction processing, adaptive systems, and integration with legacy systems is likely to require more formalized methodologies. It is therefore essential that we understand how these applications are developed, and what types of methods, tools, and techniques are used or are needed to support this process. Continuing research is needed to bring together the knowledge and experiences of Web developers in order to create and evaluate methods, tools, and techniques for this changing environment.

In particular, it is the tools and techniques that are most likely to be different in the Web environment. Entity-relationship diagrams may still be used for designing databases. But more linear process modeling tools, such as flowcharting and data flow diagramming, don't fit nicely with the non-linear, dynamic nature of many Web site designs. New tools are needed to document page designs and linkages between pages and applications. Templates for these are beginning to appear in documentation tools such as Visio and in modeling languages such as UML (Booch, *et al.*, 1998). It may also be that techniques from the graphic design area will be useful additions to the toolkit of the Web application designer. More work is needed to identify which tools are most useful in which contexts.

Conclusion

The nature of Web development is changing the development context. The development activities and processes in Web application development differ from those used in traditional systems development. The individuals involved in Web development are also likely to be different. Web application developers are likely to be non-IS professionals working outside of the structure of the IS department. Currently, most are working without any type of formal guidelines or methodologies. Few existing tools or techniques are used. Web developers are inventing their own informal methods on the fly, with little evaluation or sharing of information.

Although Web application development appears to be a more unstructured, creative process than is traditional systems development, there is still a need for tools and techniques to support the development process. Changes in the World Wide Web infrastructure and in Web development tools continue to make it easier and faster to provide more powerful Web applications to a larger audience. As Web applications take over more of the role of traditional information systems, and as new uses are found for Web applications, there will be a greater need for guidelines and methodologies to support and control the development process.

References

Bakke, B. (1998). The Intranet development strategy. Information Age, Inc. Retrieved September 17, 1998 from the World Wide Web: *http://www.informationage.com/article.htm*.

Balasubramanian, V. & Bashian, A. (1998). Document management and Web technologies: Alice marries the Mad Hatter. *Communications of the ACM*, **41** (7), 107-115.

Booch, G., Rumbaugh, J., & Jacobson, I. (1998). *The Unified Modeling Language User Guide*, Addison Wesley Longman Inc.

Conger, S. & Mason R. (1998*). Planning and Designing Effective Web Sites*, Course Technology, Cambridge MA.

December, J. (1996). Web Development Methodology. Retrieved September 17, 1998 from the World Wide Web: *http://www.december.com/present/webweave.html*.

Dennis, A. (1998) Lessons from three years of Web development. *Communications of the ACM*, 41 (7), 112-113.

Digital Focus (1998). Digital Focus Methodology. Retrieved September 17, 1998 from the World Wide Web: *http://www.digitalfocus.com/valid.html*.

Fitzgerald, B. (1994). The systems development dilemma: whether to adopt formalized systems development methodologies or not. In W. Baits (Ed.), *Proceedings of Second European Conference on Information Systems* (pp. 691-706). Nijenrode University Press.

Hardy, C., Thompson, J., & Edwards, H. (1995). The use, limitations and customization of structured systems development methods in the United Kingdom. *Information and Software Technology*, 37 (9), 467-477.

"In Search of the Perfect Market," *The Economist*, May 10, 1997, 3-6.

Network Wizards (1999). Internet Domain Survey, January 1999. Retrieved March 5, 1999 from the World Wide Web: *http://www.nw.com*.

Neubarth, M. (1996). Let's go to the videotape. *Internet World*, January, p. 8.

Russo, N. & Graham, B. (in press). A first step in developing a web application design methodology: Understanding the environment. In N. Jayaratna & A.T. Wood-Harper (Eds.), *Methodologies for Developing and Managing Emerg-*

ing Technology-Based Information Systems: Proceedings of the Sixth Conference of the British Computer Society's Information Systems Methodologies Specialist Group. London: Springer-Verlag.

Russo, N., Hightower, R., & Pearson, J. (1996). The failure of methodologies to meet the needs of current development environments. In N.Jayaratna & B. Fitzgerald (Eds.), *Lessons Learned from the Use of Methodologies: Proceedings of the Fourth Conference of the British Computer Society's Information Systems Methodologies Specialist Group* (pp. 387-394). Swindon: BCS Publications.

Russo, N. & Misic, M. (1998). Web applications: A whole new world of systems development? In M. Khosrowpour (Ed.), *Effective Utilization and Management of Emerging Technologies: Proceedings of the Information Resources Management Association 1998 International Conference* (pp. 843-844). Hershey, PA: Idea Group Publishing.

Russo, N., Wynekoop, J. & Walz, D. (1995). The use and adaptation of system development methodologies. In M. Khosrowpour (Ed.), *Managing Information & Communications in a Changing Global Environment: Proceedings of the Information Resources Management Association International Conference* (p. 162). Hershey, PA: Idea Group Publishing.

Vidgen, R. (forthcoming). Using the Multiview2 framework for Internet-based information systems development. In N. Jayaratna and A.T. Wood-Harper (Eds.), *Methodologies for Developing and Managing Emerging Technology-Based Information Systems: Proceedings of the Sixth Conference of the British Computer Society's Information Systems Methodologies Specialist Group.* London: Springer-Verlag.

Chapter 3

Planning for Effective Web-Based Commerce Application Development

Ming-te Lu
Lingnan University, Hong Kong

W.L. Yeung
Lingnan University, Hong Kong

Abstract

An ever-increasing number of businesses have established Web sites to engage in commercial activities today, forming the so-called Web-based commerce. However, careful planning and preparation are needed for those businesses to achieve their intended purposes with this new channel of distribution. This chapter proposes a framework for planning effective Web-based commerce application development based on prior research in hypermedia and human-computer interfaces, and recent research on Web-based commerce. The framework regards Web application development as a type of software development projects. At the onset, the project's social acceptability is investigated. Next, system feasibility is carried out. If the proposed project is viable, its Web-page interface is examined both from the functionality, contents, and navigability points of view. The use of the framework will contribute to more effective Web-based commerce application development.

Introduction

The Internet user population has seen tremendous growth in recent years. According to the International Data Corporation (IDC), the number of Web surfers has increased to almost 100 million by the end of 1998 and will reach 320 million by 2002 (IT Daily, 1998). The number of online shoppers on the Web will also expand from 18 million in 1997 to over 128 million in 2002. With both an increase in the number of Web shoppers and an anticipated increase in transaction volume, IDC estimated that Web-based commerce will reach more than US$400 billion by 2002. On the other hand, the Forrester Report (Kadison *et al*, 1998) forecasted that U.S. online retailers would generate US$4.8 billion in revenue in 1998 and that the figure would surge to US$17 billion in 2001. Though predictions vary, the rapidly increasing trend of Web-based commerce is apparent.

Many factors have been cited to support the claim that the Web has the potential of becoming a powerful new distribution channel for businesses; however, the work-leisure tradeoff may play the single most important role in the economics of retail surfing (Meeker and Pearson, 1997). In the U.S., the median number of hours worked per week rose from 40.6 in 1973 to 50.6 in 1995; Also, the time devoted to leisure activities has fallen from 26.2 hours per week to 19.2 hours. The increasing number of dual-earner households has also resulted in the decline of the overall family leisure time. This same phenomenon also holds true for other developed and developing nations. Since the Web-based commerce has the potential of cutting down the "main-tenance" portion of the average family's lifestyle, it is predicted that it will become a major way of shopping for many in the future.

With the great potential of Web-based commerce, many businesses have established Web sites to promote and market their products and services and to engage in all aspects of the Web-based commerce. However, no compre-hensive framework is available to help them plan for an effective Web-based commerce application development. This chapter proposes such a frame-work in order for businesses to better achieve their objectives in launching Web-based applications and to engage in Web-based commerce. After the Introduction, the Background section includes a review of the literature on hypermedia development and human-computer interface together with recent research on Web-based commerce. Next, a framework for planning Web-based commerce application development is presented, followed by a discussion on some future trends. Lastly, the Conclusion section provides final remarks on this chapter.

Background

Since Web pages employ hyperlinks and multimedia technology, they can be considered as a type of distributed multimedia hyperdocuments. Thus, previous research in hypermedia is applicable to Web application development and design. Hypermedia research generally addresses the following aspects of hyperdocuments: their user acceptability, their usability, and other quality measures (or metrics). While user acceptability is often associated with the design of the user interface, it can be generalized to the project level when an entire Web-based application is considered. Usability encompasses a wide area of research; one particular focus considered here is on the structural analysis of a hyperdocument to reflect its navigability. The equivalence of software quality models has been applied to the quality of a hyperdocument.

On the other front, online transaction processing systems (OLTP) were developed in the 1970s and 80s so that clients and customers could use terminals or special point-of-sales (POS) devices to complete transactions directly with businesses marketing goods and services. Examples include: airline reservation systems, special order entry systems, and ATMs. The nature of these systems has many similarities to Web-based commerce systems; thus, most of the human-computer interface design factors for the former may be applicable to the latter.

In recent years, due to the globalization of software market, designing interfaces for international users with different cultural backgrounds has received increasing attention from software developers and researchers. This area of research is generally referred to as international human-computer interfaces. Some of the considerations faced by international human-computer interface design are not unlike those of Web-page interface.

Key researches in the above areas that may be helpful to Web-based commerce application development and design are presented.

System Acceptability

At the project level, hyperdocument development may be considered as a special type of software development. Several frameworks or models have been proposed at this level for effective hyperdocument development. For example, Nielsen (1993, pp. 23-37; 1995, pp. 279-285) provided a framework for the so-called system acceptability for hyperdocuments. In this framework, hyperdocument acceptability is viewed as a combination of social acceptability and practical acceptability. Social acceptability refers to whether the interface is acceptable to the users in the context of the culture of the society in which the users are from; while practical acceptability considers factors such as cost, support, reliability, and compatibility with existing systems, together with the so-called "usefulness" of the interface. Usefulness as defined by Nielsen (1993, pp.23-37; 1995, pp.279-285) is the issue of whether a hypermedia system can achieve its goal. Usefulness is further divided into "utility" and "usability". Utility refers to the functionality of the system; while usability means how well the users can use the functionality in the following respects: easy to learn, efficient to use, easy to remember, few errors and pleasant to use. Usability is a combination of the usability of the underlying hypermedia system engine and the usability of the contents and structure of the hyperdocument information base, and how these two elements fit together. These same concepts are generally transferable to Web-based applications.

Structural Analysis

Along the line of usability, problems created by a hyperdocument's flexible structure and great freedom in browsing have long been recognized. Various attempts have been made to reduce the scope of the problem; for example, structural analysis looks at a hyperdocument's internal structure. Botafogo, Rivlin, and Shneiderman (1992) proposed the use of metrics as part of the structural analysis of hyperdocuments, to provide clear and precise values so that subjectivity is avoided. In addition to the readability metric, an indication of how easily one can read a hyperdocument, which may be a composite of length of words, length of sentences, and the use of passive voice, they developed an array of global and node (page) metrics. The global metrics are related to the structural properties of the directed graph representation of a hyperdocument, while node metrics center on the properties of individual nodes (pages). To capture some notions of complexity and connectedness in a hyperdocument, two global metrics, namely, compactness and stratum were developed.

The compactness metric indicates whether each node can easily reach any other node in a hyperdocument, while stratum metric suggests whether there is an order in which a hyperdocument can be read. A high compactness indicates that each node in the document can readily be reached from any other node; a low compactness indicates insufficient links and that parts of the document may be disconnected. The stratum metric measures the linear ordering of a hyperdocument and is based on the concepts of status and contrastatus defined by Harary (1959) to reveal to what degree the hyperdocument is organized so that some nodes must be read before others. Botafogo, Rivlin and Shneiderman (1992) also defined two node metrics, namely, depth and imbalance. The depth of a node is the distance between that node and the root; nodes that are deep in a hyperdocument may be hard to reach. Imbalanced nodes are those at the bottom of an imbalanced tree. It is apparent that similar structural analyses may also be performed on Web pages in order to assess their usability.

Software Quality Model

Hatzimanikatis, Tsalidis and Christodoulakis (1995) developed a quality model to determine the quality of hyperdocuments based on the Factor-Criteria-Metric hierarchical model in software engineering. First, high-level factors such as readability, maintainability, correctness, integrity, usability and testability, which determine the quality of hyperdocuments, are identified. They specifically singled out readability and maintainability to illustrate the use of the quality model. Readability refers to the degree of difficulty in navigating a hyperdocument, while maintainability measures the difficulty of extending, changing, and correcting the hyperdocument after completion.

Maintainability and readability cannot be measured directly on a hyperdocument but need to be decomposed into lower-level criteria that are measurable attributes of the hyperdocument. Criteria affecting both maintainability and readability may include: size, path complexity, tree impurity, modularity, individual node complexity, coherence, complexity of node contents, simplicity, etc. Next, metrics are developed to provide quantitative values to reflect the attainment of these criteria.

Hatzimanikatis, Tsalidis, and Christodoulakis (1995) suggest a size metric based on the software science concept of a program being a collection of *tokens* that can be classified as either *operands* or *operators* (Halstead, 1977). Keywords that describe nodes and links as well as those that describe the layout of the contents of a node (such as bold, center, etc.) in a hyperdocument may be considered as operators. The contents of nodes, lines of text or graphs, may be considered as operands. A composite formula of operands and operators can be used to represent the *volume* or the size metric of the document. Compactness and stratum metrics developed by Botafogo, Rivlin, and Shneiderman (1992) are cited as possible measures of path complexity among others.

EOS Interface Design

Lu and Song (1987) examined the role of human component in retail business transactions for interface design of extra-organizational systems (EOS) through which the clients of a business may complete transactions unassisted. For example, some of the functions performed by a sales clerk in a retail business transaction may include: providing information on merchandises; providing information on operational policies; personal selling and bargaining; individualized consultations, surveillance; packaging; collecting payments and making changes. They claim that as the level of technology advances, more and more of those functions may be replaced by a machine (i.e., a computer). Yet at the same time, the pace of automation of those functions is affected by the traditional way of life, in other words, habits or culture in a society. Based on the framework of human-dominated to machine-dominated interface continuum, Lu and Song (1987) described the key factors affecting interface design for EOS as follows:

1) Client considerations. The attributes or behavior of the target clients for the EOS should be taken into account for its interface design. These may include the skills in using the terminals, frequency of purchase, the amount of purchase, and the geographic distribution of customers.

2) Products/services considerations. The information content of products or services has an impact on the design of EOS interface. The higher the information content needed by potential clients/customers, the more difficult it is to replace the human component by a machine. These considerations may include the complexity of products/services, stability of products/services, variety of products/services, and value of products/services. As clients/customers become more familiar with the product, the need for information reduces.

3) Control and other considerations. There are ancillary operations in a normal business transaction, e.g., handling and showing merchandise, demonstrating the use of merchandise, surveillance of customers, and personalized consultations. The more a transaction requires these functions, the more difficult it is to automate.

Even though Web-based commerce has different characteristics and interface issues from those of EOS addressed by Lu and Song (1987), many of the basic design principles they proposed are still applicable to Web-based commerce, such as the client and products/services considerations.

International Human-Computer Interface

The area of international human-computer interfaces (del Galdo and Nielsen, 1996; Nielsen, 1990) has received much attention in recent years due to the globalization of the software market. del Galdo and Nielsen (1996) believe that there are three levels at which the issues of international user interface could be addressed (del Galdo and Nielsen, 1996, p. vi). The first level refers to the display and processing of the user's native language, character set, notations, and formats; the second level is about the ability to produce an interface and information that is understandable and usable in the user's language; the third level concerns the creation of an interface that accommodate the user's cultural characteristics and mindset. In other words, to achieve the third level, the interface design has to incorporate the way business is conducted and the way people communicate in the target society. Since Web pages are one kind of man-machine interface, similar considerations are applicable to Web page development.

Web-based Commerce Research

Recently, research on Web-based commerce has called for attention to the importance of better Web-page design in order to improve the look-to-buy ratio for online sales. For it is said that only 20% of the Internet users have made a purchase (Kadison et. al, 1998). The findings of some of those researches are presented below.

In a study of consumer reactions to electronic shopping on the Web, Jarvenpaa and Todd (1997) identified product perceptions, shopping experience, and customer services as factors that have important bearings on consumer behavior. Product perceptions include product variety, price and quality, while shopping experience includes shopping effort, compatibility to traditional shopping, and playfulness (a "fun or frustrating" experience). Customer services refer to responsiveness and tangibility. Responsive merchant provides customers sufficient information in a clear and informative way for purchase decision; tangibility relates to the clarity and visual appeal of information about products/services, or shops in the Web pages. Jarvenpaa and Todd advise that Web sites should be designed in such a way that they will support the way in which customers shop. The design of the site should focus on providing adequate content with tangible product/service descriptions, facilitating goal-directed shopping, making the business' policies clear, and providing mechanisms that make the ordering process straightforward.

Lohse and Spiller (Spiller and Lohse, 1997-98; Lohse and Spiller, 1998) surveyed attributes of Internet retail stores to provide a classification of the strategies pursued in Web-based commerce. Based on their studies, store attributes that influence store traffic and sales may be grouped into the following six categories:

1) Merchandise. These include attributes on the quantity, quality, and variety of products/services offered together with merchandise order information.
2) Service. These include the FAQ section, gift services, company information, feedback section, and others.
3) Promotion. These include frequent-buyer incentives, links to other product-related information sites, extra ads on the Web pages, etc.
4) Convenience. These are features such as store layout, organization features, as well as ease of use.
5) Checkout. These include the convenience, consistency and the length of the checkout process.
6) Store Navigation. These include product search functions, site maps, product indices, and the overall site design and organization.

Lohse and Spiller believe that the growth of Internet retail sales will depend on the interface design issues raised in the above categories.

The quality of a Web site was addressed by Day (1997) as "customer focused" and "customer led". Day divided notion of quality into static quality and dynamic quality. The static quality of a Web site is affected by design elements related to the purpose, content and structure of a Web site, whereas, the dynamic quality is related to customer interactivity and feedback. To ensure Web site quality, Day suggests the following procedure: (1) Identifying our customers; (2) Articulating the site's purpose; (3) Providing relevant content; (4) Creating coherent structures to mirror customers' needs; (5) Arranging visual elements to reflect (1), (2) and (3) above (housestyle); (6) Creating relevant concluding/action points; (7) Delivering the promises we made at the action points.

Concerning a Web site's purpose and content, Day advocates that the purpose should be distinctly clear and have a quantifiable customer-focused measure and that content should be based on an understanding of the target audience and how they behave.

Based on the above prior research in hypermedia, human-computer interface, and more recent research on Web-based commerce, a comprehensive framework for effective Web-based commerce application development and Web page design is formulated next. This framework examines Web-based commerce application development both at the project and at the Web-page design levels. It addresses the social acceptability, system feasibility, and the interface design of the application development with the aim to fulfill the objectives of Web-based commerce for a business. This "from general to specific" approach can be considered as an integration and synthesis of the prior research outcomes presented above.

A Framework for Effective Planning and Design

A framework for developing effective Web-based commerce applications is proposed as an extension of prior research (see Figure 1). This framework regards Web-based commerce applications as a special type of system development projects with specific target user populations on the Internet. Traditionally, the system development life cycle consists of stages such as: planning, feasibility, analysis, specification, design, implementation, and maintenance. The proposed framework addresses mainly the planning, feasibility, and design of Web-based commerce application development. For planning, which involves the proposing, selecting, and prioritizing of an organization's Web-based commerce projects, the framework offers the concept of *social acceptability* to help to screen out unsuitable projects. For feasibility, the framework addresses the economic, technical, operational,

Figure 1: A Framework for Effective Web-based Commerce Application Development

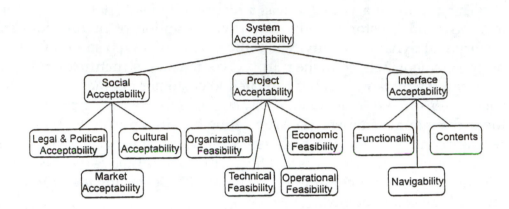

and organizational feasibility of Web-based commerce projects by highlighting several important considerations that are specific to the Web. Finally, for design, the framework focuses on issues peculiar to the hypermedia-based user interface of Web-based applications.

The framework suggests that before the development of a Web-based commerce application begins, its social acceptability should be assessed. In other words, one should ask, "Are the products/services intended for the Web-based commerce application acceptable/viable for the target population in its social context?" Next, the Web-based commerce application development effort is to be scrutinized in the same way as in other system development projects with respect to its economic, technical, operational, and organizational feasibilities. If the development project is judged as worthy of being carried out based on the results of its social acceptability and system feasibility phases, the functionality, contents, and navigability of the Web-page interface will come into play at the design stage.

Social Acceptability

When an organization embarks on a Web-based commerce application project, the project's eventual success hinges on whether its intended products and contents are acceptable by the members of the target population in the context of economic, cultural, legal and political environments of their society. The concept of social acceptability here is broader than the one defined by Nielsen (1993, 23-37; 1995, 279-285) for he was mostly concerned with hypermedia interface issues.

With the Internet's communication capability, technically speaking, the target audience of a Web-based commerce application could be the general public scattered around the world, yet in reality, it is often much smaller due to its social acceptability. Social acceptability may be viewed from market, cultural, legal and political perspectives:

Legal and political acceptability. If the messages, products or services to be promoted or sold on the Internet were prohibited by laws in certain societies, these societies would not be part of the target population for the Web application. Examples may include the sales of liquors, cigarettes, contraceptives, and political sensitive materials in some countries. Web sites engaging in illegal activities may also be censured or prosecuted by law enforcement agencies. Sometimes the products or services may be legal but politically unacceptable or incorrect, the consequences are not only loss of sales but also troubles for the business which publicizes them on the Web. Aalberts, Townsend and Whitman (1998) identified the exposure of Internet businesses to the long-arm jurisdiction of courts in 50 different states of the U.S. as one of the critical legal issues seriously threatening the continual growth of the Internet as a commerce medium. They also suggested some practical considerations that may help an organization plan its Internet presence such as limit the amount of interaction, choose an ISP carefully, and limit access to certain locales. Quelch and Klein (1996) stated that foreign government support and cooperation were critical in determining how the Internet business environment would evolve. Governments may exert influence on Web-based commerce by legislation on external access and internal use of the Internet, and on data security and taxation on transactions. Some of the obstacles put up by a government may practically exclude the country from being part of the target population for a commercial Web site.

Cultural acceptability. Messages, products or services to be promoted on the Web should be acceptable to the members of the target population in view of their ways of life, habits and religious belief. Horwitt (1997) reported that Web commerce in the European community, especially on the consumer side, remained culturally, linguistically, and monetarily fragmented. Companies seeking a continental Web presence faced the challenges to address the diverse preferences, tastes, and customs of different nationalities.

Indeed, key factors for interface design for extra-organizational systems (EOS) considered by Lu and Song (1987) are mostly shaped by the culture of the target population. For example, it would be quite difficult to sell clothing items to people in Hong Kong because sizes have not been standardized, and that they consider street shopping as a form of recreation. On the other hand, it is a good idea to sell grocery items on the Web in Hong Kong (e.g., http://imsp00l.netvigator.com/shopping/wellcome/index.html) because, unlike the U.S., most of the residents do not have cars to carry heavy grocery items home; thus, Web sites promising home delivery would be welcomed. In addition, knowledge of products and services, of course, are often culturally dependent.

Market acceptability. If the messages, products or services can reach a sufficient number of potential interested parties or target customers who have sufficient financial means to make the purchases, then the project is viable from the marketing point of view. According to a recent survey by ActiveMedia (http://www.activemedia.com), the top revenue-generating Web sites were dominated by the major online brands that had wide general appeal, such as books, travel, computers, stocks, auction houses, computer equipment resellers, and entertainment.

A study of the profiles of Web browsers and likely Web commerce customers will lead to some estimates of the size of the potential market. For example, to promote expensive condominiums on the Internet to the vast population in the PRC may not be a good idea, for most of the Internet users are either academics who do not have enough income to be the buyers of those properties or expatriates who may not in a position to acquire those properties. In fact, while the number of Internet users in the PRC may be surging, analysts believe that the lack of credit capacity amongst consumers there may hamper the development of business-to-consumer e-commerce in the country, thus limiting its market acceptability for many products and services (Internetnews.com, November 23, 1998).

Once social acceptability for the intended products or services is affirmed, it means that there would be potential demand for those products or services once they are offered on the Web. It does not mean, however, that the venture would be an economic success; additional investigation and planning are required.

Project Acceptability

Since Web-based commerce application development projects are also a kind of software development project, system feasibility including economic, technical, operational, and organizational feasibility should be evaluated (O'Brien, 1996, pp. 80-82; Whitten, Bentley and Barlow, 1994, pp. 810-831). A Web-based commerce application's acceptability hinges on whether the results of all these feasibility studies are favorable or not.

Economic feasibility. Obviously, one would like to see that perceived benefits such as increased revenue, profits, reduced costs, and other intangible benefits would outweigh the costs of creating and maintaining the Web-based commerce application. Increased revenue and profits can be estimated based on the estimated size of the potential market in the study of the market acceptability. Reduced costs may be estimated by comparing the distribution channel costs with the Web application added. Intangible benefits often derive from better image and exposure to potential customers and improved customer services (Kambil, 1995). When a business embarks on a Web-based commerce application development project, the common mistake is to underestimate the total cost of such a project over time due to the relatively low start-up hardware and software costs. A properly carried out economic feasibility study should include the cost of maintaining the Web pages current over time and the added costs of providing back-end support to online transactions. It has been reported that the annual costs of Web site maintenance may be two to four times the initial launch cost (Bernoff and Ott, 1995).

Technical Feasibility. When considering the technical feasibility, one has to assess it not only from a developer's point of view such as possible difficulties in linking the Web pages with the legacy transactional processing systems, but also from the browser's point of view. For example, including bells and whistles which will not be used by the majority of the target customers, due to their level of technical sophistication and limited capabilities of their PCs, will not only be a waste of resources but will also increase their download time and frustration.

Operational feasibility. It is important to know whether management, employees, customers, suppliers and other parties are willing to support, operate, and use the proposed system. For example, if target customers lack confidence in online payment methods, the likelihood that they will make purchases online will be diminished. To overcome this problem, telephone and fax numbers could be provided so that customers may use the normal purchasing channels. On the other hand, if employees perceive that a proposed Web application will take away their commission income, they may not be enthusiastic about the project; as a consequence, low morale and productivity may result.

Organizational feasibility. The proposed Web site should support the objectives of the organization and its strategic plan with respect to marketing channels of distribution. Some of the questions needed to be asked are: What is its relationship with the existing channels and what channel functions will it carry? (Stern, El-Ansary and Coughlan, 1996, 8-10); Are we reaching the same target market, or are we reaching a different market via the Web? Information obtained from social acceptability study would be helpful here.

Once project acceptability study is concluded with favorable findings, the design and development of the Web pages for the intended products/services may then start; major considerations in this stage are functionality, contents and navigability.

Interface Acceptability

Interface acceptability refers to whether a Web-based commerce application would be useful to browsers/customers in terms of its intended purposes, i.e., to complete the transaction. In other words, does it have the functionalities that would enable them to complete all phases of the shopping experience? Do Web pages provide sufficient information about the products and services being promoted, such as the size, color, materials, and quality? Are Web pages easy and fun to browse and navigate? Key factors that would affect consumer behavior as identified by Jarvenpaa and Todd (1997), such as product perceptions, shopping experience, and customer services, should be paid attention to in the Web page design. In urging online merchants to improve their look-to-buy ratios, a merchant should make sure that the site is fast and easy to navigate, and the checkout speed is increased among others (Kadison et. al., 1998).

Functionality. At the functionality level, a Web site should provide support for product comparison, shopping basket, checkout and payment, inquiry and feedback, and other basic functions; the availability of a secured transaction environment is generally regarded as essential for online trans-actions. Additional functions for differential treatments of repeated or val-ued customers and promotion of special items have been cited as ways to improve sales (Jarvenpaa and Todd, 1997; Kadison, et. al., 1998; Lohse and Spiller, 1998) and should be considered.

Contents. Contents refer to the information provided in the Web pages. Information about a company's history, policies, or background will help customers to know more about with whom they are dealing with and to whom they are sending their credit card information (Fram and Grady, 1995; Spiller and Lohse, 1998). To ensure that products or services are acceptable by the market, information such as production description, price, quality, and product variety should be made clear to potential customers; in addition, information about various customer services will result in positive feelings about responsiveness, tangibility, empathy, assurance, and reliability of the Web site buyers (Jarvenpaa and Todd, 1997).

Navigation. Ease of navigation is a key factor to increase the look-to-buy ratio for frustrated shoppers leave sites that are difficult to navigate (Kadison et. al., 1998). Store layout, and Web-page organization should have browsers in mind. General help or search functions should be made available for error recovery and for searching for particular items. Shopping and checkout processes should be simple, straightforward, and short. Site maps, product indices and consistent navigation links will all help reduce the pain of navigation.

In terms of easy to read, it is especially important for the Web-based commerce application developers to design an interface for the target popu-lation in the context of their culture. Even though currently Web pages are predominantly English and that English is presumed to be the business

Table 1: Interface Acceptability for Amazon.com

	Functionality
Product comparison	Book titles can be browsed by subjects. For any particular title, similar titles are brought to the attention together with reviews written by critics and other customers. Even the shopping cart page shows some recommendations.
Shopping basket	The conventional shopping basket (cart) metaphor is employed.
Checkout & payment	Apart from checking out with a shopping cart, customers can register with Amazon.com once with their credit card details; after that, all purchases can be done by simple clickings.
Secure transactions	Amazon.com uses SSL and Netscape Secure Commerce Server for handling transactions. Its Safe Shopping Guarantee protects customers from credit card frauds.
Inquiry and feedback	Customers can contact Amazon.com by e-mail or by a toll-free phone number (Canada and US only).
	Contents
Company background Security policies	The "About Amazon" section introduces the company's history and management team and provides elaborate information for shareholders and potential investors. Security and privacy policies are clearly stated online.
Product information	Book titles are furnished with reviews by critics and customers with ratings.
Customer services	Customer services are well explained while customers can always send an e-mail for inquiry.
	Navigation
Help	The "Help Desk" section, which is accessible from every page, lists help information under various topics for easy referencing.
Search	Keyword, author, title, and subject searches are provided.
Site map	None, all pages are well linked up.
Language	English. There is a separate German Web site for German books.

language of the world, to reach the majority of the potential customers worldwide necessitates the development of international interfaces for Web applications. A good example of a Web site that targets populations in the Americas and Europe is Piece Unique (http://www.pieceunique.com/class.html) which has translation capabilities for English to French, German, Italian, Spanish and Portuguese.

The minimum requirement for a Web application user interface should be that the interface and information is understandable and usable in the user's language. The goal, however, should be the creation of an interface that accommodates the user's cultural characteristics, mindset and habits. Many Web sites in the U.S. often ignore this and ask users for states and zip codes in their addresses; when their input is rejected, the users simply give up.

Amazon.com's Web site (http://www.amazon.com), "the ultimate example of online shopping" according to the *PC Magazine*, manifests many positive attributes described above for interface acceptability (see Table 1).

Validation of the Framework

For most of the system development projects, it is often recommended that users of the system be involved in the design of the new system. The involvement of system users would ensure that their points of view are incorporated into the new system and that the system's eventual acceptability is enhanced. Prototyping, one of such approaches, requires that system design goes through an iterative process during which users would provide feedback for subsequent modifications and refinements of the system design. For any system that will be used by personnel external to an organization, pilot studies and tests are often carried out to test the system's usability before the full-scale implementation is started.

For a Web-based commerce application, the validation for the framework proposed requires a similar if somewhat different approach. During the investigation of the social acceptability, it is important that the concept for the products, services, and/or contents is evaluated by representatives of the target population or customers in form of a focus group. For the project acceptability study, personnel in different departments of the organization should be involved. In other words, a Web-based commerce application should not be developed by a small group of technical or marketing personnel only. To understand the full impact of such an application, personnel in accounting, human resources, sales and other relevant departments should also be involved. For testing interface acceptability, in addition to a pilot study in which the Web pages would be accessed and appraised by a representative group of the target population, the Web pages can also be assessed objectively by quantitative measures or metrics which reflect their functionality, contents, and navigability.

For example, Spiller and Lohse (1997-98) come up with 35 descriptive measures or variables of online apparel stores. These 35 variables are grouped into Merchandise, Service, Promotion, Other Store Variables, and Interface variables. Where Merchandise would include: (1) The number of different products; (2) The number of hierarchies between home page and product page; (3) The total number of lines providing information about guarantees and the ordering process. Service information includes whether the store featured any gift services, had the FAQ's and feedback section; others include the text length on "end" product pages, phone number/e-mail of sales representatives, etc. Promotion information may include the availability of frequent-buyer schemes, What's New section, links to other sites, extra banner ads on the pages. Other Store Variables include the availability of the search or browse functions, product and/or site indices, and the number of modes to shop the store (by brand, price, and department). Interface Variables include the number of products on end-product page, availability of menu bars on all pages, background color, help on interface usage, page length of the home page, etc.

In addition, there are third-party organizations that provide objective assessment of a Web site. For example, Web Site Garage (http://www.websitegarage.com) assesses a Web site's browser compatibility, load time, dead link, link popularity, spelling and HTML design. WebTrends (http://webtrends.com) together with Web hosting companies provide user profile by regions, most requested pages and frequencies, top referencing sites, etc. Of course, the ultimate validation of the framework is the degree of success with respect to customer traffic and sales.

The application of the above framework allows Web-based commerce application developers to screen out projects with low potentials and concentrate on those with high potentials. The framework would also allow developers to evaluate a project in a systematic and comprehensive way in which effectiveness issues about the project viability are addressed first before efficiency issues associated with Web page design are. As a result, the effectiveness of the developed Web-based commerce application can be assured.

Future Trends

The social acceptability ensures that the messages, products and services to be presented are compatible with the living habits, the culture and social system of the target population. A study of the social acceptability may lead to a better understanding of the size and the attributes of the target market resulting in a more precise estimate of the potential market for the products and services. Further research in this area may identify the attributes of products or services that are suitable for Web-based commerce for different segments of the market.

Since the Web is still a relatively new technology, new functionalities would emerge in the future. Today's emerging technologies such as 3D images and virtual reality may become common scenes in the future. It could mean that in the future Web pages could provide more realistic images of products or services, and the differences between shopping in the real world and on the Web could be substantially narrowed necessitating different paradigms for Web-based commerce.

In terms of usability for hypermedia, Botafogo, Rivlin and Shneiderman (1992) cited three different fronts in an attempt to solve the problem of "lost in hyperspace": user interface, textual analysis, and structural analysis. Improvements in user interface include help menu, multiple windows, maps, tours or path mechanisms; textual analysis is often carried out by the hyperdocument authors using software aids to statistically analyze word frequencies in a document so as to index documents by significant terms; structural analysis gives a better understanding of the hyperdocument's overall structure. Further research to improve Web navigability may also be conducted in these three directions by software vendors and Web page developers.

With the increasing importance of Web-based commerce, more corporate resources are being spent on the creation of more effective Web pages that are easier to read and subjectively pleasing. As a consequence, third party agencies, not unlike the ad agencies, which have the expertise in the field, will thrive. These agencies will be quite different from the individuals and parties which are currently helping organizations design Web pages for these new agencies will conduct tasks associated with market assessment and system feasibility as outlined in the proposed framework and will emphasize the contents and structures of the Web pages with technical sophistication taken for granted.

Conclusion

The framework presented in this chapter enables an organization to examine the viability of a commercial Web application development project before it is launched. First, its social acceptability is assessed from the legal and political, cultural, and market perspectives. It ensures that the products/ services under consideration have a real market and that the messages to be disseminated on the Web are easily and clearly understood by the target population. Next, project acceptability is carried out which includes an examination of organization, economic, technical, and operational feasibilities, similar to what other system development project proposals are subject to. Subsequently, issues for Web-page interface design such as functionality, contents and navigability are critically examined. The use of quantitative measures or metrics is recommended for interface design bench-marking.

The strength of this framework lies in that design considerations can be viewed in the proper perspectives to ensure that business purposes are achieved.

References

Aalberts, R.J., Townsend, A.M., Whitman, M.E. (1998). The threat of long-arm jurisdiction to electronic commerce. *Communications of ACM*, 41(12), pp.15-20

Bernoff, J. and Ott, A. (1995). People and Technology: What Web Sites Cost. *The Forrester Report*, December.

Botafogo, R. A., Rivlin, E., and Shneiderman, B. (1992). Structural Analysis of Hypertexts: Identifying Hierarchies and Useful Metrics. *ACM Transactions on Information Systems*, 10(2), April, 142-180.

Day, A. (1997). A Model for Monitoring Web Site Effectiveness. *Internet Research: Electronic Networking Applications and Policy*, 7(2), 109-115.

del Galdo, E. M. and Nielsen J. (1996). *International User Interfaces*, John Wiley & Sons, Inc., New York.

Fram, E. H. and Grady, D. B. (1995). Internet Buyers-Will the Surfers Become Buyers? *Direct Marketing*, October, 58(6), 63-65.

Halstead, Maurice H. (1977). *Elements of Software Science*, Elsevier North Holland, New York.

Harary, F. (1959). Status and Contrastatus. *Sociometry*, 22, 23-43.

Hatzimanikatis, A. E., Tsalidis, C. T., and Christodoulakis, D. (1995). *Software Maintenance: Research and Practice*, 7, 77-90.

Horwitt, E. (1997) Europe: Cultural, language barriers challenge the Continent. *Computerworld*, pp. 21-23.

IT Daily. (1998). 3, August 19, 392.

Jarvenpaa, S. L. and Todd, P. A. (1997). Consumer Reactions to Electronic Shopping on the World Wide Web. *International Journal of Electronic Commerce*, Winter, 1(2), 59-88.

Kadison, M. L., Weisman, D. E., Modahl, M., Lieu, K. C., and Levin K. (1998). Online Retail Strategies. *The Forrester Report*, 1(1), April 1998.

Kambil, A. (1995). Electronic Commerce: Implications of the Internet for Business Practice and Strategy. *Business Economics*, 30(4), October, 27-33.

Lohse, G. L. and Spiller, P. (1998). Electronic Shopping. *Communications of the ACM*, 41(7), 81-87.

Lu, M. (1997). A Multi-Dimensional Study of WWW Use in Hong Kong. *Proceedings of The Pacific Asia Conference on Information Systems' 97*, April.

Lu, M. and Song, J. H. (1987). "Key Design Factors for Extra-Organizational Systems," *International Journal of Information Management*, 7, 159-166.

Meeker, M. and Pearson, S. (1997). *The Internet Retailing Report*, Morgan Stanley, May 28.

Nielsen, J. (1990). *Designing User Interfaces for International Use*. North Holland, Amsterdam: Elsevier Science Publisher.

Nielsen, J. (1993). *Usability Engineering*. San Diego, CA: Academic Press Inc.

Nielsen, J. (1995). *Multimedia and Hypertext: The Internet and Beyond*. Cambridge, MA: Academic Press Professional.

O'Brien, J. A. (1996). *Management Information Systems*. Burr Ridge, IL: Irwin.

Quelch, J. A. and Klein, L. R. (1996). The Internet and International Marketing. *Sloan Management Review*, Spring, 60-75.

Spiller, P. and Lohse, G. L. (1998). A Classification of Internet Retail Stores. *International Journal of Electronic Commerce*, Winter, 2(2), 29-56.

Stern, L. W., El-Ansary, A. I., and Coughlan, A. T. (1996). *Marketing Channels*, 5th ed. N.J.: Prentice Hall.

Whitten, J. L., Bentley, L. D., and Barlow, V. M. (1994). *Systems Analysis and Design Methods*. Burr Ridge, IL, Irwin.

Note: This chapter is based on a previous article: Ming-te Lu and W.L. Yeung. "A framework for effective commercial Web application development," *Internet Research*, 8 (2), 1998, pp. 166-173.

Chapter 4

Managing Web Technologies Acquisition, Utilization and Organization Change: Understanding Sociocognitive Processual Dynamics

Mathew J. Klempa
Information Systems Consultant

Abstract

This chapter presents a perspective on web technologies acquisition, utilization, organization change and transformation grounded in Gidden's theory of structuration, i.e., a contextualist analysis. A contextualist analysis is processually based, emergent, situational, and holistic, marrying both theory and practice. This chapter's paradigm affords a substantive analytical tool to the practitioner for understanding and managing not only web-based IT acquisition, utilization and organization change, but all IT-based recursive, organization changes and transformations.

Organization change associated with IT acquisition and utilization is posited as concomitantly necessary. Organization change is recursive, dynamic, multilevel, and nonlinear, i.e., an "enacted" environment. Ever present organization opposing values are treated dialectically, i.e. as paradox, operating simultaneously. The nature of the resolution of such paradox enabled/ inhibits reframing, i.e., organization transformation and change. The paradigm presented defines an organization change continuum, delineating four organization responses to contradiction and paradox.

The chapter explicates organization culture and organization learning as systemic, multiplicative metaforce underpinnings of organization change and sociocognitively-based, recursive, structurational processual dynamics.

The chapter discusses use of the IT acquisition and utilization paradigm for organization diagnosis as well as customization of organization change interventions. The chapter suggests further typologically-based research venues.

Introduction

The truest sayings are paradoxical — Lao-Tse, 6th Century B.C.

In what has become a familiar mantra, business executives are exhorted to jump aboard the WWW bandwagon. A blizzard of "normative" articles promulgate the WWW as the means to deliver competitive gains, speed up business transactions, increase customer satisfaction, deliver superior quality, and lead to improved profitability.

> If there is one thing management can count on in today's world, it's another person proclaiming the miracle that is the World Wide Web...a whole new arena for organizations to play in .... The ... opportunities are endless for creative firms willing to redefine ... who they are (Griffith and Palmer, 1999, p. 3,9)

Successive generations of information technology (IT) since 1950 witnessed a halving of the price of computing every 2-3 years, with concomitantly increased functionality — input/output modalities, storage, processing, communications, and migration from mainframe to distributed architectures, e.g., client server (Brynjolfsson, 1993). The United State's expenditures, 2.8% of GDP on IT, is highest worldwide. Notwithstanding such aggregate IT investment, price performance, and increased functionality, predicted business transformations, i.e., increased productivity and indirect benefits from IT, have not been realized (Morton, 1991). Labeled the productivity paradox, mismanagement of information and technology is cited as contributing to the productivity paradox (Strassman, 1997), (Rai, et.al., 1997), (Brynjolfsson, 1993), (Hayashi, 1997). Technological change has outstripped individual and organization rates of change (Morton, 1991), (Kanter, 1988).

> Most Fortune 500 companies are actively trying to figure out the benefits of Internet technology. The biggest challenge for companies involved...isn't the technology — it's changing the corporate culture. It requires an organization to be bold... (Haber, 1997, p. 112)
> What I want to see from computers is not newer and fancier technology ... but tools that can release the creativity ... of ... people (Hayashi, 1997, p. 47)

These organization change "gauntlets," i.e., "be able to redefine who you are," "be able to release creativity of people," "be able to change corporate culture" and "the organization needs to be bold" are set against a backdrop of organization thinking and practice dominated by mass production, bureaucracy, routinization, and control. The prior organization lens, focusing on stability, required uniformistic, hierarchical, and quantitative thinking. Planned change and punctuated equilibrium organization change models prevailed.

The new organization prism focuses attention to the expressive, ideational aspects of collective organization consciousness. This prism involves exploring, learning, and innovating, thus requiring heterogenetic, interactionist, and qualitative thinking. Organization change and transformation are the *sine qua non* in the management of web technologies acquisition and utilization.

> ...the unprecedented nature of advanced information technology and its complex interaction effects ... will generate contradictions which undermine organizational arrangements in unanticipated ways. In such contradictory developments, nonlinear change is possible ... and organizational properties may be transformed so as to be substantially different from those that existed before... (Orlikowski, 1991, p. 13).

> ... the open-ended nature of many new technologies ... assumes ... user construction of capabilities and effects (Orlikowski, 1996, p. 64).

> ... the most interesting practical questions concern change...managers want to know the best way to change organizations .... the study of change may be a good opportunity to do research that is useful both theoretically and practically (Lawler, et.al., 1985, p. 17).

These observations are more striking and pronounced in the context of web-based IT. Effective acquisition and utilization of web-based IT will likely require that substantial knowledge barriers be overcome. Efforts to transform organizations with web-based IT may meet resistance, associated with conflicting, i.e., competing values. Integral to the understanding and managing of organization change and transformation is both recognition and treatment of organization values *dialectically*, i.e., as competing values simultaneously present and equally operative within the organization.

This chapter explicates a competing values (CV) framework (Figure 3), an understructure to human knowledge (Quinn and McGrath, 1985). The CV framework, in turn, undergirds this chapter's paradigm, embodying the four paradox-based typologies (Figure 1), whose metaphysical bases are well grounded in extant organization theory, i.e., organization innovation, organization change, individual creativity, social cognition, and sociology of knowledge literatures. The paradigm addresses a deficit in prior research conceptualizations by focusing on organizations as structures of knowledge and systems of interpretation. The paradigm provides a robust, comprehensive and systemic perspective on organization change and web-based IT acquisition and utilization, previously applied[1] to IT diffusion (Klempa, 1993, 1994a, 1994b), management of technology and innovation (Klempa, 1995b), (Klempa, 1995, October), and (BPR) business process reengineering (Klempa, 1998). This paradigm delineates the continuum of organization change in response to contradiction and paradox, shown in Figure 2.

The social and technological domains are inherently intertwined, and the fusion ... by information technology makes their disconnection even more untenable" (Orlikowski, 1991, p. 35).

... a sociocognitive approach to information technology ... an understanding of people's interpretations of a technology is critical to understanding their interaction with it. To interact with technology, people make sense of it, and in this sense-making process, they develop assumptions, expectations, and knowledge of the technology which serve to shape subsequent actions toward it ... by examining these ... we can gain much insight into how technologies are developed and used and change (Orlikowski and Gash, 1994, p. 175).

A sociocognitive-based paradigm captures both orientations as well as situations simultaneously. This paradigm (Figure 1) informs the practitioner's breadth and depth of understanding of both individuals' and groups' interpretations of, and interactions with IT, by explicating:

- WHAT—two systemic organization metaforces, organization culture and organization learning, underpinning organization change processes and IT acquisition and utilization processual dynamics .
- HOW—these systemic organization metaforces multiplicatively interact synergistically, to enable or inhibit leveraging of organization change and IT acquisition and utilization.
- WHY—the recursive dynamics of organization culture, organization learning, the organization frame of reference, and reframing, essential in the dynamic of organization change and IT acquisition and utilization.
- WHY—organization resistance to change as a nonisomorphic, autopoetic[1] response, thus enabling customized, rather than monolithic organization change interventions

This chapter's paradigm (Figure 1) informs the practitioner's understanding of:

- Web-based IT propensity

Figure 1: IT acquisition and utilization paradigm

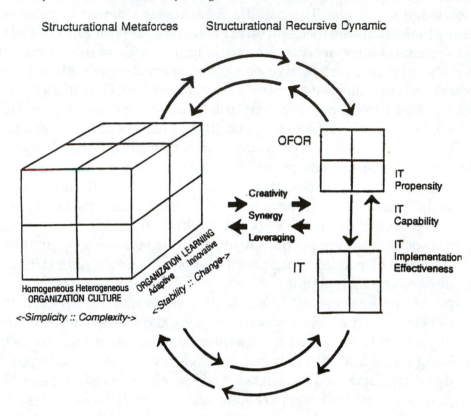

Figure 2. Organization responses to contradiction and paradox

Homogeneous Adaptive	Homogeneous Innovative	Heterogeneous Adaptive	Heterogeneous Innovative
Isolation	*Accommodation*	*Dominance*	*Transcendence*

<———————————————————————————————————————>

Homeostatic Organization (Schismogenesis)

Morphogenetic Organization (Transcendence)

Organization Change:

Beta Change

<————————————————————>

Tectonic Change

<—————————————————————————————————————>

Gamma Change

<——————————>

- Web-based IT capability
- Web-based IT implementation effectiveness

Web-based IT propensity includes the organization's environmental awareness, information gathering, and conceptualizing antecedent to Web-based IT decision making. Web-based IT capability encompasses decision analysis of the situation and solutions, as well as implementation analysis and considerations. Web-based IT implementation effectiveness includes all technical and organization operational implementation aspects.

Chapter objectives of interest to the researcher include:

- to explicate the centrist role of paradox in innovation and organization change
- to explicate four paradox-based typologies well grounded in multiple literatures
  - organization culture
  - organization learning
  - organization frame of reference
  - IT-enabled core :: linkages organization change
- to explicate organization responses to paradox, defining a homeostatic :: morphogenetic organization change continuum, identifying beta, tectonic, and gamma organization change
- to explicate the CV framework
- to focus attention to typological inquiry, a processually-based, holistic inquiry research genre.
- to propose the sociocognitive grid as a nomothetic research tool, for use concomitantly with idiographic techniques.

Background

Prior IT acquisition and utilization research is characterized by seemingly inconstant findings, inattention to construction and use of coherent theoretical frameworks, and inattention to applicable theory about organizations. More particularly, prior IT acquisition and utilization research is characterized by:

- A variance theory-basing
- Taxonomically-based research
- Mixing and crossing levels of analysis
- Linear, phased-process / incomplete models

Variance theory-basing

Multiple researchers have identified the dominance of variance-orientated prior research Markus and Robey (1988), Orlikowski (1992), Orlikowski and Robey (1991), and Orlikowski and Baroudi (1991). Orlikowski and

Baroudi's sample of published information systems research found approximately 90% were one-time, cross-sectional, rather than *processual*. Variance theories of IT acquisition and utilization posit an objectivist, deterministic relationship, both necessary and sufficient, between various IT acquisition and utilization antecedents as well as outcomes. Both antecedent and outcome variables are assumed as objective, i.e., capable of being represented by researcher-devised constructs and measures. Levels of outcome likewise are assumed predictable from levels of the contemporaneous antecedent variables. Such invariant relationships are too stringent for social phenomena, providing minimal possibility for purposive human action.

Taxonomically-based research

Typologies are differentiated from classification systems, i.e., taxonomies, which have clear differentia, are mutually exclusive, collectively exhaustive, and nonvacuous (Doty and Glick, 1994). Rather, typologies consist of ideal types. Each ideal type in a typology represents an organization composite that might exist. Actual organizations might *resemble* an ideal type but should not be *assigned* to one of the ideal types in the typology. Ideal types richly describe complex organization forms, emphasizing complex processes and associated organization outcomes. Since ideal types are complex phenomena, are described in multiple dimensions, reflect complex patterning of organization attributes, and include synergistic effects, the concomitant use of typologies in structurationally-based paradigms is both singularly appropriate and desirable. The four paradox-based typologies presented herein, anchored in the CV framework and additionally well grounded extant organization theory, constitute a beginning step toward an improved understanding of IT-enabled organization change and transformation processual dynamics.

Mixing and crossing levels of analysis

Prior IT acquisition and utilization variance-based research, both objectivist and subjectivist, researched IT acquisition and utilization antecedents at differing levels, i.e., individual, group, and the organization, e.g., Damanpour (1991), Carter (1984), Meyer and Goes (1988), Lewis and Siebold (1993), Leonard-Barton (1987, 1988), Dunegan, Tierney and Duchon (1992), and Saleh and Wang (1993). Few such researches are purposefully designed as intraorganizational, i.e., mixing individual, group, and organizational levels within the same study. The paucity of prior multilevel intraorganizational research has resulted in seemingly inconsistent findings, appearing fragmented and inconclusive, in syntheses of such research.

Linear, phased-process / incomplete models

Most prior research about organization change has been ahistorical, aprocessual, and acontextual, focusing on a "change episode", e.g., an organization's acquisition of a particular IT, rather than the *processual dynamics of changing* (Pettigrew, 1985). Additionally, prior research calling for processual models of innovation and organization change, generally employs stage (phase) models (Meyer and Goes, 1988), (Rogers, 1988), (Gersick, 1991), and (Lundberg, 1985). Such models assume stages can be identified, are not simultaneous and occur within a prescribed sequence (Pelz, 1983). In reaching an "equilibrium" state, opposing organization values, e.g., stability :: change[2] (seen as *dichotomies*) are resolved, i.e., a compromise. Large precipitating pressures and "triggering" events disturb this *static* equilibrium. Resolution (through compromise of the dichotomy), in favor of stability, results in a new, static equilibrium. The tendency to define away contradiction, i.e., to be schismogenic[3], typifies Western thinking. The treatment of competing values as dichotomies precludes capturing the "give and take" of innovation and organization change processes (Kanter, 1988).

More recent research, e.g., Cameron and Quinn (1988) provides an alternative paradigm concerning such competing values, i.e., a *dialectic*, embodying Janusian[4] thinking, in which two contradictory tensions are equally operative, i.e, simultaneous antithesis. Such a dialectic perspective enables a dynamic, recursive and multilevel processual dynamics view, i.e., structuration, of organization change and IT acquisition and utilization.

Pelz (1983), Kline(1985), Quinn (1985), and Tornatzky and Kline (1982) suggest that IT acquisition and utilization processes are better captured by the use of complex, nonlinear, recursive models, e.g., how microlevel interactions impact macrolevel interactions and vice versa. Microlevel tasks are accomplished by individuals and groups, within the context of macrolevel conditions. Such a person-situation interaction both influences and is influenced by, antecedent conditions as well as the current situation. IT acquisition and utilization processually-based paradigms should address intentions and consequences at multiple levels, including the organization, group, and individual, in order to address a complete picture of IT acquisition and utilization and organization change (Frost and Egri, 1991). Such a perspective marries two pervasive research literatures: behaviorally-based research on individual creativity and organizationally-based research on organization change, as suggested by Amabile (1988), Terborg (1981), Woodman, Sawyer and Griffin (1993), Coleman (1986) and Markus and Robey (1988).

This chapter considers IT within an "enacted" environment (Weick, 1979), i.e., IT is developed and used within social and historical circumstances, its form and functioning reflecting these circumstances. Such contextual analysis (Pettigrew, 1985) sets forth how structure and context are mobilized by individuals and groups seeking to obtain outcomes, e.g., IT acquisition and utilization. Central to IT acquisition and utilization is *individual and organization change*, occurring in either or both of the material and organization context, which involves altering of relationships and previous ways of doing things. Such cognition-based social process of change involves politics, trust, and time, each of which assists individuals, groups, and organizations in coming to terms with competing values and change (Frost, 1994). Thus, integral to this paradigm are the ever-present dialectical points of tension and instability in organizations, and how they interact to enable / inhibit IT acquisition, utilization, organization change and transformation.

Paradox and Organization Processual Dynamics

Dualities in organizations and paradox

Paradox focuses on organization opposing forces, i.e., competing values, at multiple levels. Paradox involves contradictory, mutually exclusive elements that are present, operate equally and simultaneously, i.e., a synchronic duality (Purser and Pasmore, 1992). Multiple research such of that of (Quinn and Cameron, 1988), (Ford and Backoff, 1988), (Cameron and Quinn, 1988), and (Van de Ven and Poole, 1988) identify the centrist role of paradox in innovation, creative insights, and breakthroughs, thus enabling organization change and transformations. The simultaneous consideration of contradictions enables reframing, i.e., new frames of reference[5] in which opposing sets of values can be interpreted in a new ensemble with a new logic of its own. By focusing attention on the tension associated with the contradictory, paradox provides an opportunity for organization change which is concomitantly integral to IT acquisition and utilization (Cameron and Quinn, 1988), (Siporin and Gummer, 1988), and (Bartunek, 1988).

Without the tension of such polar opposites, varying degrees of ability to reframe occur, as represented in the four responses to contradiction and paradox (Figure 2). At one end of this continuum, the organization's focus on one attribute perpetuates itself until it becomes both extreme and dysfunctional, i.e., schismogenesis (Morgan, 1981).

Resolution of paradox through structuration

An organization is a social system constructed by individuals, i.e., action in organizations is microlevel; social structure is macrolevel. An organization change paradigm must connect individual interests with social structure. In Giddens (1979, 1984) theory of structuration, purposeful individuals are guided by beliefs, values, and norms as well as constraints both created by themselves and/or imposed by the social environment. The organization's social structural properties channel individual activity, constrain action, and shape members' perspectives, perceived choices, desires, and purposes. Individuals, who are in control of their own behavior, act to achieve their self-interests and other interests, i.e., contradictory assumptions may arise.

In highly complex systems, seemingly straightforward actions may lead to unintended consequences. The desideratum is a *processual* paradigm of IT acquisition and utilization which reconstructs the meaningful connections underlying individuals' choices, embedded within multilevel historical and current contexts, at individual, group, and organization levels and reflects the inherent paradox at these multiple levels.

IT and the theory of structuration

Orlikowski (1992) has extended Gidden's theory of structuration, i.e., IT becomes one additional type of structural property of an organization. The recursive nature of technology constitutes the duality of technology, i.e., technology is socially constructed by actors, working in a given social context, through different meanings they attach to it. Once developed and deployed, technology becomes institutionalized, i.e., part of the structural properties of the organization. Thus, IT is both an antecedent and consequence of organization action.

Extension of Orlikowski's paradigm - A generalized competing values framework

This chapter extends Orlikowski's (1992) research[2] by explicating the generalized CV framework (Quinn and McGrath (1985) shown in Figure 3. The CV axes of bias help map social action enabling understanding of changing contradiction and paradox. This framework is consonant with the metaphysical orientations existentialism, idealism, rationalism, and empiricism (Mitroff and Mason, 1982), (Muller-Merbach, 1994), (Pepper, 1961), (Boland and Greenberg, 1988), and Kilmann (1983). The competing values shown in Figure 3 surface when individuals, groups, and organizations recursively and socially construct enactment processes, e.g., web-based IT acquisition, utilization, and organization change. This chapter paradigm focuses both practitioner and research attention on two interwoven and pervasive institutional properties -organization culture and organization learning which are systemic paradox underpinnings, i.e., metaforces underlying structurational processual dynamics in the organization.

Organization culture and the simplicity :: complexity paradox

Simplicity :: Complexity Paradox

<-->

HOMOGENEOUS   **HETEROGENEOUS**

The organization culture epistemology explicated in this chapter focuses on the competing values concerning the modalities by which reality is both perceived and enacted. Reality can either be perceived and enacted as a single entity, i.e., homogenous, or perceived and enacted as having a multiplicity of components, i.e., heterogeneous (Lundberg, 1985). This anchoring reflects the simplicity :: complexity innovation paradox, as embodied in the research of Ford and Backoff (1988), Cameron and Quinn (1988), Kanter (1988), Cox and Blake (1991), Miller (1993), and Sheridan (1992). Organization innovativeness and organization change are linked to complexity, i.e., heterogeneity (Martin, 1992). Simplicity, i.e., organization homogeneity is seen as impeding innovation.

Culture is about social relations, social structure, and behavior at both

Figure 3. Competing values axes of bias

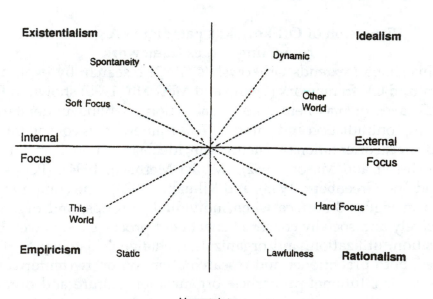

Adapted from Quinn and McGrath (1985)

macrolevels and microlevels of the organization which provide transmission of meaning, thus enabling the organization to manage uncertainty, direct attention, and shape decision making (DiTomaso, 1987). Transmission of meaning is accomplished via the culture "web" of shared ideologies, beliefs, attitudes, values, and norms (Kilmann, et. al., 1986), (Beyer, 1981), and (Sproull, 1981). Table 1 delineates characteristics of the components of the culture web. Culture shapes organization processual dynamics; processual dynamics re-create culture, in an evolving interaction, i.e., structuration (Saffold, 1988).

At both the organization and subunit levels, cultural potency and cultural dispersion can further inform analysis of culture. Cultural potency is a summative index of the power of the organization's culture to act as an influence on behavior. The dynamic and interlinked organization system of ideologies, beliefs, values, and norms is a summative index of cultural potency and integral to understanding organization change and IT acquisition and utilization processual dynamics. Cultural dispersion includes the degree to which culture manifestations are shared, as well as deeply internal-

Table 1. *Organization culture component characteristics*

Organization Culture Component	Characteristics
Ideologies	• explain cause-and-effect relationships • explain how and why of processual dynamics • basis may be internal logic or habitual courses of action • recursive - behavior affects ideologies ideologies affects behavior
Beliefs	• mental representations of human understanding • produced by active cognitive processing • social interaction influences members' beliefs • are veridical--individuals and groups "known" their world • attitudes (composed of beliefs) are dispositional-situational and based on cognitive processing
Values	• are antecedent to behavior, involve both cognitive and affective elements • are *dialectical*, express a mode of conduct preferable to an opposite mode of conduct • are emergent, evolutionary, exhibit reciprocity, synergies, and resistance to change • may have both breadth and intensity

Norms	• based in perceived realities, are unwritten and socially transmitted, prescribe ranges of behavior
	• serve to provide stability
	• shifting individuals from relative independence to interdependence impacts norm patterning
	• norms that promote innovation can be:
	  • those promoting creativity
	  • those promoting implementing creative output

ized by subcultures, groups, and individuals.

Organization Subcultures

For purposes of exposition, this chapter conceptualizes organization culture at the level of the firm. Organization culture is not monolithic, i.e., multiple subcultures may coexist, occurring along gender, education, occupational specialty, task exigency, sentient group, functional, product, or geographical lines. Schein (1993) identifies sourcing of subculture strength as: convictions of organization's founders, dynamics of a group or subculture, number and intensity of crises survived, and characteristics of the learning process. Both recognition and management of organization subcultures are necessary and critical in understanding and managing organization change processes.

Three types of subcultures are identified—enhancing, orthogonal, and counterculture (Duncan, 1989). The enhancing subculture more fervently accepts the dominant culture's values than the dominant culture does. The orthogonal subculture accepts the values of the dominant culture, as well as a nonconforming set of values that it considers its own. A counterculture challenges the values of the dominant culture. In many organizations, the informal organization, supported only by implicit norms and often regarded as unsanctioned, serves this purpose.

The capacity of an organization to innovate increases to the extent it encourages diverse but connected subcultures (Schein, 1993) and (Fine and Kleinman, 1979), i.e., a simplicity ::complexity paradox. Using political cultural analysis, Lucas (1987) identifies "structured perceptions" and "negotiated order" through which subcultures maintain and adapt their behavior and activities with respect to the organization's dominant culture. Countercultures that are innovative within a latitude of tolerance by the dominant culture can be beneficial to the organization.

Quinn and McGrath (1985) have identified the four position organization culture paradox-based typology shown in Figure 4. Salient characteristics associated with this organization culture typology are shown in Table 2.

Organization learning and the stability :: change[7] paradox

Stability :: Change Paradox

<--->

ADAPTIVE   **INNOVATIVE**

The centrality of organization learning in this chapter's structurational paradigm explicates a second significant organization paradox - stability ::

Figure 4. Organization culture paradox typology

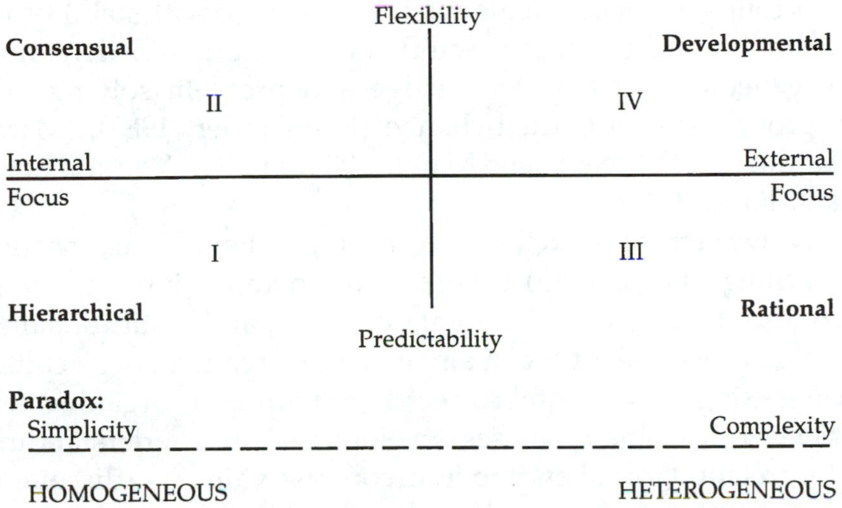

<pre>
                            Flexibility
    Consensual | Developmental

              II | IV

    Internal | External
    Focus | Focus

              I | III

    Hierarchical | Rational
                          Predictability

    Paradox:
     Simplicity — — — — — — — — — — — — — —   Complexity

     HOMOGENEOUS   HETEROGENEOUS
</pre>

Adapted from Quinn and McGrath (1985)

Table 2. Organization culture typology

Culture:	Hierarchical	Consensual	Rational	Developmental
Beliefs	Fewer, narrow focus	Focus on the organization	Focus on sub-unit, individual	Many, wide ranging
Value Orientation	Status quo - cautiousness, formality, logic, obedience	Relationship - cooperation, openness	Task - aggressive-ness, diligence	Change - creativity, experimen-tation
Norms	Rich norm structure for wide range of behaviors	Structuring reflects focus on consensus	Structuring reflects focus on maximum	Lean normative structure governs few behaviors
Sub-cultures	Orthogonal, counter-cultures function as iconoclasts	Subculture dominance - coalitions	Subculture dominance - power, resource allocation	Team empowerment moderates subculture impact
Information Processing	Formal • measurement • documentation • computation	Collective • discussion • participation • consensus	Individual • individual • judgement • decisiveness	Intuitive • insight • invention • innovation
Goal Orientation	Continuity • stability • control • accountability	Cohesion • teamwork • morale	Performance • efficiency • productivity	Revitalization • growth • resource acquisition

change. Within individual, group, and organization, there is a fundamental duality between being "learningful" and being productive and competent. Organizations, groups, and individuals must be concerned with stability, i.e., productivity, control, and efficiency. Simultaneously, organizations must deal with the generation of new knowledge and problem solving,- i.e., organization, group, and individual change (Friedlander, 1983), (March, Sproull, and Tamuz, 1991), (Leavitt and March, 1988), (Van de Ven and Poole, 1988), (Ford and Backoff, 1988).

Stability involves the construction and sharing of beliefs, i.e., meaning lower level learning (single loop) occurs through repetition, in a well-understood context, focuses on behavioral outcomes, and institutionalizes formal rules. Single loop learning maintains the organizations' culture characteristics, seeking to detect and correct error within the organization's norms. Experience in learning processes develops common understandings and makes interpretations of beliefs public. In contrast, values are discovered by experiencing more preferences, rather than less. Discovery of contrary experience permits construction of new causal relationships, i.e, change such as that integral to web-based IT acquisition and utilization. Organizations with multiple and effective higher level (double loop) learning mechanisms will likely be innovative (Argyris and Schoen, 1978).

Double loop learning seeks to understand contradictions. Realization that certain experiences cannot be interpreted within the current frame of reference contributes to higher level learning search and exploration of alternative routines, values and norms (Lant and Mezias, 1992). Such alternatives result in new ways to assemble responses and connect stimuli to responses (Hedberg, 1981) and (Lyles, 1988). Higher level learning addresses the organization's dynamic complexity, i.e., organizations "learn how to learn" by maintaining processes that critically examine key assumptions, beliefs, values, decisions, and issues (Purser and Pasmore, 1992). Potentially, reframing of both the individual and organization's underlying frame of reference, beliefs, values, and norms (Fiol and Lyles, 1985) can occur. Such search, exploration, and organization reframing processes are central to organization change processes such as IT acquisition and utilization. Types of higher level organization learning mechanisms include: rich learning (March, Sproull, and Tamuz, 1991), action learning (Morgan and Ramirez, 1984), vicarious learning (Huber, 1991), unlearning (Huber, 1991), Hedberg (1981), (Klein, 1989), and (Johannessen & Hauan, 1994b), learning by failure (Klein, 1989), experimental learning (Huber, 1991), and deutero learning (Johannessen & Hauan, 1994b).

Organization learning occurs through the medium of individual members through whom learning takes place (Shrivastava, 1983) and (Hedberg, 1981) within a system of exchanges, i.e., sharing and integration of learning done by others in interrelated roles at multiple levels - individual, group, and organization (Shrivastava, 1983), (Duncan and Weiss, 1979) and (Simon, 1991). This multilevel system of exchanges is influenced by a broad set of social, political, and structural variables utilizing both cognitive and social communication bases (March, 1991) and (Simon, 1991). Organization learning includes both processes which reflect defensive adjustments to reality and processes by which knowledge is used offensively (Hedberg, 1981).

As an organization process, organization learning is more than the sum of individual members' learning, i.e., organizations have collective cognitive capabilities and memories (Hedberg, 1981). Organization memory preserves ideologies, beliefs, values, and norms, thus impacting organization learning, innovation processes, and organization change. In turn, innovation and organization change processes identify new states of outcome for ideologies, beliefs, values, and norms, through organization learning. Thus, ideologies, beliefs, values, and norms are antecedent to, as well as a consequence of, organization learning.

Daft and Huber (1987) propose the organization learning paradox-based typology in Figure 5. Each organization learning gestalt represents a style of learning appropriate to the organization's interpretive requirements which reflect both the organization's IT and communications structures. Table 3 further delineates this organization learning typology.

Multiplicative interaction of the metaforces—
creativity, synergy, leveraging

Multiplicative interaction of the two paradoxical metaforces, organization culture and organization learning (Figure 1), is consonant with research directions called for by Saffold (1988), Walsh and Ungson (1991), Nonaka and Johansson (1985), Fiol and Lyles (1985) Tushman and Nadler (1986), Senge (1990), and Adler and Schenbar (1990). For example, Saffold advocates a research focus on the processually-based interactions of organization culture interwoven with organization processes such as organization learning. Research, including that of Saffold, Dixon and John (1989), and Frost and Egri (1991) propounds such interactions as a multiplicative model of sociocognitive dynamics, i.e., enabling higher degrees of creativity, synergy, and leveraging (morphogenetic enabling), or, alternatively, inhibiting creativity, synergy, and leveraging (contributing to schismogenesis). Such synergies are discussed in Klempa (1995, October). Multiplicative interaction of organization culture and organization learn-

Figure 5. Organization learning paradox typology

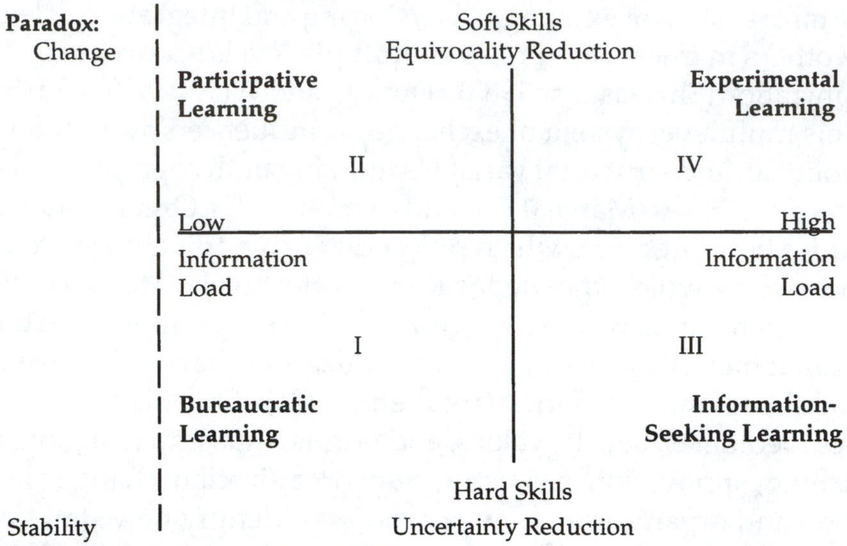

```
Paradox:  |                    Soft Skills
  Change  |              Equivalocity Reduction
          |  Participative                      Experimental
          |  Learning                           Learning
          |
          |         II                    IV
          |
          |__Low_____High
          |
          |  Information                       Information
          |  Load                              Load
          |
          |         I                     III
          |
          |  Bureaucratic                      Information-
          |  Learning                          Seeking Learning
          |
          |                    Hard Skills
 Stability|              Uncertainty Reduction
```

Adapted from Daft and Huber (1987)

Table 3. Organization learning typology

Typology Characteristic	Bureaucratic Learning	Participative Learning	Information-Seeking Learning	Experimental Learning
Learning Emphasis	Institutional Experience	Assumption Sharing & Interpretation	Development of Knowledge Base	Trial-&-error Interpretive Enactment
Rules / Structuredness	Many	Medium	Medium	Little
Type of Knowledge	Objective	Subjective / Objective Consensus	Objective, with Maximization	Subjective / Objective, Intuition Heuristics
Communications Modality	Centralized Few boundary departments	Decentralized Personal networks	Many boundary departments	Personal networks & boundary departments
Requisite Variety	Low	Moderate	Higher	Very High
Reflexivity of Inquiry	Low	Higher	Moderate	Very High
Equifinality*	Very Low	Moderate	Moderate	Very High
Organization Learning Perspective	Systems - Structural**	Interpretive***	Systems - Structural**	Interpretive***

adapted from Daft and Huber (1987)

* Equifinality - Multiple pathways through redundancy of function
** Systems structural - Understanding leads to action
*** Interpretive - Action leads to understanding

ing may have powerful effects on individuals' assumptions, expectations, and knowledge sharing about the purpose, context, importance and role of IT, thus influencing choices made regarding the acquisition and utilization of IT. Table 4 provides exemplars of such organization culture and organization learning multiplicative, sociocognitive dynamics.

The multiplicative interaction of organization culture (Figure 4) and organization learning (Figure 5) yields eight theoretical states of response to contradiction and paradox. This chapter uses, for purposes of both theoretical exposition and integration with prior research, the simplified four position typology of responses to contradiction and paradox shown in Figure 2.

This chapter identifies two additional paradox (Figure 1), convergence :: divergence (OFOR) and morphostasis :: morphogenesis (IT-enabled core :: linkages) that recursively interact to enable or inhibit IT acquisition, utilization, and organization change and transformation. Each is discussed in turn below.

Organization frame of reference (OFOR) and the convergence :: divergence paradox

Convergence :: divergence paradox

<--->

CONVERGENCE   **DIVERGENCE**

OFORs inform organization research by providing a *processual* instead of a static, i.e., episodic, approach to studying organization change (Shrivastava and Schneider, 1984). The OFOR (Appendix B) includes the epistemological, methodological, scientific, and common sense assumptions that individuals, groups, and organizations make about the conditions for acquiring, ordering, and using information (Shrivastava and Mitroff, 1983). The OFOR, a self-contained belief system, or "mindscape", serves as a basis for organization sense-making, thus bracketing, interpreting, and legitimizing issues. The OFOR's sense making capacities provide the organization's collective raison d'etre and external legitimization, thereby defining boundaries and membership.

The OFOR constitutes a recursive dynamic concerning how organization issues are created, validated, and recreated. The OFOR maps the individuals' experiences of the world, identifies their relevant aspects, and enables understanding through assumptions about event happenings and individuals' situational responses (Bartunek, 1988). OFORs cue and are cued by affect

Table 4. Multiplicative sociocognitive dynamics exemplars

| Schismogenic Contributors | | | | Morphogenetic Enablers | |
Org. Culture	Org. Learning			Org. Culture	Org. Learning
			Divergence		
Culture passively managed	Management does not listen to subordinates		High Ref. Inq., Req. Variety	Culture proactively managed	Unlearning from dissent
Deductive thinking	Minimal experimental learning			Inductive thinking	Learning by failure
First order feedback	Compartmentalized learning	OFOR		Multilevel, multidimensional feedback	Cross-functional learning
Specifically skilled individuals	Few higher level learning mechanisms			Multifunctionally skilled individuals	Much higher level learning
Linkages mechanistics, static	Individual, non-collaborative learning			Systemic linkages, interpersonal	Collaborative learning
Weak subculture linkages to organization	Learning characterized by event orientation	Low Ref. Inq., Ref. Variety		Subcultures recognized, managed proactively	Learning focus is systemic
		Convergence			

and behavior. OFORs are not simply individual predispositions, but rather social cognitive schema, i.e., intersubjective and reflecting a common knowledge and mutual understanding of the organization's members. Such sense-making occurs through complex and recursive interactions with individuals, groups, organization, and environment, i.e., a structuration process. Shrivastava and Mitroff (1983) propose the OFOR typology shown in Table 5.

Various researchers identify two critical dimensions of the OFOR: reflexivity of inquiry (Shrivastava and Mitroff, 1984), (Wilkins and Dyer, 1988) and requisite variety (Ashby, 1956), (Sitkin and Pablo, 1992), (Weick, 1987), (Wilkins and Dyer, 1988), and (Morgan and Ramirez, 1984). Reflexivity of inquiry is shaped by the domain of inquiry characteristics, i.e., domain of inquiry limits access to alternative frames of reference, specific instances of

Table 5. OFOR typology

OFOR Characteristic	Bureaucratic	Political	Pragmatic	Prospective
Cognitive Elements	Objective Information	Subjective, interest group/ coalition commitment	Intersubjective Information & Objective Information	Inter-subjective Personal commitment
Cognitive Operators	Computa-tional Analysis	Negotiation Interpersonal Problem Solving	Long range problem formulation & solution	Judgement, intuitive analysis
Reality Tests	Organization Rules & Procedure	Social & organization norms	Empirical proofs, methodo-logical rigor	Self-experience
Domain of Inquiry	Departmental, well defined boundaries	Changes with shareholder interests	Organization, fixed boundaries	Changing contin-uously
Degree of Articulation	Explicit statement of assumptions and rules	Through rhetoric and metaphorical communication	Explicit through knowledge base utilized for decision making	Through empowered enactment

*adapted from Shrivastava and Mitroff (1983)

Figure 6. OFOR paradox typology

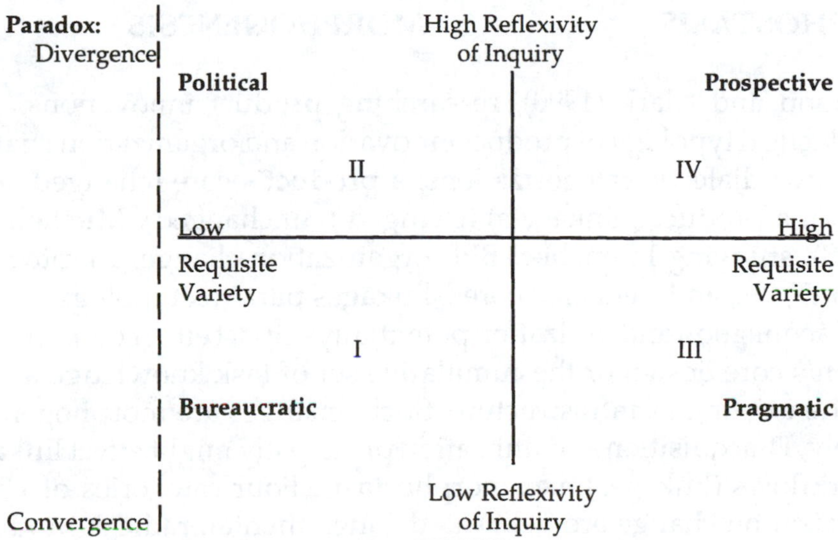

Adapted from Shrivastava and Mitroff (1983)

inquiry, and the entire set of cognitive maps that individuals use in inquiry in general. The capacity to map other OFORs depends on the complexity and sophistication of one's own frame of reference. Reflexivity of inquiry is a function of both the existing knowledge base and appreciation of alternative reference frames. Complex and sophisticated OFORs enable heterogeneity, in turn enabling opportunities for innovation and change. Organizations with high reflexivity of inquiry exhibit a systemic resilience quality.

Requisite variety specifies that in order for the organization to deal with changing circumstances, e.g., IT acquisition and utilization, the organization must possess an internal variety equal or greater than the variety in its changing external circumstances. Holographic organization principles suggest building as much variety into every element of the organization as possible, i.e., organization elements should be designed as multiskilled, interchangeable, and allow for errors arising in other parts of the system. Requisite variety should be built into the system where it is needed for interacting directly with a problem. In such an organization, decision-making processes are spread as widely as possible, gaining a wide range of perspectives on a given issue, hence maximizing the range of knowledge acquired. Treating reflexivity of inquiry and requisite variety dialectically yields the OFOR paradox-based typology shown in Figure 6.

IT and the morphostasis :: morphogenesis[8] paradox

Morphostasis :: morphogenesis paradox

<--->

MORPHOSTASIS   **MORPHOGENESIS**

Henderson and Clark (1990), researching product innovations, proposed a dialectical typology of product innovation and organization change, identifying two dialectic categorizations: a product's core (changed :: unchanged) and a product's linkage(s) (changed :: unchanged). Mitchell and Zmud (1998), studying IT-enabled BPR organization change, adapted this typology to IT, i.e., an IT-enabled core :: linkages paradox typology.

Both IT acquisition and utilization potentially impact either or both of the organization's core design or the cumulative set of task knowledge associated with the existing IT infrastructure. Such changes are morphogenetic. Alternatively, IT acquisition and utilization principally might effect linkages among workflows (linkages), i.e., morphostasis. Four categories of IT-enabled organization change are delineated - incremental, radical, modular, and architectural (Figure 7).

Figure 7. IT-enabled core::linkages paradox typology

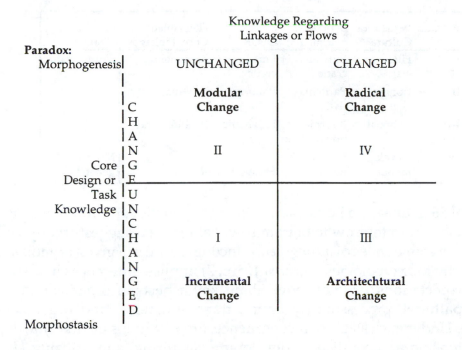

Adapted from Henderson and Clark (1990).

An incremental change makes modest refinements and extensions to the core design or task knowledge as well as the linkages or flows, i.e., both are fundamentally unchanged (Quadrant I). Radical change (Quadrant IV) establishes a new dominant design, i.e., a new set of core design concepts linked together in a total new and different linkage architecture. Quadrant II (modular change) changes core design or task knowledge only, leaving linkages unchanged. Quadrant III (architectural change) changes linkages only, leaving core design or task knowledge unchanged. Architectural change, although morphostatic in character, nonetheless may present challenges to the organization, e.g., knowledge regarding linkages or flows is likely to be contextually, processually, and historically embedded.

Organization's responses to contradiction and paradox

Multilevel, sociocognitive-based structurational enactments are better understood with respect to the concept of congruency. Congruency is a theoretical state characterized by conditions such that contradiction and paradox are less prevalent than in states of incongruence. Quinn and McGrath (1985) identify four organization responses (Figure 8) to contradiction and paradox.

Table 6. *Homeostatic::morphogenetic states of congruence continuum*

Quadrant	Organization Culture	Organization Learning	OFOR	IT-enabled Core::Linkages	Organization Change
I	Hierarch-ical	Bureau-cratic	Bureau-cratic	Incremental	Homeostatic
II	Consen-sual	Participa-tive	Political	Modular	
III	Rational	Informa-tion Seeking	Pragmatic	Architectural	
IV	Develop-mental	Experi-mental	Prospective	Radical	Morpho-genetic

Table 6 delineates a homeostatic :: morphogenetic continuum of congru-ency states, from top row to bottom row. Table 6 also suggests many wide-ranging possible states of *incongruence*. Incongruence in a given organization among the four typologies (Figures 4, 5, 6, 7) implies differences in assump-tions, expectations, or knowledge about key aspects of organization rela-tional patterns, processual dynamics, transformations, and organization change. Under such states of incongruence, organizations are likely to expe-rience tension and conflicts in developing, acquiring, and utilizing IT. By focusing attention on incongruencies, ever present in organizations faced with complexity and change, the CV framework informs our understanding of organization transformation and change, i.e., the *processual* dynamics arising from resolution of contradiction and paradox, such as that associated with web-based IT acquisition and utilization. Understanding paradox-based processual dynamics, as well as incongruence which may arise out of organization paradox, is integral to both attempting and customizing organi-zation change interventions, as well as dealing with unanticipated circum-stances arising from organization change interventions. Paradox and incon-gruence analyses for Sterkoder, Ltd. are presented below.

Organization change — beta, tectonic, gamma

Homeostatic (Figure 2) organizations exhibit autopoetic responses to change. Such organizations are oriented toward morphostasis, i.e., stability. Homeostatic organizations are likely to engage in beta[9] organization change efforts. Attempted organization change efforts are likely to require less elapsed time and be more selectively directed within the organization.

Morphogenetic organizations are change oriented, i.e., involving trans-formations at the core of the organization, i.e., gamma[10] organization change. Attempted organization change efforts are likely to require longer lead times, many iterations, and be broadly-based within the organization. A midrange level of change, tectonic[11] change, sufficiently large to overcome the organization's autopoetic responses and schismogenetic tendencies, yet not "so great that it overwhelms the organization" (Reger, et. al., p. 577) is also identified.

Beta, tectonic, and gamma change overlap (Figure 2). In structurational enactment processes, IT-enabled change depends upon a combination of technical and social influences that are only partially controllable. Organization processual paradox-based dynamics must be receptive to attempts to change. A diversity of consequences may be realized, e.g., intended transformations may occur, pre-existing processual dynamics may persist, or unanticipated combinations of new and old practices may emerge. Tectonic change may arise through multiple recursive enactments over time, i.e., a series of "situated change" enactments (Orlikowski, 1996).

Typological analysis of an organization's or organization subunit's resemblance to the theoretical congruency states of *isolation, dominance, accommodation, and transcendence* is not for "closest fit" as suggested by contingency theory, but rather for purposes of intensive focus on multilevel contextual and processual dynamics within the organization. Such a contextual understanding of the processual dynamics should be concomitantly considered with the organization / individual change curve (Klempa, 1998) shown in Figure 9.

Individuals' and organization subunits' responses to the ambiguity associated with organization change is not isomorphic. Rather than monolithic organization change interventions, customized organization change interventions are possible, reflecting organization culture, organization learning and the OFOR. In addition, such individual and organization unit responses are dispositional, in part, impacted by the individual's cognitive style, locus of control, incongruity adaptation level, and defense mechanisms. For each individual and organization units impacted by proposed IT acquisitions, diagnosis and assessment of those individuals' and organization units' location on the individual / organization unit change curve needs to be undertaken. Such assessments are explicated below for Sterkoder, Ltd.

IT-Enabled Organization Change and Transformation Application of Multilevel Paradox Analysis, Sterkoder, Ltd.

Sterkoder, Ltd. is a medium-sized shipyard (see Appendix A and Johannessen & Hauan, 1994a, 1994b), with substantive investments in IT, which enabled radical organization change (Figure 8). This chapter's paradigm (Figure 1) is a *generalized* paradigm applicable to all IT, e.g., CAD/CAM at Sterkoder Ltd. Sterkoder Ltd. fully exemplifies the diagnosis / assessments of, and multilevel processual dynamics analyses proposed, in this chapter's IT acquisition and utilization paradigm.

Figure 8. Organization response to contradiction typology

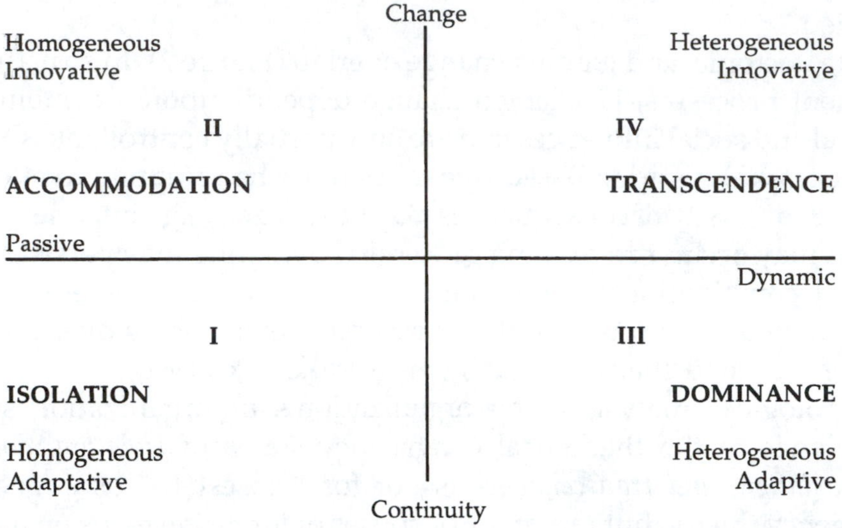

Change

Homogeneous Innovative	Heterogeneous Innovative
II	**IV**
ACCOMMODATION	**TRANSCENDENCE**
Passive	
	Dynamic
I	**III**
ISOLATION	**DOMINANCE**
Homogeneous Adaptative	Heterogeneous Adaptive

Continuity

Adapted from Quinn and McGrath (1985)

Isolation	Passive	seeks to maintain one of the competing values, and closing off the other. Mechanisms, e.g., denial, concealment, altering, ignoring, and buffering, may be used.
Accomodation	Passive	subordinates one of the competing values through compromise. Mechanisms used include placating, negotiating, and bargaining.
Domination	Dynamic	maintains continuity through conquest of opposing positions. Mechanisms used include challenging, controlling, influencing, and coopting.
Transcendence	Dynamic	permits reframing of contradictions, enabling creativity, synergy, and leveraging. Enables gamma organization change.

The new owner, Jens Ulltveit-Moe was willing to provide financial resources sufficient to invest in construction as well as new technology including "massive investments in integrated IT systems" (Johannessen & Hauan, 1994a, p. 43). A major shift in technology was needed, reflecting Ulltveit-Moe's desire to transform the shipyard from artisan in nature to a modern industrial mode of operation, constituting a shift in both the "core" of Sterkoder's construction methods, i.e., a restructuring of both the construction philosophy itself, and Sterkoder's "linkages".

Sterkoder, Ltd. focuses the reader's attention to the processual dynamics of organization transformation and change concomitantly necessary to acquisition and utilization of IT. These processual dynamics enabled organization transformation and change including:

Figure 9. Organization/individual change curve

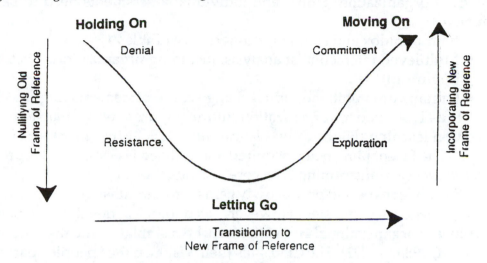

From <u>Business Process Change: Reengingeering Concepts,</u>
<u>Methods, and Technologies</u> (p. 108) by V.Grover and W. Kettinger (Eds.)
1998. Harrisburg. Idea Group Publishing. Copyright 1998 by
Idea Group Publishing. Reprinted with permission.

- redistribution of work from individual to shared responsibility
- nature and texture of work from tacit, private, and unstructured to articulated, public, structured
- emergence of proactive forms of collaboration among specialists
- emergence of knowledge-based, shared understanding, with both breadth and depth, in conjunction with organization learning
- patterns of interaction from reactive to proactive and experimental
- evaluation of performance from output focused to focus on process
- forms of accountability from manual, functional, local, sporadic to cross-functional and continuous.

Over a two year period, these transformations were enacted as individuals and groups incorporated the IT into work practices, experimented with localized innovations, responded to unanticipated circumstances, and initiated organization learning-based processual initiatives which enabled Sterkoder's recursive use of the IT. By way of comparison, the above-cited organization changes and transformations also were identified by Orlikowski (1996) who researched Lotus notes software acquisition and utilization in a large U.S. company. Orlikowski provides an extensive examination of the recursive nature of IT acquisition and utilization.

Organization Assessments

Prior to an organization's acquisition and utilization of an IT, several types of organization, group, and individual assessments need to be conducted:

- Four paradox and states of incongruence (Table 7)
- Multilevel, interactionist analysis, including organization subcultures (Figure 10)
- Organization unit, individual change curve placements (Figure 11)

Pre-IT, Sterkoder's organization culture (Figure 4) was *hierarchical*, organization learning (Figure 5) was *bureaucratic*, OFOR (Figure 6) was *bureaucratic*. The IT-enabling being acquired and utilized is classified (Figure 7) as *radical change*, transforming both core and linkages.

Sterkoder expected productivity gains through substantive investments in IT, a necessary first step. However, "technological developments, in the absence of organizational innovation, will be assimilated into the status quo" (Zuboff, 1988, p. 392). The CEO, Nils Juell, visioned the "people" part of the change effort as

> ...producing an understanding of the social...requirements of such change in terms of individual and group behavior.
>
> people need to know more about what was supposed to happen ... CAD/CAM ... provides a feedforward structure...dependent on continuous communication ... communicative practices were expected to produce this... .
>
> ...the new mode of production ... created high degree of technological interdependence....[requiring]...the system to cope with the added complexity
>
> ...communicative routines were needed...based on redundancy of function and a multiskilled workforce...and exchange of experience and problem-solving
>
> ...the job situation...facing each person is more explicit and less equivocal in terms of expectations and consequences of actions
>
> ...[the] information system was linked to a 'local initiative/central synthesis' philosophy (Johannessen & Hauan, 1994a, pp. 47-48, 50, 51)

Although Sterkoder's organization culture, organization learning are OFOR are congruent, collectively they are incongruent with IT-enabled radical change, i.e., gamma organization change. Gamma organization change interventions require longer lead times and multiple, recursive, nonlinear change. Although Sterkoder Ltd. may, in part, exhibit aspects of planned change, the transformations are more clearly understood as structurational enactment processes over time. Such a perspective incorporates a situated change perspective (Orlikowski, 1996), i.e., multiple, recursive, nonlinear tectonic organization change transformations.

Table 7. Sterkoder, Ltd. Characteristics impacting paradox, pre-IT and post-IT

Paradox	Pre-IT Characteristics	Post-IT Characteristics
Simplicity::Complexity	Limited Mission, Multiple subcultures	Empowering, Shared knowledge
Stability::Change	Craft skills, Power coalitions	Local Initiative, Central synthesis
Convergence::Divergence	Tacit knowledge, Isolated social position	Structured job expectations, Multi-skilled
Morphostasis::Morphogenesis	Top-down communication, Policy dictates change	IT-enabled core knowledge, Self-organizing flexibility

Pre-IT, resolution of paradox primarily utilized *isolation, dominance*

Table 8. Sterkoder, Ltd. Organization culture pre-IT and post-IT

Organization Culture Component	Pre-IT Characteristics	Post-IT Emerging, transitioned to
Ideology	• Limited perspective of what a shipyard is • Functional specialization with downward communication only	• Shared, visibility of activities • Knowledge elicitation from below and two-way communication
Beliefs	• Specialized local unit knowledge • Senior manager never appeared on shop floor • "Dumb work" unquestioned • Operators do not rely on engineers	• Knowledge system made explicit & accessible to all • Paradox leverages creativity, synergy • Empowered employees enables self - organizing
Values	• Upward influence-peddling; in-fighting • Middle managers turf-protecting • Authority patterns required fault finding	• Encouraging unplanned search activities • To do the "correct" thing more important • To be "innovative" • Extension of trust to other people
Norms	• Operators generally did not fill out reports • Operators did not give out "secrets of the trade" to engineers	• Problem definition from operational level • Redundancy of functions • Multi-skilled workforce • Budgets are a group planning device, not just control

Table 9. Sterkoder, Ltd. Organization learning pre-IT and post-IT

Organization Learning Characteristic	Pre-IT Characteristic	Post-IT Emerging, transitioned to
Learning Emphasis	Departmental, unit experience	Trial-and-error Interpretive enactment
Rules/ Structuredness	Few cycles, many rules	Few rules, many cycles
Type of Knowledge	Objective	Subjective / Objective Consensus, Intuition, Heuristics
Communications Modality	Centralized, few boundary units	Personal networks, many boundary units
Requisite Variety	Low Minimal, segmented information	Very High Inputs from multiple sources, perspectives
Reflexivity of Inquiry	Low Objective data, narrow domain	Very high Shared enactment, visiblity, diverse domain
Equifinality *	Nonexistent	Multifunctional, multiskilled individuals
Minimal Critical Specification **	Nonexistent	Predominant Decision-making at operator level
Organization Learning Perspective	Understanding leads to action	Action leads to understanding

adapted from Daft and Huber (1987)

  * equifinality - multiple pathways through redundancy of function
  ** minimal critical specification - no more should be specified than what is essential

Table 10. Sterkoder, Ltd. organization OFOR pre-IT and post-IT

OFOR Component	Pre-IT Characteristics	Post-IT Emerging, transitioned to
Cognitive elements	Objective, quantifiable data from formalized systems	Subjective, personal experiences; data from personal sources
Cognitive operators	Problem formulation institutionalized in formal systems; limited perspective	Ability to shift perspectives; choice is through feedback guided by recognition
Reality tests	Data acquisition and analysis of environment viewed as objective	Personal experience through shared definition and enactment of environment
Domain of inquiry	Organization self-image is stability; coalitions determine power distribution; narrow domain	Organization self-image is innovative; change is valued; diverse domain
Degree of articulation	Low degree of articulation is formal through policies and procedures	High degree of articulation & sharing of OFOR is through personal example, visibility to others

Adapted from Klempa (1998)

Two additional analyses (Figures 10 and Figure 11) are needed. Figure 10 is a multilevel, interactionist analysis. Sterkoder was a highly functionally specialized, loosely coupled organization with ideologies, beliefs, values, and norms as shown in Table 8. At least three subcultures were prominent in the established work routines -- engineering, production (operators), and middle management. Engineering "handed down" decisions via design specifications. Operators viewed themselves as highly skilled artisans whose "secrets of the trade" were not shared with engineering. Recommendations from operators, when "passed up" to engineering, were often vetoed, citing "policy" reasons. A sizable core of middle managers mediated between these two subcultures.

Assessments of each significant organization unit's, work group's, and individuals' placements on the organization unit / individual change curve is shown in Figure 11.

Karlsson enlisted the help of a number of "change agents" internal to the company as well as external suppliers of goods and services. The change agents were already at the *commitment* stage, i.e., able to reframe. The union leaders were willing to *explore* new work dynamics and processes associated with the new IT. The operators, who had the most dreary job situations, were willing to *explore and commit* to the evolving and unfolding work process dynamics.

In contrast, at the opposite position on the change curve (Figure 11), were the engineers and middle managers. The new IT adjusted the old reality of handed-down, one-way information flow from the engineers and the associated mediating role of middle management. The middle managers were at the stage of *denial*. They perceived themselves to "bear the brunt" of the organization transformations associated with the new IT. The engineers, while having moved beyond denial, were at the stage of *resistance*.

Individuals' and groups' responses to ambiguity and organization change are not isomorphic. Both individuals' and groups' ideologies/beliefs, values, and norms must be transitioned into the organization's new ideology/ beliefs, values, and norms. Such OFOR transitions occur at both a rational and emotional level (Sheldon, 1980). Although often conceptualized as "willful", i.e., a negative model of resistance, resistance is a homeostatic response, when viewed cybernetically. Such an autopoetic response by the system (individual, group, or organization) attempts to maintain equilibrium by carrying out established patterns of behavior in order to survive in a stressful and difficult situation (Goldstein, 1988). An autopoetic organization, group, or individual will resist changes, perceived as a threat to that individual's, group's, or organization's frame of reference.

Rather than direct confrontation, new tasks need to be found, employing

Figure 10. Sterkoder, Ltd. Multilevel Interactionist Analysis

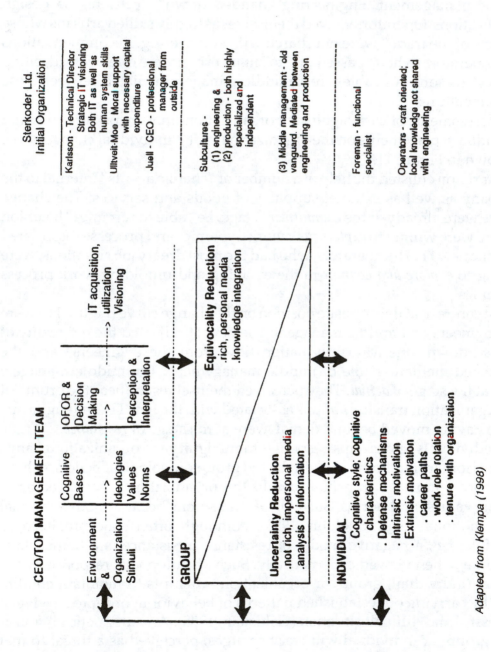

Adapted from Klempa (1998)

the homeostatic resistances, but placing them within a new context, thus permitting new experiences to emerge. Such tasks allow change from within and provide the individual, group, or organization the ability to express responses within new contexts that consequently change the responses' communicational meaning and impact, i.e., reframing (Hirschhorn and Gilmore, 1980). By using "difference questioning", i.e., contrasting the autopoetic identity and the targeted identity desired, information can be surfaced about alternative ways of achieving the targeted identity. Looking at IT acquisition and utilization as an "opportunity" contributes to the individual's sense of control, facilitates search and use of external information, contributes to internalized values of progressiveness, and focuses on the future (Dutton, 1992).

These conceptual approaches to organization and individual change and reframing were utilized at Sterkoder, Ltd. The earliest change interventions by Karlsson included:

> an uncompromising devotion to the needs of the operators...he would engage in dialogues with ... operators on the floor... emphasized ... the importance of allocating more resources to accommodate these needs (Johannessen & Hauan, 1994a, pp. 45-46).

The appearance of Karlsson, a top manager, on the shop floor broke established norms. Another new norm established was the practice of always having at least three different levels of the company represented when decisions were made that directly affected production activities. Karlsson edited the company newsletters about changes underway and engaged in "hammering out" sessions with trade union leaders who carried legitimacy. These sessions formulated actions, evaluated resulting dynamics, and adjusted actions over time.

In transforming Sterkoder's organization processual dynamics into two-way communication including knowledge elicitation from below, Sterkoder was guided by:

> ...turning managers into coworkers and workers into knowledge workers challenged their conception of imperial authority
> unlearning seems to be a ... social phenomena...and ... predominantly organizational
> lack of interaction between groups gives rise to a locally constructed view of reality...occupational subcultures are formed ... and perpetuated...as group cohesion strengthens, groups ... become aware of how their patterns of relationships are changing and ... consequences.
> when people see that changes are taking place, they will be more inclined...to accept vision or philosophy that underlie these

Figure 11. Sterkoder, Ltd. Organization Unit/Individual Change Curve Placements

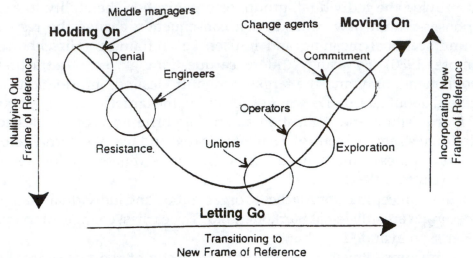

changes...as the pattern of reality changes, behaviors change ... affect the alliances and communicative practices ... concentrating on ... groups of people [rather than individuals] ...makes change efforts more resistant to counteractive actions.

the social web has...openness and solidarity conducive [to a] sense of security to arouse propensity to change (Johannessen & Hauan, 1994a, pp. 48-50).

Paradox-based tensions coexisted in Sterkoder, Ltd. as shown in Table 7. Pre-IT, two modalities for resolution of paradox, *isolation and dominance* were prevalent. These modalities were recursively transformed over time to *transcendence.*

For example, those who regarded the organization transformations underway as threatening their interests formed an emerging network referred to as "the alliance which separates." Karlsson referred to them as "my amplifiers". These forces within Sterkoder were not seen as functioning in a reactive manner. Rather, "they only regard the change process in a historic perspective...and add...a new dimension to the change process" (Johannessen & Hauan, 1994a, p. 47), i.e., the paradox of stability :: change was managed dialectically. Other examples of dialectical management of paradox at Sterkoder, Ltd. include the linkage of the acquired IT to a "local initiatives, central synthesis philosophy". This illustrates the simplicity :: complexity paradox as well as the convergence :: divergence paradox. "Local initiatives" foster both complexity and divergence. Yet simultaneously, "central synthesis" of the locally sponsored initiatives fosters both simplicity and convergence. All three illustrate the proactive, dialectically-based management of paradox enabled organization transformation and change at Sterkoder.

Organization learning at Sterkoder Ltd. utilized action learning, experimental learning and deutero learning, which took place through a variety of coordination mechanisms, all of which enabled new behaviors to be learned, encouraged, and rewarded. For example, the position of "leading skilled worker" (LSW) was established, a position, knowledge-wise, somewhere "between" the traditional foreman and skilled workers. This position helped bring about new learning behaviors on the part of both foreman and skilled workers. Another formal position created was that of "Change Report Coordinator".

Change reports were initiated as part of the IT system. But more importantly, this mechanism reinforced the earlier change efforts of Karlsson, who wanted to encourage a two-way flow of information, with a focus on information flows upward from the operators, i.e., getting all people involved in physical production and bringing problem definition to the operational level of the company. The recursive nature of such action learning and experimental learning processes is illustrated by the subsequent funneling of change reports through "production coordinators", a different position whose functional responsibility bridged production (operators) and engineering. Multidiscipline groups (MDGs) were created, subsequently, as well. An MDG consisted of no more than 6 or 7 people, one of whom had to be an LSW. The people on the MDG team were supported by the production coordinators, who acted as a two-way information flow conduit between the operators and engineering. Using job rotation, people on the MDG team became multiskilled. The MDG team concept is consonant with the research of Lim et. al. (1997), who found that codiscovery learning methods formed mental models with higher inference potential than self-discovery learning. The MDG team concept also illustrates dialectical management modalities— convergence :: divergence and simplicity :: complexity. Over time, and through a series of recursive processes, these organization learning approaches provided mechanisms by which old behaviors were unlearned, and pathways to new behaviors were explored and commitment gained.

Future Trends

Implications for Practice

The chapter's paradigm is a generalized paradigm, applicable to all information technologies. For example, structurationally-based paradigms have been applied to a range of diverse information technologies, e.g., from geographic information systems (GIS) within county government (Robey and Sahay, 1996) to an application involving Lotus Notes supporting the Technical Services Division of a large U.S. software products company (Orlikowski, 1996).

The paradigm herein is particularly useful for examining individuals' and groups' interactions with IT and organization change and transformation over time. The paradigm affords the ability to explain and anticipate outcomes that are not captured, for example, by structural contingency models, which inherently provide a dichotomous treatment of competing values. The paradigm considers organization change as anticipated, perceived and enacted by individuals as well as organization units, thus enabling examination of both intended and unintended organization transformations. As such, it enables the complexities and subtleties of IT-enabled organization change to be addressed in a manner not possible with variance-based theories.

Sociocognitive Grid

Dunn and Ginsberg (1986) propose a replicable methodology, the sociocognitive grid, that enables quantifying differences in organization frames of reference, monitoring of diverse learning processes, measurement of the sociocognitive connectedness of organization members, and both identification and monitoring barriers to organization change and transformation. The sociocognitive grid transforms data across multiple levels: intrapersonal, interpersonal, and organizational.

As has been shown with Sterkoder, Ltd., diagnosis and assessments of incongruence enables the organization to be proactive, i.e., to potentially reduce the unintended consequences of acquisition and use of a new IT, by attempting customized, rather than monolithic, organization change interventions. Contrast the recursively changing processual dynamics and the diminishing role of middle managers at Sterkoder, which prevented clashes with operators with expanding job responsibilities to that reported by Zuboff (1988). In that situation, managers were unable to accept IT that would increase workers' autonomy and decision-making authority, resulting in social clashes around worker grievances and union action. Diagnosis and assessment of incongruencies provides not only baseline benchmarks, but also insights into the nature of appropriate congitive as well as affective organization interventions. The sociocognitive grid can be used to assess both intraunit and interunit incongruencies.

Implications for Research
Application to other areas

This chapter's paradigm is a fundamental organization change paradigm, applicable to other organization change processual dynamics, e.g., BPR and IT diffusion. An expanded structurational metaforce underpinnings conceptualization (Figure 12) has been applied to BPR (Klempa, 1998) and IT diffusion (Klempa, 1993, 1994a, 1994b). In these earlier evolutionary conceptualizations of this chapter's structurational metaforce underpinnings, organization competing values were treated as dichotomies, i.e., a contingency paradigm, rather than dialectically.

The third structurational metaforce underpinning, knowledge sharing, constitutes a differentiation :: integration paradox. Differentiation reflects an intrinsic value system, focusing on variety and individual autonomy, employing a coactivational view of organizations, stressing recurrent patterns of interaction among organizational participants. Such organizations use a concurrent model of innovation characterized by simultaneous and spontaneous communication, with transfer into and out of the collective knowledge pool of the organization. Integration reflects an extrinsic value system,

Figure 12. Expanded structurational metaforce underpinnings

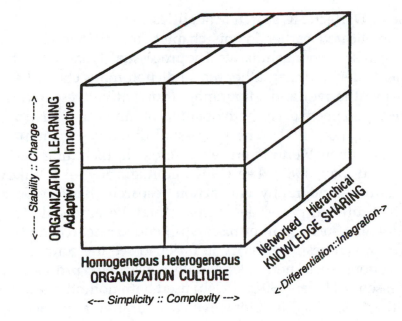

Adapted from Klempa (1998)

focusing on order, uniformity, and collective choice, employing a configura-tional view of organizations, emphasizing integration of work tasks under common managerial authority. Integration employs a "sequential" model of innovation, a phased transformation of information across boundaries.

Further research exemplars

This chapter's paradigm identifies a set of four paradox-based, processual dynamics typologies that can serve as the basis for future research. The four typologies are a beginning step towards explicating and articulating organi-zation processual dynamics. Further research will serve to explore the robustness of each of the four typologies. The four typologies can be applied to diverse organization settings, thus permitting interorganization compari-sons for a given web-based IT.

Such interorganization comparisons might include contrasting web-based IT acquisition and utilization in organizations whose OFOR requisite variety and reflexivity of inquiry are dramatically different. Tracking an organization's OFOR over time can provide insights into underlying ideol-ogy, belief, value, and norms shifts as linked to both qualitative and quanti-tative organization change. Research is needed to examine the breadth and depth of incongruence, e.g., how incongruence varies by context and time. For example, sourcing of incongruence, e.g., ambiguity, inconsistency, lack of articulation can be addressed.

Use of Dialectic Research Modalities

As explicated earlier in this chapter, most prior IT acquisition and utilization research is quantitative. The processual dynamics of structurational enactments demand that rather than a dichotomous choice between nomo-thetic (quantitative) and idiographic (qualitative) research modalities, a dialectical perspective, i.e., both quantitative and qualitative approaches be melded, e.g., Lee (1991). The processual dynamics of human action, for example, is amenable to interpretive research, including hermeneutics — (Boland and Day, 1989), Lee (1994), ethnography — (Orlikowski, 1991), hermeneutic ethnography and action research (Baskerville and Davies, 1992). Institutional properties, in part, may be amenable to quantitative methodologies such as survey research. Blended research modalities provide the level of synthesis necessary in order to see the connectedness among human actions, social networks, socially constructed processes, and context. Johannessen & Hauan(1994a, 1994b) used both nomothetic and idiographic modalities, i.e., a highly interactive collaborative approach, with various kinds of "diversity inquiring models, ranging from multiple question de-signs to auto-communicative inquiry" Johannessen & Hauan (1994a). Indi-viduals were encouraged to express fully affective elements, e.g., enthusiasm, joy, frustration experienced during the two-year organization change transformations.

Conclusion

This chapter's paradigm is consonant with Markus and Robey's (1988) call for paradigms of IT and organizations utilizing detailed understanding of dynamic organization processes, knowledge about the intentions of actors, and characteristics of IT, i.e., emergent perspective paradigms. As such, the paradigm grounds IT acquisition and utilization processes in organizations in both their socio-historical context, as well as in IT acquisition and utilization's dual nature as both objective reality and socially constructed product. Further, the structurational enactment paradigm proposed herein provides improved opportunity for future research with empirical fidelity, i.e., the ability to faithfully mirror the phenomena under study.

The chapter's paradigm is an additional step toward addressing a more complete picture of the IT acquisition and utilization dynamic and organization change than is presently found in the literature. As such, it responds to some of the theoretical and methodological difficulties that have persisted in the prior IT acquisition and utilization literature, including level of analysis, a preponderance of deterministic-in-nature research, prior processually-based research which has not considered the inherently contradictory and paradoxical nature of organizations, insufficient attention paid to interpersonal communication activities through which interpretations are developed and maintained among organization participants, lack of integration of the underlying individual creativity, organization innovation, and organization change theory constructs underlying IT acquisition and utilization processes.

Author Notes

Lao-Tse was a Chinese philosopher, believed to be the father of Taoism.

The application, by the author, of this chapter's paradigm is based on available published information about Sterkoder in the two *Creativity and Innovation Management* journal issues, as cited.

Appendix A
Sterkoder, Ltd.

Sterkoder, Ltd., ... in Kristiansund....Norway was established in 1816 ... It is now a medium sized shipyard, employing about 650 people [March, 1993], and specializing in construction of advanced trawlers, special tank/chemical carriers, and offshore supply vessels. ....the company has been through major reorganizations influencing its markets, organizational and technological procedures. The company has been changed from a conservative, hierarchical state-subsidized shipyard to a modern, profitable shipyard, competitive by virtue of its market orientation and increased productivity .... through productivity gains from using information technology [CAD/CAM].

Top management wants knowledgeable and reflective employees ... to develop a highly competitive and highly specialized shipyard ranking among the best in the world in the knowledge intensive, 'high-price-per-kilo' segments of the market ... supported by massive investments in integrated information technology systems and a people-orientation producing a shift away from hierarchical organization...in the first three decades of the post-war era.

....it became apparent ... that the mode of production and management style hitherto pursued did not meet the requirements of performance necessary to compete in the market. ... Karlsson was hired as Technical Director ... to "redesign and reorganize the shipyard to meet future demands". ...an ... entrepreneur, Ulltveit-Moe ... took over the shipyard...provided strong moral support that was backed up by financial resources and a willingness to invest in construction ... and new technology... Ulltveit-Moe ...was an influential insider in the shipping industry...the management of the company was headed by a professional manager from outside the company, Juell [CEO]....

Trade unions ... had a direct impact on policy decisions... wage and price controls imposed ... enabled the union to concentrate on management and issues of strategic ownership rather than bargaining...for wages.

[A] feature of the traditional shipyard is separation of...construction [engineering] and production, in relation to work activities and also socially. Contracts came into being through informal conversations between owner/managers and shipowners about ... specifications and features...engineers' sketches were used to establish price...then worked out the details ... [the normative order] of what was to be built. The [descriptive order], the building itself was left to foremen and their workers ...Traditionally information systems in shipyards are designed and developed to accommodate the construction departments' [engineers) need for perfecting drawing procedures. These are then converted to work-related information through an elaborate system of blueprints [with] a high degree of disciplinary differentiation.

Workers ...often relied more on their experience and craftsmanship than the theoretical recommendations from the engineers...changes were seldom reported to the engineers...the gap widened between what was supposed to be going on and what actually took place.

Prior to reorganization, the foreman was in charge of all activities relating to his functional field on the entire ship... trying to finish work at the same time...a lot of dumb work was done...not benefitting the system as a whole .... when something went wrong, ...foremen would....find someone to pin the blame on... chains of events could not be reconstructed... the organization 'form'... rested on a taken-for-granted collective understanding of what kind of worlds shipyards are....

Mediating between Construction [engineering] and production used to be the prime task of a core of middle managers...placing them in a powerful position. Exercising complete control over subordinates, they would protect their territories against each other.

Reprinted and excerpted from:
Johannessen, J. & Hauan, A. (1994). *Creativity and Innovation Management*, 3(1), 43-51.
Johannessen, J. & Hauan, A. (1994). *Creativity and Innovation Management*, 3(2), 96-103.
Copyright 1994 by Blackwell Publishers. Reprinted and excerpted by permission.

Appendix B

Organization Frame of Reference

Characteristic	Focus	Description
Cognitive elements	Experiential Bases	Preference for experiential bases that constitute sourcing of information
Cognitive operators	Ordering/Arranging Information	Methods of ordering information to arrive at meaning/understanding
Reality tests	Legitimization of Process of Inquiry	Legitimization of process of inquiry through connection with past experiences/practices
Domain of inquiry	Scope of Inquiry, Boundaries	Definition of: • Organization itself • Individual - organization relationships • Organization - environment relationships
Degree of articulation	Modalities of Dissemination and Codification	Modalities by which OFOR made known and codified to organization members

adapted from Shrivastava and Mitroff (1984)

Endnotes

[1] These earlier, recursive conceptualizations treated competing values dichotomously.

[2] The symbol :: indicates opposition.

[3] Schismogenesis is a process of self-reinforcement where one action or attribute perpetuates itself until it becomes dysfunctional.

[4] Named for the Roman god, Janus, who looked in opposite directions at the same time.

[5] Other terminology in the literature, with similar (although not identical) constructs, includes ideology, world view (weltanschauung), master script, organization paradigm, cognitive map, interpretive frames, interpretive schemes, and thought worlds.

[6] Orlikowski provided exemplars of "institutional properties" of IT, e.g., ideology, culture, control mechanisms, operating procedures, communication patterns, etc. (p. 409).

[7] The stability::change paradox is also referred to as the reliability :: validity paradox.

[8] The term morphogenesis is from biology. Morphogenesis...is of a form that penetrates so deeply into the genetic code that all future generations reflect these changes. Change occurs in the very essence, i.e., the core. Morphostasis consists of those adjustments that occur as the system grows and develops.

[9] Beta change - moderate level of organization change. Organization or organization subunit norms (evaluation criteria) shift. Minimal change in ideologies/beliefs and values.

[10] Gamma change - highest order organization change. Requires radical shift in the organization's frame of reference, i.e., ideologies, beliefs and values. Other essentially synonymous terminology - second order change.

[11] Seismologists hope for moderately powerful earthquakes, significant enough to overcome the inertia preventing the plates from moving, yet not cataclysmic.

References

Adler, P.S. & Shenbar, A. (1990). Adapting your technological base: The organizational challenge. *Sloan Management Review, 32*, 25-37.

Amabile, T.M. (1988). A model of creativity and innovation in organizations. *Research in Organizational Behavior, 10*, 123-167.

Argyris, C. & Schoen, D.A. (1978). *Organization learning: A theory of action research.* Reading, MA: Addison-Wesley.

Ashby, W.R. (1956). *An introduction to cybernetics.* London: Chapman and Hall.

Bartunek, J. (1988). The dynamics of personal and organizational reframing. In R.Quinn & K.Cameron (Eds.), *Paradox and Transformation: Toward a Theory of Change in Organization and Management*, Cambridge, MA: Ballinger Publishing.

Baskerville, R.L. & Davies, L. (1992, December). A workshop on two techniques for qualitative data analysis: Action research and ethnography (a workshop). *Thirteenth International Conference on Information Systems*, Dallas.

Beyer, J.M. (1981). Ideologies, values, and decision making in organizations. In P. Nystrom & W. Starbuck (Eds.) *Handbook of Organizational Design, Volume 2*. England: Oxford University Press.

Boland, R. & Day, W. (1989). The experience of systems design: A hermeneutic of organizational action. *Scandinavian Journal of Management*, 5(2), 87-104.

Boland, R. & Greenberg, R. (1988). Metaphorical structuring of organizational ambiguity. In L. Pondy, R. Boland, and H. Thomas (Eds.) *Managing Ambiguity and Change*. Chicester: John Wiley.

Brynjolfsson, E. (1993). The productivity paradox of information technology. *Communications of the ACM*, 36(12), 67-77.

Cameron, K. & Quinn, R. (1988). Organization paradox and transformation. In R.Quinn & K.Cameron (Eds.), *Paradox and Transformation: Toward a Theory of Change in Organization and Management*, Cambridge, MA: Ballinger Publishing.

Carter, N. (1984). Computerization as a predominate technology: Its influence on the structure of newspaper organizations. *Academy of Management Journal*, 27(2), 247-270.

Coleman, J.S. (1986). Social theory, social research, and a theory of action. *American Journal of Sociology*, 91, 1309-1335.

Cox, T. & Blake, S. (1991). Managing cultural diversity: implications for organizational competitiveness. *Academy of Management Review*, 5(3), 45-56.

Daft, R.L. & Huber, G.P. (1987). How organizations learn: A communications framework. *Research in the Sociology of Organizations*, 5, 1-36.

Damanpour, F. (1991). Organizational innovation: A meta-analysis of effects of determinants and moderators. *Academy of Management Journal*, 34(3), 555-590.

DiTomaso, M. (1987). Symbolic media and social solidarity: The foundations of corporate culture. *Research in the Sociology of Organizations*, 5, 105-134.

Dixon, P.J. & John, D.A. (1989). Technology issues facing corporate management in the 1990s. *MIS Quarterly*, 13(3), 247-255.

Doty, D. & Glick, W. (1994). Typologies as a unique form of theory building: Toward improved understanding and modeling. *Academy of Management*

Review, 19(2), 230-251.

Duncan, W.J. (1989). Organizational culture: 'Getting a fix' on an elusive concept. *Academy of Management Executive, 3*(3), 229-236.

Duncan, R. & Weiss, A. (1979). Organization learning: Implications for organizational design. *Research in Organizational Behavior, 1,* 75-123.

Dunegan, K., Tierney, P. & Duchon, D. (1992). Perceptions of an innovative climate: Examining the role of divisional affiliation, work group interaction, and leader / subordinate exchange. *IEEE Transactions on Engineering Management, 39*(3), 227-236.

Dunn, W.N. & Ginsberg, A. (1986). A sociocognitive network approach to organizational analysis. *Human Relations, 40*(11), 953-976.

Dutton, J.E. (1992). The making of organizational opportunities: An interpretive pathway to organizational change. *Research in Organizational Behavior, 15,* 195-226.

Fine, Gary A. & Kleinman, S. (1979). Rethinking subculture:An interactionist analysis. *American Journal of Sociology, 85*(1), 1-20.

Fiol, C.M. & Lyles, M.A. (1985). Organizational learning. *The Academy of Management Review, 10*(4), 803-813.

Ford, J. & Backoff, R. (1988). Organizational change in and out of dualities and paradox. In R.Quinn & K.Cameron (Eds.), *Paradox and Transformation: Toward a Theory of Change in Organization and Management,* Cambridge, MA: Ballinger Publishing.

Friedlander, F. (1983). Patterns of individual and organizational learning. In P. Srivastava et. al. (Eds.) *The Executive Mind: New Insights on Managerial Thought and Action*: San Francisco: Jossey-Bass.

Frost, P. (1994). Leading with innovation in mind. *Creativity and Innovation Management, 3*(2), 79-84.

Frost, P. & Egri, C. (1991). The political process of innovation. *Research in Organization Behavior, 13,* 229-295.

Gersick, J.G. (1991). Revolutionary change theories: A multilevel exploration of the punctuated equilibrium paradigm. *Academy of Management Review, 16*(1), 10-36.

Giddens, A. (1979). *Central problems in social theory.* Berkeley: University of California Press.

Giddens, A. (1984). *The constitution of society: Outline of the theory of structure.* Berkeley, CA: University of California Press.

Goldstein, J. (1988). A far-from-equilibrium systems approach to resistance to change. *Organizational Dynamics, 17,* 16-26.

Griffith, D.A. & Palmer, J.W. (1999). Leveraging the web for corporate success. *Business Horizons, 42*(1), 3-10.

Haber, L. (1997). Truck stops on the web. *Datamation, 43*(7), 110-112.

Hayashi, A. (1997). Squeezing profits from IT. *Datamation, 43*(7), 42-47.

Hedberg, B.L. (1981). How organizations learn and unlearn. In P.C. Nystrom & W.H. Starbuck (Eds.) *Handbook of organizational design.* New York: Oxford University Press.

Henderson, R. & Clark, K. (1990). Architectural innovation: the reconfiguration of existing product technologies and the failure of established firms. *Administrative Science Quarterly, 35,* 9-30.

Hirschhorn, L. & Gilmore, T. (1980). The application of family therapy concepts influencing organizational behavior. *Administrative Science Quarterly, 25,* 18-37.

Huber, G.P. (1991). Organizational learning: The contributing processes and the literatures. *Organization Science, 2*(1), 88-115.

Johannessen, J. & Hauan, A. (1994a). Organizational unlearning. *Creativity and Innovation Management, 3*(1), 43-51.

Johannessen, J. & Hauan, A. (1994b). Information, innovation, and organizational learning. *Creativity and Innovation Management, 3*(2), 96-103.

Kanter, R.M. (1988). When a thousand flowers bloom: structural, collective, and social conditions for innovation in organization. *Research in Organizational Behavior, 10,* 169-211.

Kilmann, R. (1983). A typology of organization typologies: toward parsimony and integration in the organizational sciences, *36*(6), 523-548.

Kilmann, R., Saxton, M., & Serpa, R. (1986). Issues in understanding and changing culture. *California Management Review, 28*(2), 87-94.

Klein, J.I. (1989). Parenthetic learning in organizations: Toward the unlearning of the unlearning model. *Journal of Management Studies, 26,* 291-308.

Klempa, M.J. (1993, April). Management of IT innovation: A heuristic paradigm research perspective. In M. Tanniru (Ed.) *Proceedings of the 1993 ACM SIGCPR Conference,* St. Louis.

Klempa, M.J. (1994a). Managing information technology: An integrative acquisition / diffusion contingency model. In M. Khosrowpour (Ed.) *Information technology and organizations: Challenges of New Technologies.* Harrisburg, PA: Idea Group Publishing.

Klempa, M.J. (1994b). Management of information technology diffusion: A meta-force integrative contingency diffusion model. In L. Levine (Ed.) *Diffusion, transfer, and implementation of information technology (A-45).* Amsterdam: North-Holland.

Klempa, M.J. (1995). Information resource management, innovations, and schismogenesis. *Information Management, 8*(1/2), 16-17.

Klempa, M.J. (1995, October). Management of innovation: Organization culture and organization learning synergistic implications. In Quingrui, X. & Jin, C. (Eds.) *Proceedings of the Multinational Symposium on Management of*

Technology and Innovation. Hangzhou, People's Republic of China.

Klempa, M.J. (1998). Understanding business process reengineering: A sociocognitive contingency model. In Grover, V. & Kettinger, W. (Eds.) *Business Process Change: Reengineering Concepts, Methods, and Technologies.* Hershey, PA: Idea Group Publishing.

Kline, S.J. (1985). Innovation is not a linear process. *Research Management, 28*(4), 36-45.

Lant, T. & Mezias, S. (1992). An organizational learning model of convergence and reorientation. *Organization Science, 3*(1), 47-71.

Lawler, E., Mohrman, A., Mohrman, S., Ledford, G., & Cummings, T. (1985). *Doing research that is useful for theory and practice.* San Francisco: Jossey-Bass.

Lee, A.S. (1991). Integrating positivist and interpretive approaches to organizational research. *Organization Science, 2*(4), 342-365.

Lee, A.S. (1994). Electronic mail as a medium for rich communication: An empirical investigation using hermeneutic interpretation. *MIS Quarterly, 18*(2), 143-158.

Leonard-Barton, D. (1987).Implementing structured software methodologies: A case of innovation in process technologies. *Interfaces, 17,* 6-17.

Leonard-Barton, D. (1988). Implementation characteristics of organizational innovations. *Journal of Communications Research, 15*(5).

Levitt, B. & March, J. (1988). Organization learning. *American Review of Sociology, 14,* 319-340.

Lewis, L. & Seibold, D. (1993). Innovation modification during intraorganizational adoption. *Academy of Management Review, 18*(2), 322-354.

Lim, K.H., Ward, L.M. & Benbasat, I. (1997). An empirical study of computer system learning: Comparison of co-discovery and self-discovery methods. *Information Systems Research, 8*(3), 254-272.

Lucas, R. (1987). Political-cultural analysis of organizations. *Academy of Management Review, 12*(1), 144-156.

Lundberg, C. (1985). On the feasibility of cultural intervention in organizations. In P.J. Frost, L.F. Moore, M.R. Louis, C.C. Lundberg, & J. Martin (Eds.) *Organization Culture.* Beverly Hills, CA: Sage Publications.

Lyles, M.A. (1988). Learning among joint venture sophisticated firms. *Management International Review, 28,* 85-98.

March, J.G. (1991). Exploration and exploitation in organizational learning. *Organization Science, 2*(1), 71-87.

March, J.G., Sproull, L., & Tamuz, M. (1991). Learning from samples of one or fewer. *Organization Science, 2*(1), 1-13.

Markus, M.L. & Robey, D. (1988). Information technology and organizational change: Causal structure in theory research. *Management Science, 34*(5),

583-598.

Martin, J. (1992). *Cultures in organizations: Three perspectives.* New York: Oxford University Press.

Meyer, A.D. & Goes, J.B. (1988). Organizational assimilation of innovations: A multilevel contextual analysis. *Academy of Management Journal, 31*(4), 897-923.

Miller, D. (1993). The architecture of simplicity. *Academy of Management Review, 18*(1), 116-138.

Mitchell, V. & Zmud, R. (1998). Strategy congruence and BPR rollout. In V. Grover & W. Kettinger (Eds.) *Business Process Change: Reengineering Concepts, Methods, and Technologies,* Harrisburg: Idea Group Publishing.

Mitroff, I. & Mason, R. (1982). Business policy and metaphysics: some philosophical considerations. *Academy of Management Review, 7*(3), 361-371.

Morgan, G. (1981). The schismatic metaphor and its implications for organizational analysis. *Organizational Studies, 2,* 23-44.

Morgan, G. & Ramirez, R. (1984). Action learning: A holographic metaphor for guiding social change. *Human Relations, 37*(1), 1-28.

Morton, M.S. (Ed.). (1991). *The corporation of the '90s: Information technology and the organizational transformation.* New York: Oxford University Press.

Muller-Merbach, H. (1994). A system of system approaches. *Interfaces, 24*(4), 16-25.

Nonaka, I. & Johansson, J. (1985). Japanese management: What about the "hard" skills?. *Academy of Management Review, 10*(2), 181-191.

Orlikowski, W.J. (1991). Integrated information environment or matrix of control? The contradictory implications of information technology. *Accounting, Management, and Information Technology, 1*(1), 9-42.

Orlikowski, W.J. (1992). The duality of technology: Rethinking the concept of technology in organizations. *Organization Science, 3*(3), 398-427.

Orlikowski, W.J. (1996). Improvising organizational transformation over time: A situated change perspective. *Information Systems Research, 7*(1), 63-92.

Orlikowski, W.J. & Baroudi, J.J. (1991). Studying information technology and the structuring of organizations. *Information Systems Research, 2*(1), 1-28.

Orlikowski, W.J. & Gash, D. (1994). Technology frames: Making sense of information technology in organizations. *ACM Transactions on Information Systems, 12*(2), 174-207.

Orlikowski, W.J. & Robey, D. (1991). Information technology and the structuring of organizations. *Information Systems Research, 2*(2), 143-169.

Pelz, D.C. (1983). Quantitative case histories of urban innovations: Are there innovating stages. *IEEE Transactions on Engineering Management, EM-30*(2),

60-67.

Pepper, S. (1961). *World hypotheses: A study in evidence*. Berkeley: University of California Press

Pettigrew, A. (1985). Contextualist research: A natural way to link theory and practice. In E. Lawler et. al. (Eds.) *Doing Research That Is Useful for Theory and Practice*, San Francisco: Jossey-Bass.

Purser, R.E. & Pasmore, W.A. (1992). Organizing for learning. *Research in Organizational Change and Development*, 6, 37-114.

Quinn, J.B. (1985). Managing innovation: Controlled chaos. *Harvard Business Review*, 73-84.

Quinn, R.E. & Cameron, K.S. (1988). Paradox and transformation: A framework for viewing organization and management. In R.Quinn & K.Cameron (Eds.), *Paradox and Transformation: Toward a Theory of Change in Organization and Management*, Cambridge, MA: Ballinger Publishing.

Quinn, R.E. & McGrath, M. (1985). The transformation of organizational cultures: A competing values perspective. In P.Frost, L.Moore, M.Louis, C.Lundberg, & J.Martin (Eds.), *Organizational culture*. Newbury Park, CA: Sage Publications.

Rai, A., Patnayakuni, R., & Patnayakuni, N. (1997). Technology investment and business performance. *Communications of the ACM, 40(7)*, 89-97.

Reger, R., Gustafson, L., Demarie, S., & Mullane, J. (1994). Reframing the organization: Why implementing total quality is easier said than done. *Academy of Management Review, 19(3)*, 565-584.

Robey, D. & Sahay, S. (1996). Transforming work through information technology: A comparative case study of geographic information systems in county government. *Information Systems Research, 7(1)*, 93-110.

Rogers, E. (1988). Information technologies: How organizations are changing. In G.Goldhaber & G.Barnett(Eds.) *Handbook of Organization Communication*. Norwood, NJ:Ablex.

Saffold, G.S., III. (1988). Culture traits, strength, and organizational performance: Moving beyond "strong" culture. *The Academy of Management Review, 13(4)*, 546-558.

Saleh, S. & Wang, C. (1993). The management of innovation: Strategy, structure, and organization climate. *IEEE Transactions on Engineering Management, 40(1)*, 14-21.

Schein, E. (1993). Innovative cultures and organizations. In T. Allen & M.S. Morton (Eds.) *Information Technology and the Corporation of the 1990s*. Oxford University Press.

Senge, P.M. (1990). The leader's new work: Building learning organizations. *Sloan Management Review, 32*, 7-23.

Sheldon, A. (1980). Organizational paradigms: A theory of organizational change. *Organizational Dynamics, 8*(3), 61-80.

Sheridan, J. (1992). Organizational culture and employee retention. *Academy of Management Journal, 35*(5), 1036-1056.

Shrivastava, P. (1983). A typology of organizational learning systems. *Journal of Management Studies, 20*(1), 7-28.

Shrivastava, P. & Mitroff, I. (1983). Frames of reference managers use: A study in applied sociology of knowledge. *Advances in Strategic Management, 1*, 161-182.

Shrivastava, P. & Mitroff, I. (1984). Enhancing organizational research utilizations: The role of decision maker's assumptions. *Academy of Management Review, 9*, 18-26.

Shrivastava, P. & Schneider, S. (1984). Organizational frames of reference. *Human Relations, 37*(10), 795-809.

Simon, H.A. (1991) Bounded rationality and organizational learning. *Organization Science, 2*(1), 125-134.

Siporin, M. & Gummer, B. (1988). Lessons from family therapy: The potential of paradoxical interventions in organizations. In R.Quinn & K.Cameron (Eds.), *Paradox and Transformation: Toward a Theory of Change in Organization and Management*, Cambridge, MA: Ballinger Publishing.

Sitkin, S.B. & Pablo, A.L. (1992). Reconceptualizing the determinants of risk behavior. *Academy of Management Review, 17*(1), 9-38.

Sproull, L.S. (1981). Beliefs in organizations. In P. Nystrom & W. Starbuck (Eds.) *Handbook of Organizational Design, Volume 2*. England: Oxford University Press.

Strassman, P. (1997). Will big spending on computers guarantee profitability? *Datamation, 43*(2), 75-85.

Terborg, J.R. (1981). Interactional psychology and research on human behavior in organizations. *Academy of Management Review, 6*(4), 569-576.

Tornatzky, L. & Klein, K. (1982). Innovation characteristics and innovation adoption-implementation: A meta-analysis of findings. *IEEE Transactions on Engineering Management, EM-29*(1), 28-45.

Tushman, M. & Nadler, D. (1986). Organizing for innovation. *California Management Review, 28*(3), 74-92.

Van de Ven, A. & Poole, M. (1988). Paradoxical requirements for a theory of organizational change. In R.Quinn & K.Cameron (Eds.), *Paradox and Transformation: Toward a Theory of Change in Organization and Management*, Cambridge, MA: Ballinger Publishing.

Walsh, J.P. & Ungson, G.R. (1991). Organizational memory. *The Academy of Management Review, 16*(1), 57-91.

Weick, K.E. (1979). Cognitive processes in organizations. *Research in Organizational Behavior, 1*, 41-74.

Weick, K.E. (1987). Organizational culture as a source of high reliability. *California Management Review*, 24(2), 112-127.

Wilkins, A. & Dyer, W. (1988). Toward culturally sensitive theories of culture change. *Academy of Management Review*, 13(4), 522-533.

Woodman, R., Sawyer, J., & Griffin, R. (1993). Toward a theory of organizational creativity. *Academy of Management Review*, 18(2), 293-321.

Zuboff, S. (1988). *In the age of the smart machine*, New York: Heinemann.

Chapter 5

The Five Stages of Customizing Web-Based Mass Information Systems

Arno Scharl
University of Economics and Business Administration, Austria

Abstract

Web-enabled standard software for electronic commerce incorporating adaptive components will reduce the barriers between productive data processing and dispositive data processing like market analysis, Web-tracking, or data warehouses. A conceptual research framework for analyzing the evolution of electronic markets as well as their business ecosystem represents the foundation of a document-oriented modeling technique for analyzing and designing (adaptive) Web-based Mass Information Systems. A Java prototype based on this meta-model is presented which supports cooperative efforts of academic research, IS departments, top-level management, and functional units to map and classify individual and aggregated customer behavior. The symbolic visualization of user clickstreams based on this analysis is intended to streamline the decision processes necessary for implementing, updating and maintaining complex Web-enabled applications.

Introduction

The commercialization of the Internet and the exponential growth of the World Wide Web in particular introduce communication channels to millions of consumers and computer users that previously were not utilized. While mass media channels are essential to disseminate initial information about an innovation, personal channels are essential to ensure acceptance of this innovation (Rogers, 1995). Web-enabled applications provide the unique advantage of simultaneously supporting both types of channels. The success of the World Wide Web, therefore, was not only grounded on the graphical user interface provided, but also in the simple but effective and very flexible underlying communication architecture. By analyzing the evolution of electronic markets, the first part of this chapter builds the foundation for a subsequent outlook into future trends regarding modeling and designing Web-enabled applications. In contrast to systems supporting Electronic Data Interchange (EDI) and wholesale trading, Web-based mass information systems (WMIS) exclusively target individual customers. Mass information systems in general are systems that support on-line information retrieval and routine tasks by way of self-service for a large number (thousands or millions) of occasional users who are spread over various locations (Hansen, 1995; Hansen and Scharl, 1998). WMIS as a subcategory of mass information systems – next to kiosk systems or ATMs, for example – rely on the distributed hypertext functionality and transfer mechanisms of the World Wide Web. Being characterized by interactivity, dynamic updating, hypertextuality, and global presence are very similar to the concept of electronic catalogs (Palmer, 1997) which include any Web-page "that contains information about the products and services a commercial entity offers" (Segev, Wan and Beam, 1995, p. 11).

The strong specialization of academic research and practice in formulating, analyzing, and implementing marketing strategies for WMIS was a direct result from the insight that abstract marketing instruments cannot generally be applied to different sectors and industries without taking into account the specific features of these heterogeneous segments. The necessary consideration of these features as well as an organization's core competencies is reflected in a number of highly specialized approaches for analyzing market-oriented decision behavior (Haller, 1997). Such an analysis represents the basic requirement for tailored solutions at a cost level comparable to that of mass marketing, increasing the degree of freedom for price policy, attracting new customers, reducing price elasticity of demand, and creating barriers to market entry for potential competitors (Reiss and Beck, 1995). The convergence of information retrieval and usage as far as adaptive WMIS are concerned makes the usual distinction between market research and market management obsolete. Nevertheless, isolated and sequential approaches are still quite common in practice. Seen as a closed loop consisting of conceptual design, pretest, stimulus, customer response, performance analysis, and adaptive systems contribute to a more realistic, dynamic user model and a more efficient allocation of an organization's limited marketing resources.

Due to the immaterial, nontangible, and transitory nature of services and due to the fact that production and consumption take place synchronously, the value of product oriented market research in the traditional sense is drastically reduced. The focus on products has to be replaced by an in-depth analysis of customers and target groups including personal needs, preferences, and expectations which provides essential feedback for product design as well as for strategic and operative decisions of the sales department (Huettner, 1997). The customer oriented regular gathering of stimulus-response-data and its integration with stored information for creating dynamic user models in conformity with observable real-world access patterns help an organization to map and classify the user's behavior, to describe its geographic and temporal distribution, and to predict future behavior as accurately as possible (Link and Hildebrand, 1995; Jaspersen, 1997). The research project described in this chapter focuses on commercial electronic transactions between a company and its online customers. It supports technology-oriented business decisions by providing a user-centric, document-oriented visualization framework for this specific type of transactions. The object types of this framework, the extended World Wide Web Design Technique (eW3DT), will be presented. In addition to that, a platform-independent, prototypical implementation of eW3DT in Java enables organizations to analyze access patterns of active and potential online customers, thus enhancing the current, in most cases only statistically oriented representations of commercially available analysis software with a map-like view analogous to customer tracking in traditional retailing outlets ("Web-Mapping"; see Figure 6).

Evolution Of Electronic Markets

Economic View: The Emergence of Business Ecosystems

To understand the complex dynamics of modern companies, JAMES F. MOORE provides an ecology-oriented framework. He concludes that businesses are not just members of certain industries but parts of a particular business ecosystem that incorporates a whole bundle of different industries. The driving force is not pure competition but co-evolution, implying that companies work cooperatively and competitively at the same time. Their efforts are centered on innovation and the development of new products in order to create and satisfy individual customer needs (Moore, 1993). Such a business ecosystem may be regarded as "an economic community supported by a foundation of interacting organizations and individuals – the organisms of the business world. This economic community produces goods and services of value to customers, who are themselves members of the ecosystem. ... Over time they co-evolve their capabilities and roles, and tend to align themselves with the direction set by one or more central companies" (Moore, 1997, p. 26).

By analyzing the chronological development of such business ecosystems four distinct stages can be identified (Moore, 1993, 1997): Birth, Expansion, Authority, and Renewal (or Death). The process of co-evolution is a complex interplay between cooperative and competitive business behavior. In the pioneering stage (Birth) cooperative behavior usually represents the preferable option. In the expansion stage, however, the ecosystem has to broaden its concept in order to reach a global audience. The authority stage is characterized by the fight for control in that particular business ecosystem, while in the renewal stage tracking new trends and anticipating them with corporate strategies deserves highest priority. In addition to companies with their active and potential customers, the business ecosystem also includes government agencies, regulatory organizations, and a number of additional stakeholders mentioned in the shaded areas of Figure 1. All members of such an ecosystem are responsible for the prosperity of this particular system. For establishing a new business ecosystem even competitors have to cooperate (they are allies in the competition with other business ecosystems but rivals within the boundaries of their own system).

Assuming that the development of electronic markets follows the stages identified by Moore we currently find ourselves at the beginning of the expansion stage (Scharl and Brandtweiner, 1998a). The most important task in this stage is the creation of a world-wide critical mass of customers in electronic markets. To create this critical mass the marginal costs of doing business online (regarding, for example, communications and customer service) have to be reduced substantially in comparison with traditional retailing networks (Tenenbaum, 1998). These reductions can only be provided by customizable solutions which have to co-evolve with the changing and heterogeneous demands of electronic markets. Delivering customized contents with adaptive WMIS aims at identifying profitable potential customers and presenting them an offer tailored specifically to their individual needs and preferences. While being motivated by a user-centered design perspective, the question goes beyond the scope of WMIS interfaces or document presentation and includes the development of flexible software architectures and corresponding business models to take advantage of adaptive system behavior. However, due to the heterogeneous character of customer profiles and market allocation mechanisms, it remains difficult to adequately consider them using traditional system architectures.

Technological View: Changes in the Infrastructure for WMIS

Change in information technology, organizational structure and the

Figure 1. The business ecosystem of electronic markets

corporate value chain strongly influence electronic commerce as a new business paradigm. Since the emergence of the World Wide Web in 1991, adaptability has represented an inherent feature of WMIS (see figure 2). In the first stage (S1), stand-alone servers deliver simple hypermedia compound documents subsequently being displayed by the browser. The *Hypertext Markup Language (HTML)* used for specifying the structure and layout of these documents provides rich facilities for display, but no standard way to manage meta-data. At least to some extent every user is able to specify the general appearance of documents by setting standard browser preferences. But with the progressive commercialization of the Internet and the integration of additional layout options, companies increasingly try to determine the exact design of their documents due to strategic marketing considerations and in order to maintain a consistent corporate identity. But adaptability is not limited to visual design. Available attributes and preferences of registered users may be stored in profile databases and incorporated into WMIS using simple rule-based constructs. Granting different access privileges according to IP domain, personally addressing customers with dynamically generated documents, or determining purchase conditions according to user category are typical scenarios which require the server-side database and application interfaces of stage two (S2). *Perl (Practical Extraction and Report Language)* is by far the most popular interpreted language for programming applications based on the *Common Gateway Interface (CGI)*.

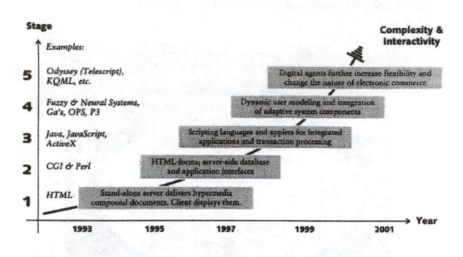

Figure 2. Evolution of the WMIS infrastructure
(Scharl, 1997; Hansen & Tesar, 1996; compare Rogers, 1995)

Integrating the Economic and Technological Perspective

Comparing the evolution of the WMIS infrastructure from S1 to S5 as depicted in Figure 2 with Moore's sequential approach, strong similarities are revealed. S1-S2 correspond to the pioneering stage of the Moore model since WMIS create new value for customers and deliver this value in an innovative and highly efficient way. However, in most cases little is known about the users themselves. Although customer profiles frequently remain incomplete and do not reflect economic reality, they have to be processed instantly within the expected WMIS response time. It goes without saying that scaling such a task becomes difficult to handle with exponentially increasing numbers of on-line users. Therefore, *Java-applets* and client-side scripting languages like *JavaScript* for integrated transaction processing gain popularity in stage three (S3), overcoming the poor performance and other functional limitations of S2-applications solely based on Perl, CGI, and HTML. More ambitious efforts focus on intelligent digital agents of stage five (S5), especially as far as information retrieval and complex negotiations are concerned. General Magic's *Odyssey* (the Java-successor of *Telescript*), for example, provides the necessary infrastructure for such a scenario. The *Knowledge Query and Manipulation Language (KQML)* is a language and protocol for exchanging information and knowledge between digital agents. Based on such languages, mobile agents as proactive, intentional systems promise to further increase flexibility and will radically change inherent characteristics of electronic commerce. In the meantime, adaptive technologies like *neural networks*, *genetic algorithms* (GA's), or related soft computing approaches represent an established field and will start to influence electronic commerce substantially in stage four (S4) – increasing the functionality of deployed applications, independent of the complex infrastructure being necessary for mobile agents – see section "Gathering Customer Information" for a description of the *Open Profiling Standard (OPS)* and the *Platform for Privacy Preferences (P3)*.

Considering the recent infrastructural developments as far as electronic markets are concerned, S3-S5 belong to the expansion stage of Moore's framework. In order to develop all these new technologies, cooperation as a precondition of co-evolution is absolutely necessary. The business ecosystem of electronic markets has not reached the stages authority or renewal until now. Obviously, some companies are prospering very well and may be regarded as innovators or technical leaders, but up to now there is no formal or informal leader in the ecosystem of electronic markets. A lot of ambitious efforts may be observed in this field, but the real battle for leading the whole ecosystem has not even started yet. With the reduced barriers between productive data processing (transactions) and dispositive data processing like market analysis, WMIS-tracking or data warehouses, the widespread consideration of dynamic user models for customizing WMIS, will become a necessity for every serious commercial project and – in contrast to mobile agent technology – does not require a complete redesign of the underlying IS architecture.

Analysis & Design Of Web-based Mass Information Systems
WMIS Reference Modeling

People have to deal with the problem of filtering and processing more and more information in order to make the right decisions in a rather short period of time. The increased dynamics of the environment as well as the cognitive demand of multidimensional problems put a lot of internal and external pressure on them and may reduce the efficiency of decision processes. In order to cope with the complexities involved managers need to reduce the multidimensional problem space to a manageable personal conceptual framework (Meyer and Grundei, 1995). As a consequence, the visualization of data remains a crucial factor in the design process of every WMIS. For this reason the extended World Wide Web Design Technique (eW3DT) has been developed. Focusing on consumer-to-business transactions, the document-oriented modeling framework is intended to remove existing communication barriers between academic research, IS departments, and the management (top-level management as well as functional units). One of the main problems regarding modeling and developing hypermedia applications is the strong interdependency between presentation (user interface) and representation (explicit structuring) of published information. Many meta-models and design methodologies for WMIS lack the necessary object types for modeling this interdependency and are only suited for highly structured segments. In order to serve as an efficient interface to people with very heterogeneous knowledge and expectations, visual representations of hypermedia architectures intended for the general public have to include the essential information in an illustrative, clearly arranged, and comprehensible way.

Effective means of gathering customer feedback and the availability of hierarchical description formats for WMIS, therefore, are the most important prerequisites for an in-depth analysis and for the formulation of conceptual design guidelines. This chapter provides a detailed analysis of these prerequisites. Design guidelines usually are presented as industry-specific reference models. Company-specific implementation models follow these guidelines and apply them to the strategic plans and situational parameters of a specific company (see Figure 3).

According to these assumptions, reference modeling of WMIS with eW3DT facilitates the exchange and dissemination of information in two ways:

- The meta-model serves as a common symbolic language, clearly understandable for the management and easy to handle for technical experts and authors of reference models. Specifications for any WMIS project should include a preferred meta-model and standardized procedures for applying it to the specific problem domain.
- In addition to that, the replacement of intuitive by scientific criteria facilitates coordination between organizations. Reference solutions support the cooperation between academic institutions, business partners and departments within an organization. The information transfer between these groups is improved by integrating group-specific patterns of communication.

Gathering Customer Information

Collection of information about customers is a necessary prerequisite for any form of relationship marketing, from face-to-face contact to globally distributed electronic media (Bauer and Scharl, 1999). A cornerstone and major obstacle of relationship marketing on the Internet, therefore, is the availability (or lack) of data about potential online customers. Consumers use anonymous Web clients, and communication is provided through stateless

HTTP (Hypertext Transfer Protocol). However, online customers usually agree to fill out questionnaires about themselves under certain circumstances. Nevertheless, the quality of this feedback source remains disputable and companies rely on the willingness of Internet users to provide personal information. Consequently, a consistent framework including operational guidelines for assembling accurate profiles is needed. Customers, third parties, as well as the Web client or the relevant network parameters constitute potential information sources. Various methods are available to obtain customer information. These (implicit or explicit) acquisition methods obviously depend on where the data is sourced from with information gains being closely related to the efficiency and the scope of the acquisition method being employed.

The role of customers is getting transformed in the virtual marketspace of WMIS. Guttman, Moukas and Maes (1998) identify six fundamental stages guiding consumer behavior: need identification, product brokering, merchant brokering, negotiation, purchase and delivery, as well as product service and evaluation. In comparison with these stages, Schmid and Lindemann (1998) offer a more transaction-oriented perspective. Methodologies for efficient tracking, mapping, and interpreting customer navigation patterns and individual decisive factors should be based on a detailed taxonomy for categorizing the attributes necessary respectively beneficial for an adaptive design of electronic trading systems. Such a taxonomy has to consider the obligatory negotiation mechanisms which generally may be defined as computer assisted form of decision making where two or more parties jointly search a space of possible solutions with the goal of reaching a consensus (Rosenschein and Zlotkin, 1994; Guttman et al., 1998).

Efficient ways to implement the functionality for each market transaction phase (information, agreement, and settlement) require standardized description models for user profiles like the *Open Profiling Standard (OPS)* or the *Platform for Privacy Preferences (P3)*. Being somewhat similar, the specific focus of each technology is different. While OPS deals with secure transport and control of user data, P3 concentrates on enabling the expression of privacy practices and preferences. The commercially available product Cupcakes, for example, is one of the first products built upon the OPS foundation [http://www.cupcakes.com].

Hypertext Design Methodologies
Due to limitations found in existing WMIS design concepts, BICHLER and NUSSER developed the World Wide Web Design Technique (W3DT) together with a working prototype called WebDesigner which supports the graphical, interactive design of complex WMIS (Bichler and Nusser, 1996). Comparable

Figure 3: Conceptual WMIS reference modeling

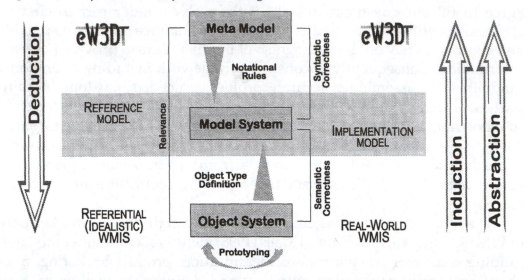

academic or commercial modeling tools like the WebArchitect, SchemaText, or FrontPage98 from Microsoft, to name just a few, provide similar "authoring-in-the-large" functionalities but lack the semantic richness of (e)W3DT. Other database-centric modeling approaches like the widely accepted RMM ("Relationship Management Methodology"; Isakowitz, Stohr & Balasubramanian, 1995) based on entity relationships or the object-oriented OOHDM ("Object-Oriented Hypermedia Design Model"; Schwabe and Rossi, 1995) are especially suited for providing database interconnectivity with regard to highly structured information domains. In most cases they succeed traditional hypermedia design techniques like HDM or HDM2 ("Hypermedia Design Model"; Garzotto, Paolini and Schwabe, 1993; Garzotto, Mainetti and Paolini, 1995, 1996) which themselves are under constant development. In contrast to these database-oriented methodologies, W3DT was built from scratch to support the requirements of unstructured, hierarchical systems. Utilizing practical experiences in developing such systems, the graphical notation of the design tool was further refined and used to document a number of deployed WMIS. With special regard to reference modeling of commercial WMIS, the extended World Wide Web Design Technique (eW3DT) was developed (Scharl, 1997). As far as database-centric hypermedia applications are concerned, however, there is no adequate substitute for entity relationship respectively object-oriented approaches. In this sense both W3DT and eW3DT are not intended to replace modeling techniques like RMM but to act as hierarchically oriented, complementary communication tools between researchers, system analysts, and the management responsible for the decision to implement WMIS.

Developers usually try to find ways to conceptualize the World Wide Web as new medium with rather unique features. The familiar layout of a physical store, for example, becomes "a maze of pull-down menus, product indices, and search features. Now more than ever, the promise of electronic commerce and online shopping will depend to a great extent upon the interface and how people interact with the computer" (Lohse and Spiller, 1998, p. 81). A sound theoretical framework for these interactions is provided by discourse analysis, describing the structures between conversations in general and between authors of published WMIS documents and their target audience in particular (Jasper, Ellis and Wajahath, 1996). In this context, utterances are either examined as pairs (sequential accountability) or larger groups of utterances (distributional accountability). Single HTTP requests (hits) provide less information than the functional group with which those requests are associated. In case of sequential accountability, this association is represented by a multimedia compound document. Consequently, discourse analysis provides an additional rationale for using document-oriented models in WMIS analysis and will be employed to specify a document-oriented analysis framework on the basis of eW3DT.

Object Types Provided by eW3DT

The meta-model of eW3DT provides a framework for the construction of both abstract reference and company-specific implementation models during the software development process of commercial WMIS. Note the difference regarding the level of abstraction between meta-models (eW3DT), reference models, and implementation models (Scharl, 1997; Hars, 1994; see Figure 3). Conceptual data and navigational models for WMIS should support structured as well as unstructured information. They serve as interpretative guidelines for people with very heterogeneous technical expertise and professional responsibilities. Diagrams relying on eW3DT are a user-centric combination of structural and process diagrams (Lohse, Biolsi, Walker and Rueter, 1994) which require an explicit explanation of symbols. This explanation respectively notation will be presented in the following paragraphs.

Every eW3DT data object type represents a special variation of a standard symbolic element and is equivalent to an atomistic unit of the Dexter Hypertext Reference Model (Halasz and Schwartz, 1994). In the following the data object types will be referred to as information object types, the objects themselves as information objects or documents.

Independent of iconic similarity and real equivalence to a given object (hypertext compound document), every information object type defines a general profile for describing the characteristic attributes of this object. Each

114 Scharl

of these profiles corresponds to a set of abstractions commonly found in WMIS. The attributes assign information on structural position, maintenance intensity and organizational integration to the modeling constructs. Together with an (optional) differentiation by color, the sub-symbol [S] on the right side of the object name signals the basic type of the information object. The hierarchical level where the document in question usually can be found within a hypertext application has to be specified in the bottom left field [x]. The second digit [y] describes optional subcomponents. An interaction, implemented as part of the homepage, would receive the value 1.1. The eW3DT meta-model distinguishes between technical and content-specific responsibilities for designing, implementing and maintaining WMIS. Two abbreviations next to the hierarchical level refer to functional units responsible for content [CNT] and technical implementation [TEC]. In the bottom right field, one to three '☆'-symbols represent the maintenance intensity of information objects (initial efforts to implement documents are not considered). Interfaces to existing (marketing) databases influence this value substantially.

Figure 5 categorizes the object types of eW3DT into the three functional

Figure 4. Standard Symbolic Elements of eW3DT (left) and WebMapper (right)

Figure 5. Object types of eW3DT, categorized into the functional segments information, navigation, and structure

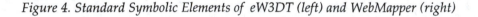

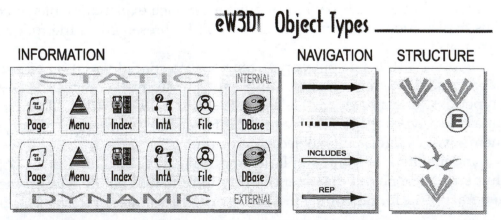

segments information, navigation, and structure. With the help of these elements it is possible to visualize WMIS models of variable complexity, no matter if they are intended for a real organization (implementation model) or for an industry-specific analysis (reference model). For each information object type with the exception of <DBase> there is a static class and a class for dynamically generated documents. A detailed description of eW3DT object types can be found in Scharl (1997, 1998). In the case of <DBase>, internal and external data structures are distinguished since the content structure itself is inherently dynamic – a fact which does not require explicit visualization. Structural variability is the relevant characteristic to separate static from dynamic objects. If the structure is changing, the dynamic process becomes part of the architecture, independent of technical realization. Even being automatically generated via database queries, the inherent character of information objects might be of static nature.

Visualizing Aggregated WMIS Clickstreams

The customer-oriented regular gathering of stimulus-response-data and its integration with stored information for creating dynamic user models in conformity with observable real-world patterns help the information provider to map and classify the customer's behavior, to describe its geographic and temporal distribution, and to predict future behavior as accurately as possible (Link and Hildebrand, 1995; Jaspersen, 1997). The granularity and quality of the resulting database entries determine the degrees of freedom for the information provider, the ability to maximize the customer delivered value, as well as the overall economic potential of every single project relying on this important source of information. For this reason the document-oriented eW3DT meta-model was modified and — as a prototypical, platform-independent Java implementation called WebMapper — employed to provide a visual framework for analyzing access patterns of WMIS customers.

In its early stages this "clickstream" application exclusively focuses on the processing of HTTP log-file data, enhancing the representations of commercially available analysis software for WMIS. Some examples for this category of applications based on HTTP log-file data are presented by (Malchow and Thomsen, 1997). These tools, however, only provide statistically oriented representations embedded in various reports (including tables, bar charts, and so forth) usually being generated directly in HTML or in a file format compatible with popular word processing software. In contrast to that, WebMapper provides a graphical overview based on eW3DT and analogous to traditional customer tracking (Becker, 1973) which is quite common for real-world retailing outlets (see Figure 6). The structure of the site's hierarchical document tree is automatically generated from the hyperlink information found within existing HTML documents. WebMapper supports organizations running commercial WMIS in their efforts to map and classify the individual as well as aggregated customer behavior. It enables them to predict future trends, to advertise more effectively, and to maximize the customer delivered value of electronic transactions (Scharl and Brandtweiner, 1998b).

As already mentioned previously, every information object type of eW3DT defines a general profile for describing the characteristic attributes of WMIS documents. With regard to the application domain of the Java prototype, however, the rectangular symbols representing different types of hypertext compound documents incorporate a completely different set of attributes in comparison with the eW3DT design meta-model (Figure 4). While the color respectively the shading of objects represents their number of HTTP requests [N_Hits], the style of connecting links between the documents represents the frequency with which these links were followed by customers. In addition to that, the average viewing time of WMIS documents in seconds is displayed in the field [Avg_VTime]. With the [Info] button, detailed information about the object in question is accessible (for example a list of host names, respectively, IP addresses of the most important visitors, aggregated number of entries and exits, and so forth). Being part of the user interface, the two arrow symbols in the bottom right corner do not represent an attribute of the object but provide the analyst with the option to move between lower-level and upper-level diagrams.

Outlook & Future Trends

Online retailing is among the most active commercial applications of WMIS (Segev et al., 1995). The selective segmentation of markets in particular has high priority for retailers since it enables them to counteract the increasing fragmentation of consumer markets. This fragmentation is equally responsible for the renaissance of direct-access media and will speed up the implementation of adaptive electronic media. Case studies of commercial WMIS applications as template for an organization's strategic decisions will be developed using the meta-model described above – including, for example, the segmentation of electronic markets according to implicitly or explicitly obtained customer attributes or the integration of external information sources (addresses acquired from list brokers and publishing companies) and internal database systems (historic data about customers, transactions, distribution channels, and so forth). Innovation tends to reduce the practical value of traditional communication models. With the continuing introduction of new technologies, strategic management decisions have to consider innovation as a crucial parameter, particularly as far as information and communications technologies are concerned.

Conclusion

This chapter purported to propagate the use of hierarchically oriented WMIS development tools and to examine the role of document-oriented WMIS modeling as a primary means of standardized communication between academic research, management, and the designers of WMIS. The development and potential of eW3DT as the symbolic language for analyzing WMIS and consistently communicating industry-specific knowledge has been presented. Complementary to hypertext design methodologies based on the entity-relationship model, eW3DT is intended to drive structural design and to streamline the decision processes necessary for implementing, updating, and maintaining complex WMIS. Due to technological advances the simple one-way communication of stage 1 (S1; see figure 2), respectively, asynchronous two-way communication (S2-S3) will be replaced by synchronous two-way communication between a company and its (potential) customers (S4-S5). By extending the syntactic richness of the eW3DT metamodel the visualization of this discourse, as well as its optimization by adaptive system components utilizing stored user profiles will become possible in a very intuitive way. In this context, further research will focus on analyzing and comparing key attributes and dominant algorithms of deployed knowledge-based applications for managing electronic consumer markets. The identification of the commercial potential of these applications will answer, among others, the following questions: Is it economically and technically feasible to provide adaptive solutions? How many domains or documents should be customized? Which attributes should be incorporated into the user model? Based on the answers to these questions and the availability of adaptive system components in Web-enabled standard software, it will become necessary to validate and further extend modeling guidelines and to incorporate them into development and visualization tools like the presented "WebMapper". This platform-independent prototype already provides a visual framework for analyzing access patterns of WMIS customers, enhancing the limited, statistically-oriented representations of commercially available Web-tracking software with a map-like view similar to customer tracking in traditional retailing outlets (see Figure 6). Future versions will provide increased functionality, sets of attributes for user profiling, and additional object types required for modeling adaptive system components. From a practical, industry-specific perspective, the objectives stated above will result in a model-based description of scenarios to utilize customer information for managing electronic consumer markets, focusing

Figure 6. Customer tracking for traditional retailing outlets versus eW3DT and WebMapper (compare Becker, 1973)

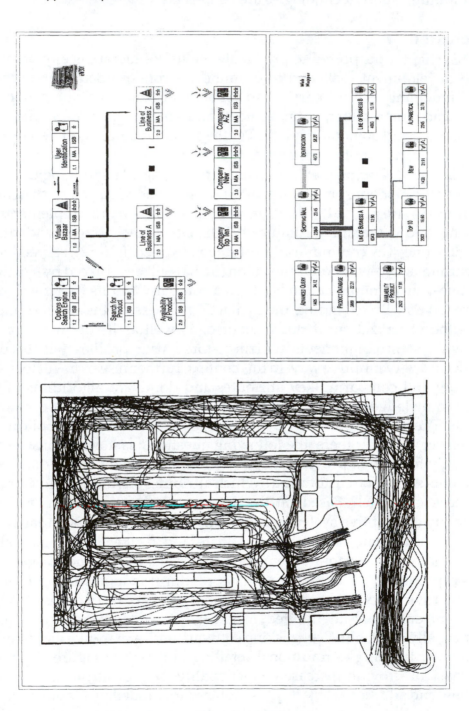

on the increased convergence of productive and dispositive business processes. In this context the relevance and suitability of existing consumer behavior models will have to be evaluated and modified in conformity with the manifold requirements and situational parameters of electronic markets.

References

Bauer, C. & Scharl, A. (1998). Acquisition and Symbolic Visualization of Aggregated Customer Information for Analyzing Web Information Systems. *Proceedings of the 32nd Hawai'i International Conference on System Sciences (HICSS-32). Volume V: Internet and the Digital Economy.* Los Alamitos: IEEE Computer Society Press.

Becker, W. (1973). *Beobachtungsverfahren in der demoskopischen Marktforschung.* Stuttgart: Ulmer.

Bichler, M. & Nusser, S. (1996). Modular design of complex Web-applications with W3DT. *Proceedings of the 5th Workshops on Enabling Technologies: Infrastructure for Collaborative Enterprises (WET ICE '96).* Stanford: IEEE Computer Society Press, 328-333.

Garzotto, F., Mainetti, L. & Paolini, P. (1995). Hypermedia design, analysis, and evaluation issues. *Communications of the ACM, 38 (8),* 74-86.

Garzotto, F., Mainetti, L. & Paolini, P. (1996). Navigation in Hypermedia Applications: Modeling and Semantics. *Journal of Organizational Computing and Electronic Commerce, 3,* 211-237.

Garzotto, F., Paolini, P. & Schwabe, D. (1993). HDM – a model-based approach to hypertext application design. *ACM Transactions on Information Systems, 11,* 1-26.

Guttman, R., Moukas, A. & Maes, P. (1998). Agent-mediated Electronic Commerce: A Survey. *Knowledge Engineering Review, 13(2),* 147-160.

Halasz, F. & Schwartz, M. (1994). The Dexter hypertext reference model. *Communications of the ACM, 37 (2),* 30-39.

Haller, S. (1997). *Handels-Marketing.* Ludwigshafen: Kiehl.

Hansen, H.R. & Scharl, A. (1998). Cooperative Development of Web-based Mass Information Systems. *Proceedings of the 4th Americas Conference on Information Systems (AIS-98),* 994-996.

Hansen, H.R. & Tesar, M.F. (1996). Die Integration von Masseninformationssystemen in die betriebliche Informationsverarbeitung. *Beitrag zur Fachtagung „Data Warehouse" an der Gerhard-Mercator-Universitaet GH Duisburg.* n.a.

Hansen, H.R. (1995). Conceptual framework and guidelines for the implementation of mass information systems. *Information & Management, 31,* 125-142.

Hars, A. (1994). *Referenzdatenmodelle – Grundlagen effizienter Datenmodellierung.*

Wiesbaden: Gabler.

Huettner, M. (1997). *Grundzuege der Marktforschung* (5th ed.). Munich, Vienna: Oldenbourg.

Isakowitz, T., Stohr, E.A. & Balasubramanian, P. (1995). RMM: A methodology for structured hypermedia design. *Communications of the ACM, 38 (8)*, 34-44.

Jasper, J.E., Ellis, R.D. & Wajahath, S. (1998). *Towards a Discourse Analysis of User Clickstreams on the Web.* [On-line]. Available: http://giw.iog.wayne.edu/manuscripts/webdiscourse/.

Jaspersen, T. (1997). *Computergestuetztes Marketing: Controllingorientierte DV-Verfahren fuer Absatz und Vertrieb* (2nd ed.). Munich, Vienna: Oldenbourg.

Link, J. & Hildebrand, V.G. (1995). Wettbewerbsvorteile durch kundenorientierte Informationssysteme – Konzeptionelle Grundlagen und empirische Ergebnisse. *Journal fuer Betriebswirtschaft, 45*, 46-62.

Lohse, G.L., Biolsi, K., Walker, N. & Rueter, H.H. (1994). A classification of visual representation. *Communications of the ACM, 37 (12)*, 36-49.

Lohse, G.L. & Spiller, P. (1998). Electronic Shopping. *Communications of the ACM, 41 (7)*, 81-87.

Malchow, R. & Thomsen, K. (1997, September). Web-Tracking. *Screen Multimedia.* 57-61.

Meyer, J.-A. & Grundei, J. (1995). Akzeptanz visueller Informationsdarstellung im Management. *Journal fuer Betriebswirtschaft, 45*, 366-380.

Moore, J. F. (1993, March). Predators and Prey: A New Ecology of Competition. *Harvard Business Review*, 75-85.

Moore, J.F. (1997). *The death of competition – leadership and strategy in the age of business ecosystems.* New York: Harper Collins.

Palmer, J.W. (1997). Retailing on the WWW: The use of electronic product catalogs, *International Journal of Electronic Markets, 7 (3)*, 6-9.

Reiss, M. & Beck, T.C. (1995, February). Performance-Marketing durch Mass Customization. *Marktforschung & Management*, 62-67.

Rogers, E.M. (1995). *Diffusion of Innovations.* 4th ed. New York: Free Press.

Rosenschein, J. & Zlotkin, G. (1994). *Rules of Encounter: Designing Conventions for Automated Negotiation among Computers.* Boston: MIT Press.

Scharl, A. & Brandtweiner, R. (1998). A Conceptual Research Framework for Analyzing the Evolution of Electronic Markets. *International Journal of Electronic Markets, 8 (2)*, 39-42.

Scharl, A. & Brandtweiner, R. (1998). Maximizing the Customer Delivered Value with Web-based Mass Information Systems. *Proceedings of the 4th Americas Conference on Information Systems (AIS-98).* pp. 453-455.

Scharl, A. (1997). *Referenzmodellierung kommerzieller Masseninformationssysteme:*

Idealtypische Gestaltung von Informationsangeboten im World Wide Web am Beispiel der Branche Informationstechnik. Frankfurt, Vienna: Peter Lang.

Scharl, A. (1998). Reference Modeling of Commercial Web Information Systems Using the Extended World Wide Web Design Technique (eW3DT). *Proceedings of the 31st Hawai'i International Conference on System Sciences (HICSS-31)*, 476-484.

Schmid, B. F. and Lindemann, M. A (1998). Elements of a Reference Model for Electronic Markets. *Proceedings of the 31st Hawai'i International Conference on System Sciences (HICSS-31)*, 193-201.

Schwabe, D. & Rossi, G. (1995). The object-oriented hypermedia design model. *Communications of the ACM, 38 (8)*, 45-46.

Segev, A., Wan, D. & Beam, C. (1995). Designing electronic catalogs for business value: results of the CommerceNet pilot. *CMIT Working Paper*. Berkeley: Fisher Center for Management and Information Technology, University of California.

Tenenbaum, J. M. (1998). WISs and Electronic Commerce. *Communications of the ACM 41(7)*, 89-90.

Chapter 6

Viability through Web-Enabled Technologies

Dirk Vriens
University of Nijmegen, The Netherlands

Paul Hendriks
University of Nijmegen, The Netherlands

It is often claimed that the Internet and associated technologies have paved the way for new types of businesses, new types of consumer behavior, and new types of services (cf. Cameron, 1996; Cronin, 1996; Laudon and Laudon, 1997). The emergence of virtual, office-less organizations, enabled by similar technologies, will—so it is said—profoundly affect both the way we work and the structure and culture of organizations (e.g., Ciborra and Suetens, 1996). Communication technologies and applications have led to the globalization of businesses, opening up new markets as well as new competition, even for small businesses (e.g., Sterne, 1995). The new technologies, brought together under the common denominator of web-enabled technologies (WETs), seem to offer great opportunities for those who recognize them, and severe threats for organizations that have awakened too late. Simultaneously, more deliberate voices call for caution. Anderson (1997, p. 5), for instance, asserts that "few companies are as yet making any money on-line, but plenty are trying." He points out that this is only one example of the fact that "practically everything that was predicted about electronic commerce three years ago has turned out to be wrong" (ibid., p. 4). According to Anderson, it is a major mistake to equate the market potential of the Internet with its sheer size. Partly because of its size, "today's Internet is, far from being a perfect market, the high street from hell" (ibid.). Such contradictory signals are bound to puzzle organizations and leave them struggling with questions like: "Could WETs significantly improve our current way of doing business?"; "Could these technologies enable us to define a new business model?" or "Is it just hype and should it better be ignored?" In short, organizations are struggling with questions concerning the usefulness of WETs applied to their own situation. In a sense, this is nothing new since similar questions arise every time a new form of information and communication technology (ICT) is launched. For WETs the need for organizations to address this issue, however, may be more imperative, because their impact on organizations seems to be extremely diverse, highly complex and cannot be compared so easily to that of earlier forms of ICT.

What is called for, then, are guiding principles for relating the specific nature of WETs to questions of organizational impact. If, as the asserted impact of WETs suggests, these technologies affect the very existence of organizations, the focal point for assessing the organizational value of WETs should address questions of an existential nature. We suggest that the concept of 'viability of organizations' may provide this focal point. If WETs are really as fundamentally influential as claimed, using them or ignoring them will affect the viability of the organization and should, consequently, be addressed in the strategies that maintain this viability. The question, therefore, becomes how organizations can systematically approach the assessment of their viability through WETs. This question is the focus of this chapter. Such a 'systematic approach' consists of three elements. First, it involves an elaboration of the notion of viability as far as organizations are concerned. Secondly, it includes a description of the specific features of WETs. Thirdly, it presents a framework that ties viability to the specific features of WETs so that an individual organization can use it to assess the impact of the technology. This may be called a 'generic framework'. The objective of this chapter is to present such a framework.

The chapter is organized as follows. First, the existing methods for analyzing the strategic impact of ICT will be discussed briefly to illustrate that they do not adequately connect the idea of viability to specific forms of ICT. Next, a framework for assessing the strategic organizational value of WETs will be developed following the three elements mentioned above. First, based on Beer's (1979, 1981) Viable Systems Model (VSM), the concept of 'viability' is presented to direct discussions on the strategic potential of ICT, such as WETs. Secondly, a model is developed that structures the specific features of WETs. Thirdly, combining the model of organizational viability and that of the peculiarities of WETs results in a generic framework tailored to the specific features of WETs. This framework is discussed at a general level, in which directions for its use are also given. The application of the framework is illustrated in the penultimate section by presenting some case studies. The final section concludes the argument and presents additional researchable issues related to the application of the framework.

Frameworks for Assessing the Strategic Value of ICT

Two bodies of literature can be used to assess the strategic value of WETs. The first deals with frameworks for assessing the strategic value of ICT in general. The rationale for considering these frameworks is that they may be applied to WETs as well. The second body of literature consists of the rapidly expanding number of books and articles dealing with WETs in particular. In this section, we will discuss bot, and point out several drawbacks.

Concern with the general impact of ICT on organizations has led to many frameworks guiding the search for an effective ICT strategy (for overviews, see Earl, 1989; Robson, 1995; or Laudon and Laudon, 1997). Well-known models for assessing the possible strategic value of ICT are Porter's value-chain and competitive forces model (cf. Porter and Millar, 1986), the Strategic Opportunities Framework (Benjamin *et al.*, 1987) and the Client-Product Life Cycle (Ives and Learmonth, 1984). It is beyond the scope of this chapter to give a comprehensive review of all these models. In this chapter, we merely to assess the value of WETs - and one may, therefore, ask whether one of these frameworks can do the job. We feel that most of the existing general frameworks suffer from two drawbacks. The first is that they lack an explicit reference to viability—that is, most models state what seems to be important in or for organizations without explicitly stating why. What seems to be important in or for organizations is always an implicit translation of the notion of organizational viability. Porter, for instance, uses the value-chain and the competitive forces model as vehicles for this translation. Our contention is the following: why not make this underlying notion of viability more explicit? After all, determining the strategic value of ICT is nothing more than ensuring the viability of an organization. Consequently, it makes sense to deal explicitly and directly with viability. After such an explication, an organization can still decide that some 'translation' or other may suit its needs. The second drawback of these general frameworks is that they are not tailored to the specifics of WETs. A thorough analysis of the potentials of WETs should rest on an understanding of their specific features —not on the recognition that they belong to the broad class of ICT.

The second drawback of the general frameworks is seemingly countered by a growing number of books and articles on the strategic impact of WETs (e.g., Maitra, 1996; Andersen, 1997; Cappel and Myerscough, 1997). Although this literature deals with the specific, mostly technological features of WETs, a number of problems still crop up with regard to the analysis of strategic impact. One of these problems is that the reason for assessing the strategic value of WETs is even more implicit in this literature than in the general frameworks. An assessment of the technological specifics of WETs does not generate knowledge about strategic impact. The impact analysis is also often an 'assessment by example, involving for instance, discussions based on success stories (for a typical example, see Cappel and Myerscough, 1997). The problem with this kind of assessment is that it does not lead to a general model of the value of WETs for organizations, but at best, to a large list of situations in which they worked (not even: why they worked).

Both bodies of literature seem to lack a thorough analysis of the strategic impact of WETs. For assessing the value of WETs, there is not yet a model that explicitly deals with the notion of viability *and* ties this to the specific features of WETs. This chapter is meant to fill this gap.

A Model of Organizational Viability

This chapter aims at a model for ensuring the viability of an organization through WETs. A prerequisite, then, is an understanding of the notion of organizational viability. One rich theory on this subject, if not the only one, is advanced by Stafford Beer (Beer, 1979; 1981; 1985), and it may be useful to explore his ideas somewhat further. Viability, Beer explains, is "being able to maintain a separate existence" (Beer, 1979, p. 113). The key task for any organization is to strive for viability. To maintain a "separate existence" in an environment, any viable system should have five functions. The first function of a viable system is the function that produces it, that is, the function that produces the identity of the system (Beer, 1985, p. 14). For an organization this function may be realized by different business units. Together, the different clusters of operations realizing this function (e.g. business units) constitute what is called 'system one' (1979, p.174). At a university, system one may be seen as consisting of two clusters of operations producing the university: teaching and conducting research (cf. Beer, 1985, p.14). The system one of a local bicycle-shop may consist of selling bikes and repairing bikes. A large oil-producing organization may have a system one that — among other things — consists of one cluster of operations that focuses on oil refinery and another in which drilling for oil is the primary activity. In short, system one contains the primary activities of an organization — its *raison d'être* (cf. Espejo *et al.*, 1996, p. 110).

An important aspect of the clusters of activities in system one is that "they can in principle be hived off - sold as going concerns" (Beer, 1985, p.8). As such, these clusters can be viewed as viable systems. The operational activities of the different activity clusters (henceforward: divisions) of system one should be aligned. If not, oscillations are bound to occur. The alignment function is the second function of a viable system. Planning the use of shared resources is an important example. Other examples include house style or a set of safety regulations. Decision making on these matters goes beyond the boundaries of the management of the individual divisions and should, therefore, take place at another level.

The individual divisions are part of one organization and, their activities should be coordinated. Yet for the same reason, their activities should be monitored and controlled — the third function of a viable system. The monitoring and control function ensures that the current goals of the organization are met by the different divisions. As Beer puts it: "It should ensure synergy among the divisions" (Beer, 1979, p. 202 ff.). The monitoring and control function is embodied in organizations by means of direct commands to the management of the individual divisions by means of occasional audits of the operational activities of the divisions and by means of determining the criteria for alignment (function two).

The fourth function called '"intelligence" (Beer, 1979, p. 225 ff.) is responsible for ensuring that the organization "does the right thing." It is responsible for aligning the activities of the organization with environmental needs. Thus, it ensures the adaptation of the organization. This function scans the environment and translates trends, changes or other environmental developments into organizational goals, hence its name: intelligence. Typical activities of this type are carried out by RandD-departments trying to come up with ideas for new products.

The third and fourth functions represent two different modes of thinking about operational activities in organizations; the third function highlights how the activities of the divisions meet the *current* goals of the organization, whereas the fourth function focuses on new goals - thereby implying the implementation of new operations. According to Beer, these two functions should be coordinated. If they are not, two problems may occur. The first is that the organization adheres too strongly to the current way of "doing business", i.e. function three (representing the status quo) is 'stronger' than function four. The second problem is that the innovative ideas of function four are overvalued, leading to products that cannot be sold profitably. It goes without saying that both problems can lead an organization to disaster. Beer states therefore that a function is needed to "balance the interaction between function three and four" (cf. Beer, 1979, pp. 251-256). This fifth and last function of a viable system is called the 'policy' function. Balancing the interaction between "maintaining the status quo" (function three) and "embarking on a changing environment" (function four) is typically done by a board of directors, directing the discussion between proponents of the two functions. Other function five activities are the formulation of a long-term strategy and the determination of an organization's identity.

Beer asserts that these five functions are necessary and sufficient for any viable system. Given the proper implementation of these functions, an organization should be able to survive. The question then is: How to implement them properly? Beer makes clear that the answer to this question relates to "dealing with complexity". The complexity of an entity is defined as the possible number of states of that entity. As the environment of an organization is characterized by a tremendous complexity, an organization must learn to cope with it in order to survive. Not only is the environment complex, but also the organization itself is complex, and this internal complexity should be dealt with, too. The notion of dealing with complexity is at the heart of the VSM: "What is going on in organizations is the management of complexity" (Beer, 1985, p.21). A successful management of complexity may be achieved by means of a correct implementation of the five functions in an organization. Following Ashby's Law of Requisite Variety, Beer mentions two general strategies for dealing with complexity. The first is the attenuation or "cutting down" of the complexity of the entity that is to be regulated. Market research, for instance, may cut down environmental complexity, if one chooses to focus on the outcomes of the research (Beer, 1985, p. 25). Ignorance, too, cuts down environmental complexity: one just does not notice the relevant environmental cues. Proper use of the attenuation strategy ensures that some sources of environmental complexity no longer disturb the organization. The other strategy for dealing with complexity is amplification of the complexity of the regulatory entity. Management information systems typically amplify the number of things a manager can handle by combining data in summaries, graphics, etc. The crux of 'correctly' building or maintaining a viable system is to design the five functions and the proper attenuators and amplifiers for the different functions in such a way that they can handle complexity. Table 1 gives an illustration of possible attenuators and amplifiers for the five different functions.

To summarize what has been stated in this section: organizational viability is maintained by means of five functions. These functions may be implemented in an organization using two strategies for dealing with complexity: attenuation and amplification. In section 5, these ideas will be used to assemble a tool for identifying WETs applications enhancing the viability of an organization. There are several reasons why Beer's Viable Systems Model seems appropriate for designing such a tool. The first is that it explicitly deals with viability —something that is implicit in most models oriented towards a successful implementation of ICT. The second reason is that the model is applicable to all kinds of organizations as long as they strive to be viable organizations. The last reason why Beer's model is appropriate has to do with its recursiveness. It is not only useful for analyzing viable system functions at the level of an organization as a whole, but also at the level of, say, a department or business unit. These may be treated as viable systems too, generating different functions and complexity strategies.

Table 1. Examples of attenuation and amplification of viability functions

	Attenuator	Amplifier
Function 1: primary activities	Outsourcing physical distribution	More production facilities
Function 2: alignment	Making divisions self-sufficient	IT for planning
Function 3: monitoring and control	Delegation of command	Management information systems (for monitoring & controlling different divisions)
Function 4: intelligence	Hiring an information broker	World Wide Web
Function 5: policy	Corporate strategy	Executive information systems (combine data from function 3 and 4 and help simulation of strategies)

Features of Web-Enabled Technologies

Using the VSM for WETs comes down to figuring out how WETs can help in carrying out the five different functions and/or seeking WETs to amplify or attenuate the complexity with regard to these functions. Applying the model of organizational viability to assess the strategic value of WETs presumes an understanding and classification of the specific features of WETs. As illustrated in the other chapters of this book, these features may be defined in several ways. For instance, from a technological point of view, WETs are defined by hypertext, network technology, concurrency control, sound and video support, etc. From an application point of view, WETs may be defined as comprising facilities for enabling electronic messaging (e-mail), chat systems, electronic meeting systems, bulletin-board systems, coauthoring systems, etc. (Ter Hofte, 1998, pp. 9 ff). For the present discussion a suitable description is easily found when WETs are seen as the means to connect people. A common trait of all WETs is that they can be used in a technical sense to establish links between individual people, places, departments, organizations, or between organizations and their customers, competitors or potential partners. The provision of such links can be seen as an important step towards facilitating already existing or newly formed groups (either conventional groups also meeting in face-to-face situations or virtual groups whose existence is enabled by the technology).

The specific features of WETs derive from how the basic idea of providing cross-links (i.e. supporting group formation) takes shape given the various types and uses of these technologies. The different aspects that may be involved in group work are represented by the following four C's:

1. *Circulation*: distributing information to a broader audience, without attempting to establish some form of interactivity with the audience.
2. *Communication*: establishing interaction between senders and receivers of information.
3. *Coordination*: dealing with correspondences and conflicts between individual tasks resulting from the fact that group members work on different tasks contributing to a larger task.
4. *Collaboration*: working together on the same task.

The strength of most WETs is that they "deliver" or facilitate one or more of these C's. It should be noted that these four concepts are used in disparate ways both in the literature and in practice (see, for instance, Vennix, 1996, Nunamaker *et al.*, 1995, Jankowski *et al.*, 1997; Roschelle and Teasley, 1995).

Before elaborating the four concepts, a few remarks need to be made. First, it may be noted that sometimes a fifth 'C' is discerned, namely that of cooperation (e.g. Roschelle and Teasley, 1995). Here, cooperation is seen as an umbrella term covering both collaboration and coordination. Second, these four concepts are to some extend interrelated. Collaboration, for instance, presupposes communication. Tools that may support communication may, therefore, also prove useful for supporting collaboration. Third, it is hardly, if at all, possible to draw a sharp demarcation line between the four concepts. For instance, in situations where people collaborate they usually do not all perform the same task or play the same role. These situations may, consequently, also be studied from a coordination point of view. These concepts are therefore best treated as focal points for characterizing activities, rather than distinct classes. Individual activities may combine features of more than one 'C', or may depend on the relations between them.

The most basic use of WETs is to provide means for circulating. publishing or distributing information to a broader audience. The group involved is then simply defined by all those who either publish the information or pluck it from the network. Usually such a group is of a virtual nature; the individual group members are typically not even aware of each other's existence, their "interaction" is nonparallel and asynchronous. This type of link is sometimes identified as one form of 'communication' (our second 'C'; see Lotus Corporation, 1995). We explicitly distinguish these two concepts, however, because of the passive nature of the relations between senders and receivers in information circulation. That using WETs may involve strategically important activities, even for passive relations, is suitably illustrated by Kassler (1997). She describes how using the Internet greatly enhances the critically important business intelligence function of tracing company profiles, news facts, and locating primary sources (such as experts). All these search activities refer to situations where the Internet was used in a purely passive sense for circulating information (similar examples can, for instance, be found in Cronin *et al.*, 1994).

If attempts are made to attune information sent and information received, circulation of information becomes communication. This is perhaps the functionality group that first comes to mind when thinking of situations where WETs may prove useful. As an example, refer to Internet-sites that guide the visitor towards those parts of the site most relevant for this user and in the process gather information on characteristics of the visitor (for instance, by asking age or preferences). Through this accumulated information, and by registering purchases, the company can build a profile of individual customers. This may lead to a next communication step as it allows the firm to alert its customers far more effectively than through direct mail when relevant new products or services become available. As another example of how WETs support communication, consider sites that invite their customers to contribute to the site, for instance, by sending their book or music reviews. Subsequently, the site may stimulate communication between customers about these reviews, for instance, via chat applications. Both for communication within organizations (intranets), between organizations and selected groups of external parties (extranets), and between organizations and all external parties or between external parties (the Internet) WETs may induce dramatic changes, both concerning range and content of the communication. Most current discussions about electronic commerce concern the use of WETs to generate or support communication (Anderson, 1997).

If a task is segregated into different subtasks, the need for coordination of the individual contributions arises. The need for coordination is contingent either upon the separation of a larger task into smaller chunks, or upon the use of the same resources by disparate tasks (Malone and Crowston, 1993, p.381). The coordination effort centres on how the individual tasks relate to each other (Are they to be performed simultaneously or sequentially? Does one subtask need the output of another task as its input? etc.). Perhaps the best known example of ICT support for coordination is to be found in the concept of workflow management (WfM); for an example of using WETs to implement WfM, see Gebauer and Schad (1998). It should, however, be noted that WfM is based on a specific coordination model that is not generally applicable to all coordination tasks, and, as such, represents just one possible class of WETs support. The role of WETs in supporting coordination efforts may vary depending on the conception of how to deal with the interdependencies involved. For instance, distinct functions for WETs become apparent when focusing on the transfer of intermediate products (as does WfM) versus fostering dialogue (Malone and Crowston, 1993).

The highest level of group formation occurs when the individual group members work together on a common task. Nunamaker *et al.* (1995) compare collaborative efforts in workgroups with the concerted efforts of, for instance, rowing crews. The integration of common functionalities for supporting idea generation and group brainstorming present in Group Decision Support Systems with Internet standards may serve to illustrate how WETs may play a part in facilitating collaborative efforts. A perhaps technically somewhat less advanced example of supporting collaboration occurs when the Internet is used as a platform for negotiations or for inviting bidding (e.g., General Electric's Trading Post Network, see Anderson, 1997, p. 24).

Within the four C's a further specification of the types of WETs applications to be considered may be achieved by introducing additional classification schemes. The best known of these is probably the time-place matrix (Johansen, 1988) which distinguishes between local and remote applications, and synchronous and asynchronous applications. Also, within each 'C', the appropriateness of restrictive versus permissive applications (Galegher and Kraut, 1990), or applications focusing on information sharing versus information exchange (McGrath and Hollingshead, 1994) may be considered. Here the four C's are only used as a starting point for identifying types of WET applications. Exploring a further specification of types of WETs within the C's is beyond the scope of this chapter.

A General Framework for Linking Web-Enabled Technologies to Viability

This section combines the viability functions, the complexity strategies and WET features from the previous sections to construct a generic framework for assessing 'viable' WET applications. Given the relevant notions from the previous sections, the overall logic of this framework is very straightforward:

1. Identify viable system functions and related complexity strategies.
2. Find out how one or more C's can support these functions or strategies.
3. Search for technical possibilities, i.e. actual or possible WET applications, for implementing the support in 2.

Searching for viable WET applications can be conceived as filling the matrix shown in Figure 1. In our view, three distinct strategies for filling this matrix may be discerned. These strategies differ in accordance with their starting point in the matrix and may be called 'routes' through the matrix. The first route starts with functions and complexity strategies; the second with the four C's, and the last route takes an existing WET application as a touchstone for envisaging the possible value of WETs.

The first strategy for assessing the value of WETs with the use of the above matrix comprises the following steps:

1. Work out how the different functions are performed and try to enumerate attenuations and amplifications.
2. See whether one or more C's can support:
   a. performing the different functions;
   b. attenuating complexity with regard to the functions;
   c. amplifying complexity in relation to the functions.
3. Translate the above analysis into more tangible technical possibilities (specific uses of WETs: intranet, Internet, etc.)

This strategy focuses on the current implementation of the functions and complexity strategies. The possibilities of WETs are 'only' used to support these. When looking at the matrix, this route works from 'the outside to the inside' of the matrix, starting with the viability functions, and may therefore be called a 'viability-driven' strategy.

The second strategy for assessing the possibilities of WETs does not take the current functions and strategies as an anchor, but uses knowledge of the four C's to generate implementations of functions and complexity strategies. This route through the matrix is driven by the knowledge of WET functionalities and can therefore be called a 'functionality-driven' strategy. The steps to be taken are now:

1. Work out how one or more C's can be used to construct implementations of:
   a. the different functions;
   b. attenuation regarding the different functions;
   c. amplification regarding the different functions.
2. Translate the above analysis into more tangible technical possibilities (specific uses of WETs -intranet, Internet, etc.).

The third route through the matrix starts off with existing WET applications (existing in practice - not necessarily within the organization). The question is then: how can these WET applications support the current implementations of functions/complexity-strategies or how can these applications be used to construct new implementation of the functions/complexity strategies? A typical answer may be: 'This particular instance of WETs may be used for our purposes, but it needs some modification...' This third route embodies what may be called a 'technology-driven' strategy, and consists of the following steps:

1. Take an existing WET application.
2. Using the 4 C's, analyze its possible use for:
   a. the different functions;
   b. the two complexity strategies.
3. Adjust the prospective WET application to the specific needs of the organization.

In terms of our matrix this way of assessing the use of WET may be called 'inside-out' (for it starts with an application -in the centre of the matrix and tries to find out how that application can be adjusted to current implementations of functions or strategies). We suspect that taking some allegedly successful WET application as a starting point for assessing the value of WETs is the most common way of exploring the possibilities of WET use (e.g. "Competitors are using it - can we?"). Starting the analysis from an existing WET application may seem rather coincidental, but we feel that its exploration may be worthwhile if it explicitly includes the viability functions, the complexity strategies and the four C's.

Although the above draws a distinction between three different routes for tying WETs to the viability of an organization, it does not mean that these routes are mutually exclusive. For the sake of clarity, we find some logic in delineating three distinct, 'ideal-typical' ways of tying WETs to viability. In practice, however, more than one route may be followed simultaneously, it may be possible to switch between routes and it may even be possible to mix different routes. For example, suppose that one lists some of the functionalities of a possible WET application using route 1, then recognizes an existing WET application that has some of these functionalities, and subsequently uses this application in a 'route-3' fashion, i.e. one tries to find out how this particular application can be used to enhance viability functions or complexity strategies. Please bear this in mind because the rest of this chapter will only make reference to the three different routes.

Application of the Framework

The framework for linking WETs to the viability of organizations may be used in several ways. These include descriptive, evaluative and normative applications. We will only explore a descriptive application in this chapter. For an evaluative use, aimed at establishing whether WET applications live up to their expectations, an exploration of additional evaluation methods and measurement techniques would be called for. If the framework is used for directing future uses of WETs, it is applied in a normative way. Here too, additional theorizing is needed (for instance, to explore the contingencies within the organization determining the appropriateness of selected applica-

Figure 1: A general framework linking organizational viability to WETs.

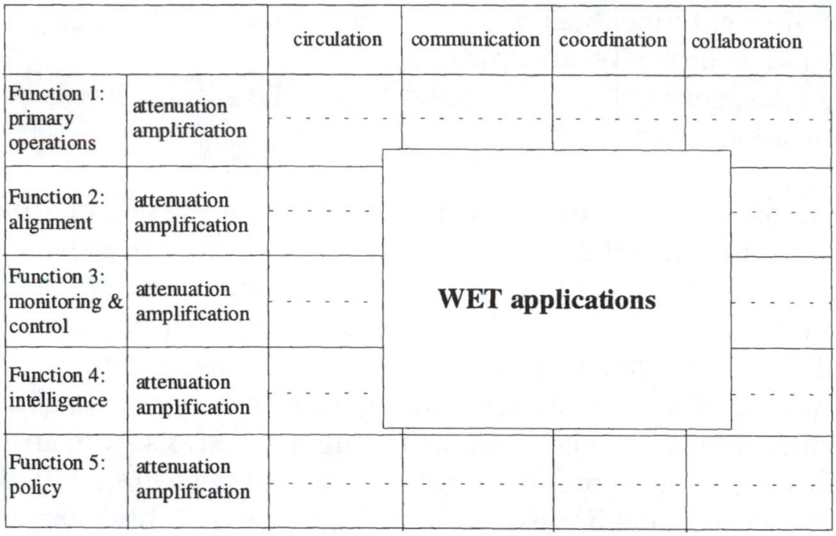

		circulation	communication	coordination	collaboration
Function 1: primary operations	attenuation amplification				
Function 2: alignment	attenuation amplification				
Function 3: monitoring & control	attenuation amplification		**WET applications**		
Function 4: intelligence	attenuation amplification				
Function 5: policy	attenuation amplification				

tions and implementation strategies). Within the class of descriptive applications of the framework, two distinct approaches can be identified. One is to fill each cell of the matrix of Figure 1 with examples of WET applications. This approach is likely to result in an extensive list of applications. An alternative approach is to describe cases in which organizations took one of the three routes for filling the matrix. This approach is superior to listing applications and for several reasons. It allows the user to explicitly start from the context of an individual organization and link its efforts to the viability functions, four C's and complexity strategies. Also, it gives additional insight in the process of assessing WET applications along the lines proposed here. This section will therefore follow the latter approach and discuss three cases in more detail. Each case illustrates one of the three strategies discussed above and covers different cells in the matrix that represents our general framework. Figure 2 identifies which cells of the matrix are covered in each example.

Example 1: The viability-driven route

Our first case deals with an example of the *viability-driven route* through the matrix. It describes how a large pharmaceutical multinational implemented a 'business intelligence' function. The aim of this function is to scan the environment for data useful for the formulation of a corporate strategy. Business intelligence requires the formulation of different product-market-technology combinations (PMTs) that direct the scanning process. These combinations may be existing (actual) PMTs or possible — virtual — PMTs.

Figure 2: Place of the examples in the framework-matrix (see text).

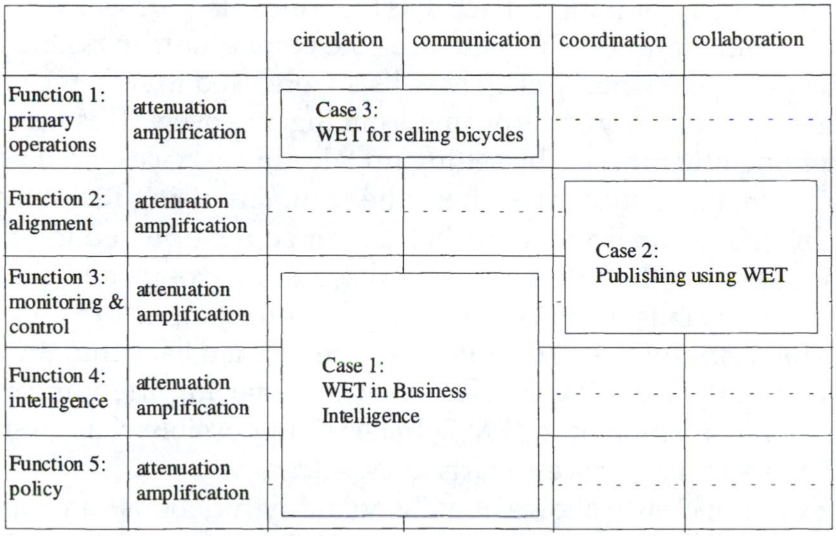

		circulation	communication	coordination	collaboration
Function 1: primary operations	attenuation amplification	Case 3: WET for selling bicycles			
Function 2: alignment	attenuation amplification			Case 2: Publishing using WET	
Function 3: monitoring & control	attenuation amplification				
Function 4: intelligence	attenuation amplification	Case 1: WET in Business Intelligence			
Function 5: policy	attenuation amplification				

When there are several PMTs, the environment is scanned for data that might support the continuation or implementation of a specific PMT, or for data that demonstrate its fallibility. One may hope that somewhere during this process a set of more or less viable PMTs emerges, forming the base for a corporate strategy. However, this does not imply that the business intelligence process stops; it should continue to generate possible PMTs and scan the environment to explore their viability. Strategy formulation is thus seen as a dynamic process. To implement the business intelligence function, a cycle of three processes may be discerned:

1. Generation of PMTs,
2. Scanning the environment and
3. Ihe interpretation of data.

These three processes are interlinked as follows. The PMTs are used to direct the scanning process; the results of the scanning process are the input for interpretation, that is, for determining the value of the PMT used for scanning. The outcomes of the interpretation process may influence further generation of PMTs, etc. The implementation of this business intelligence cycle in the multinational relied heavily on the use of WETs. To begin with, the existing intranet was used for the generation of PMTs. An internal site was started to support the discussion on the plausibility of PMTs. Among the participants were seniors from production control, marketing, and some CEOs (responsible for strategy). When a set of relatively plausible PMTs was agreed upon, these PMTs were used as an anchor for generating lists of possibly relevant information. Each PMT defines its own set of relevant information items, among which are possible competitors, possible clients, trends, technological aspects, etc. These lists were used to scan the environment—the second activity of the business intelligence cycle. This was accomplished, among other things, by setting up 'alerting services' on the net; by extending search activities throughout the company using its intranet (for example, by using e-mail and a site that contained the updated information items); by searching the Internet (using discussion groups and search engines) and by establishing network links to information brokers on the Internet. The results of these scanning activities are fed back into the discussion on the value of the PMTs used, thereby, starting the interpretation process. After evaluation of the PMTs in use (and possibly changing the set of PMTs), the scanning process starts anew, etc.

This example clearly shows how the viability functions can trigger the use of WETs. Although not explicitly stated in the example, functions three (monitoring and control), four (intelligence), and five (policy) are the focal ones. The intelligence function is relevant, because the goal of the business intelligence function is to scan the environment in order to formulate a corporate strategy. Monitoring and control play a role, because the plausibility of PMTs is not established by 'intelligence' alone: it is discussed with members of production control and marketing units and CEOs - thereby taking into account how possible PMTs might fit in with the current way of doing business. The coordination of the discussion between members of intelligence and monitoring and control is an instance of the policy function and may be carried out by the participating CEOs.

WETs are used to enhance the three viability functions as a device for both attenuation and amplification. In Figure 3, the different forms of WET use are linked to the three functions and the complexity strategies.

The internal discussion site is mainly used for communication purposes. The site amplifies the coordination activities of function five: it supports the alignment of functions three and four. It also amplifies the capacity of functions three and four: it makes it easier to participate in the discussion on what counts as a viable PMT. The other WET tools are used for scanning the environment (function four). The use of a search engine amplifies search activities and focuses on circulation. Alerting services and hiring information brokers are examples of using WETs as a device for the attenuation of search activities, because part of these activities are performed by a third party. These two WET uses emphasize circulation (of data) and communication (with the services and brokers). Participating in discussion groups also refers to these two WET functionalities.

Figure 3: Place of different Business Intelligence WET applications and functions in the framework, illustrating the viability-driven route

		circulation	communication
Function 3: monitoring & control	attenuation		
	amplification		Discussion site
Function 4: intelligence	attenuation	Alerting services Information broker	Alerting services Information broker
	amplification	Searching on the Internet: search engines discussion groups	Discussion site; Searching on the Internet: discussion groups
Function 5: policy	attenuation		
	amplification		Discussion site

Example 2: The functionality-driven route

To illustrate how the *functionality-driven route* can be conceived, the case of a publishing company will be considered. In general, publishing companies are best known for the fact they explore new markets very actively and offer new products through WETs, including abstracting services, the publication of electronic journals, and other on-line publishing activities (cf. Cox, 1997; Heath, 1997). The case presented here concerns a more specific situation in which a publisher has explored the means to support the coordination and collaboration between multiple authors of one volume. The common situation for such volumes is that an editor or editing committee directs the individual authors and evaluates their contributions. The editors are like spiders in the web. All communication between individual contributors usually passes via the editor's desk. Even in situations where individual authors interact directly without intervention from the editors, this is usually done on a bilateral basis for subjects or problems identified beforehand. The publisher, if not represented in the editing committee, is typically present in the publication process as a monitor of the process, a discussion partner and supervisor of the editors. This is a satisfactory situation if the contributions

Figure 4: Place of WET applications and functions of a publishing company in the framework, illustrating the functionality-driven route.

		circulation	communication
Function 2: alignment	attenuation	web-enabled co-authoring system; web-enabled electronic conferencing system	web-enabled co-authoring system; web-enabled electronic conferencing system
	amplification	web-enabled electronic conferencing system; e-mail	web-enabled electronic conferencing system; discussion server; e-mail
Function 3: monitoring & control	attenuation	web-enabled co-authoring system; web-enabled conferencing system; discussion server	web-enabled co-authoring system; web-enabled conferencing system; discussion server
	amplification	web-enabled co-authoring system; web-enabled conferencing system; e-mail	web-enabled co-authoring system; web-enabled conferencing system; e-mail

are of a stand-alone nature, and their link to the overall theme and to the other contributions is not problematic. If, however, the contributions should form links in a chain, the model of coordination through a central editing function is flawed. This situation occurs, for instance, if multiple authors work together to produce a monograph (consider, for instance, a textbook on a new subject addressed by experts from different places). Ideas are usually developed during the writing process. Potential links between chapters or possible disputes between authors can therefore only be identified while the work is in progress. In these situations the need for collaboration between authors and for ongoing coordination increases. Collaboration is called for because the individual contributions are no longer assessed as different subtasks that can be addressed sequentially. Instead, they are considered as integral parts of a larger task, i.e. writing a book. If writing a book is considered a collaborative task then, obviously, also the coordination of the steps to be taken in producing the book takes on new meaning. Assigning at least part of the responsibility for both the collaboration and coordination tasks to the authors instead of the editors may be expected to have positive impacts both on the efficiency of the proceedings and on the quality of the work (e.g. the risk that the editors filter out potentially useful suggestions is reduced).

The publisher in question (a medium-sized company specialized in scientific publications) decided to institute a test case in which it offered WET applications to facilitate both the collaboration between authors and their mutual coordination. These included coauthoring systems, electronic conferencing systems, e-mail and a discussion server. The decision to explore the option of offering such tools rather than encouraging the authors to use their own tools, was induced by the publisher's wish to learn and to enhance their presence in the production trajectory. Two columns of the framework in Figure 1 are considered in the example: coordination and cooperation. In the example these concern the tasks involved in conceiving and writing a book (by the authors, editors, designers, etc). The rows (VSM functions and strategies) refer to the functions within the publishing company (e.g. the alignment function addresses the interplay of such primary functions as project planning and management, production, sales and marketing, and graphical design). Only two VSM functions are given attention: alignment (function two) and monitoring (function three), although other functions are affected by the WET applications as well. Figure 4 positions the individual WET applications in the cells of the matrix.

Changes in the coordination of tasks through WETs affect the attenuation and amplification strategies for both functions considered. Particularly the use of the co-authoring system has notable effects. It attenuates the need for alignment and control. The fact that authors are able to inspect each others work and are thus able to coordinate their individual contributions themselves and to discuss matters of coordination themselves, reduces the need to align the publishers' functions (project management, production, graphical design, etc.). Authors have direct insight into the links between their work and that of their coauthors thus also relieving the publisher from some of his monitoring tasks. The coauthoring system also amplifies the publisher's control function: the publisher can check more easily whether individual contributions are well aligned. New ways of coordination also follow from the use of the electronic meeting system, affecting the attenuation and amplification of both functions. For example, the project managers, graphical editors, etc. may take part in scheduled meetings of the authors and editors, thus enhancing their capability of mutual alignment (amplification of the alignment function). The minutes of meetings of authors and editors are stored automatically and available for inspection by the publisher, enabling him to assess the coordination of the authors' work (amplification of the monitoring and control function). Additionally, alterations in coordination because of the use of e-mail, and a discussion server affects the functions considered. Through the use of e-mail, the coordination of graphical work across chapters is more easily discussed, allowing the graphical editor to stimulate and direct the individual authors in preparing their illustrations according to a standard format (amplification of the alignment function). The

Figure 5: Place of three WETbased functions for a producer of bicycles in the framework, illustrating the technology-driven route.

		circulation	communication
Function 1: primary activities	attenuation	stock checking; ordering facilities	exchange-request facilities
	amplification		
Function 3: monitoring & control	attenuation		
	amplification	stock checking	

amount of activity on the discussion server may serve to assess the need for active intervention by the editor/publisher; the nature of the discussions may help to establish whether the task coordination of the individual authors needs any attention (attenuation of the monitoring and control function).

The WETs also support the collaboration between the authors, leading to changes in the attenuation and amplification strategies for both functions. Because of the use of the coauthoring system and electronic conferencing system the production of a multi-author volume becomes increasingly a collaborative effort of the authors. This takes a substantial burden off the individual functions of the publisher, and off their alignment (attenuation of alignment function). If more people consider themselves intellectually responsible for the overall product, the need for the publisher to tackle the authors about their individual responsibilities diminishes (attenuation of the monitoring and control function). Also amplifications of both functions follow from the enhanced means of cooperation. For instance, departments such as the production department and the drawing office may take part in discussions regarding issues affecting the work of multiple authors, thus enhancing their mutual alignment capabilities (amplification of alignment function). The automatically stored minutes of meetings allow an easy assessment of the status of cooperation within the team of authors and editors (amplification of monitoring and control function).

Example 3: The technology-driven route

The third case describes the *technology-driven route* through the matrix. This route starts with an existing WET application and then tries to find out how it can be moulded in the existing organizational functionalities, using the viability functions, the four C's and the complexity strategies. The existing application in this case was a successfully used web-based application that enabled car dealers to communicate with an importer. The system was mainly used to check the stock of the importer and to order a certain amount of cars. A producer of bicycles took this application as a starting point for trying to find out how it could be tailored to his own trade. It did so by focusing on its primary operations and on attenuating complexity regarding these operations. This was done by establishing a WET based dealer network to regulate stock control - an HTML-based extranet connecting producers and dealers. This extranet had several functions. First, it enabled dealers to order bikes from the production plant. This function was directly 'taken' from the car-dealer system. It was implemented in a fairly standard web-based fashion. The second function of the network was that dealers could check the stock of other dealers on-line, and, if necessary, request the exchange of bikes, bike-parts and accessories. For implementation of this function, the network was connected to several databases at the level of individual dealers. Through an interface, dealers could take a glimpse into each other's stock. Also, e-mail facilities were used to support the communication between dealers concerning stock exchanges. In addition to these two functions, the network made it possible for the producer to gain a more detailed insight into stocks of the associated dealers and hence in stock fluctuations. In Figure 5, three extranet features ('stock checking', 'exchange-request facilities' and 'ordering facilities') are given a place in our framework.

From a producer's point of view, this example deals with Beers' functions one (it changes primary activities regarding the producer's stock and production flows) and three (it enhanced the control of the stock and production flow). The features of the system emphasize circulation and communication. To make the system work, information about stocks should be circulated. Ordering is another form of circulation of information. Communication about stock items is needed to request an exchange of stock items. The extranet was used for both attenuation and amplification of the producer's activities. By enabling dealers to look into the stock of other dealers and negotiate on the exchange of stock items, the environmental complexity for the producer was reduced. Stock fluctuations could thus be resolved among different dealers, thereby attenuating the 'stock complexity' for the producer. The network also amplifies the control function of the producer: by monitoring the individual dealer's stock, the producer gained more insight into sales and fluctuations.

Conclusion

No linear scale of organizational value exists on which WET applications can be placed (despite suggestions of the opposite frequently found in appraisals from the WET industry, and also in some academic disputes, see, for instance, Dutta *et al.*, 1997). More tools for electronic commerce, more gadgets for interactivity, etc., do not necessarily result in organizationally more valuable WET applications. Neither is an organization that has adapted its business model to the potential of WETs by definition smarter than one that aims to integrate WETs into its existing business model, or even one that completely ignores WETs. Making the most of WETs is not simply a matter of making up a list of possible WET uses and picking the appropriate ones from this list. For one thing, drawing up such a list seems hardly possible since a full understanding of the potential of WETs is firmly beyond the horizon. WETs are much like Aladdin's lamp. A WET application fulfills the wishes of its user, but has none of its own. Creativity is core business for organizations considering how WETs may help them. Although successful examples of WET use may boost this creativity, these examples in themselves do not have the potential of distinguishing between possibly useful and probably useless applications. The framework presented in this chapter, centering on functions and strategies for organizational viability, offers the perspective needed here. It may, for instance, be used to evaluate the experiences of others. It may also offer the touchstone for directing and valuing activities aimed at envisaging how WETs may support the current strategies of the organization, or introduce radically new ones.

Looking at WETs from an organizational viability perspective is a challenging, and also momentous undertaking. This chapter has made only a modest contribution to such an undertaking by sketching the pillars of a viability-centered framework, and some of these only in outline. Although the framework is still under construction, we feel that applying it may be worthwhile for several reasons. Because the framework explicitly tries to link features of WETs to the viability of organizations, it forces us to make apparent how WETs contribute to organizations. The framework also provides some insight into how this contribution is to be conceived (the particular cells in the matrix). In our experience, the framework facilitates communication and covers quite recognizable issues. Furthermore, because of its general (it discusses matters at the level of organizational 'systems') and recursive nature (it can be applied to an organization as a whole; to its divisions; or even at the level of departments or teams), it seems to offer possibilities for any organization or smaller unit.

However, to fine-tune the framework theoretically so that it can be applied more adequately, some issues will have to be tackled first. Firstly, the translation of viability-related needs and challenges into specific types of WETs requires some elaboration. As has already been suggested, exploring an appropriate combination of alternative classification schemes for WETs may prove useful for this purpose. Secondly, additional insight into how descriptive case studies fit into the framework is needed. Thus, a well-defined database may be set up for guiding future creative applications of the framework. Also, sorting individual case studies into the meshes of the framework may help test the appropriateness of the vocabulary for recognizing and labelling these case studies. Thirdly, further empirical studies of an evaluative and normative nature, for instance in the form of experiments, are needed to gain insight into the contingencies directing the application of the framework. For all these purposes, the combined experiences and insights regarding WET applications collected in a volume such as the present, may prove very useful. The reader may, for instance, classify the case studies presented in the other chapters of this volume with the use of the categories in the framework. This exercise can both be performed for testing the completeness and workability of the framework and for gaining an additional understanding concerning these case studies.

Despite the limitations of this study we feel that the notion of viability, and its elaboration in five functions and two strategies offer a conceptually fertile basis for assessing the strategic potential of WETs. The framework based on this notion offers a more rewarding and organizationally useful perspective on WETs than that generated by a standard method for assessing the strategic value of ICT or a technology-centered approach, focusing on the technical features of WETs.

References

Anderson, C. (1997). Electronic commerce. In search of the perfect market. *The Economist, 343* (Supl. 8016), 1-26.

Beer, S. (1979). *The heart of enterprise.* Chichester: Wiley.

Beer, S. (1981). *Brain of the firm.* Chichester: Wiley.

Beer, S. (1995). *Diagnosing the system.* Chichester: Wiley.

Benjamin, R.I., Rockart, J.F., Scott Morton, M.S.,, and Wyman, J. (1984). Information technology: a strategic opportunity. *Sloan Management Review,* 25(3), pp. 17-28.

Cameron, D. (1996). *The world wide web: strategies and opportunities for business.* Charleston, SC: Computer Technology Research.

Cappel, J.J., and Myerscough, M.A. (1997). Using the World Wide Web to gain a competitive advantage; *Information Strategy,* 13(3), pp. 6-14.

Ciborra, C.U., and Suetens, N.T. (1996). Groupware for an emerging virtual organization. In C.U. Ciborra (Ed.), *Groupware and teamwork; invisible aid or technical hindrance* (pp. 185-210). New York: Wiley.

Cox, J.E. (1997). Publishers, publishing and the Internet: How journal publishing will survive and prosper in the electronic age; *The electronic library*, 15(2), 125-132.

Cronin, M.J. (Ed). (1996). *The Internet strategy handbook: lessons from the new frontier of business*. Boston, MA: Harvard Business School Press.

Cronin, B., Overfelt, K., Fouchereaux, K., Manzvanzvike, T., Cha, M., and Sona, E. (1994). The Internet and competitive intelligence: a survey of current practice. *International Journal of Information Management*, 14(3), 204-222.

Dutta S., Kwan S., and Segev, A. (1997). *Competing in the marketspace: an empirical study* (Working Paper No. 97/99/TM). Fontainebleau: INSEAD.

Earl, M.J., (1989). *Management strategies for information technology*. Englewoods Cliffs: Prentice Hall.

Espejo, R., Schwaninger, M., and Schumann, M. (1996). *Organisational transformation and learning*. Chichester: Wiley.

Galegher, J., and Kraut, R.E. (1990). Technology for intellectual teamwork: perspectives on research and design. In J. Galegher, R.E. Kraut, and C. Egido (Eds.) *Intellectual teamwork: social and technological foundations of cooperative work* (pp. 1-20). Hillsdale, NJ: Lawrence Erbaum Associates.

Gebauer, J., and Schad, H. (1998). *Building an Internet-based workflow system. The case of Lawrence Livermore National Laboratories' Zephyr project* (Working Paper No. 98-WP-1030). Berkeley, CA: Fisher Center for Management and Information Technology.

Heath, R.P. (1997). In so many words: how technology reshapes the reading habit; *American Demographics*, 19(3), pp. 38-44.

Ives, B. and Learmonth, G.P. (1984). The information system as a competitive weapon, *Communications of the ACM* 27(12), pp. 1193-1201.

Johansen, R. (1988). Current user approaches to groupware. In R. Johansen (Ed.), *Groupware: computer support for business teams* (pp. 12-44). New York: Free Press.

Jankowski, P., Nyerges, T.L., Smith, A., Moore, T.J., and Horvath, E. (1997). Spatial group choice: a SDSS tool for collaborative spatial decision-making. *International Journal of Geographical Information Science*, 11, 577-602.

Kassler, H.S. (1997). Mining the Internet for competitive Intelligence. How to track and sift for golden nuggets. *Online: the magazine of online information systems*, 12(5), 34-45.

Laudon, K.C., and Laudon, J.P. (1997). *Management information systems* (2nd ed.). Upper Saddle River: Prentice Hall.

Lotus Corporation. (1995). *Groupware white paper: executive summary*. Cambridge, MA: Lotus Corporation.

Maitra, A.K., (1996). *Building a corporate internet strategy*. New York: Van

Nostrand Reinhold.

Malone, T.W., and Crowston, K. (1993). What is coordination theory and how can it help design cooperative work systems. In R.M. Baecker (Ed.), *Readings in groupware and computer-supported cooperative work; assisting human-human collaboration* (pp. 375-388). San Mateo, CA: Kaufmann.

McGrath, J.E., and Hollingshead, A.B. (1994). *Groups interacting with technology. Ideas, evidence, issues, and an agenda.* Thousand Oaks: Sage.

Nunamaker, J.F., Briggs, R.O., and Mittleman, D.D. (1995). *Electronic Meeting Systems: ten years of lessons learned.* In D. Coleman, and R. Khanna (Eds.), *Groupware: Technology and Applications* (pp. 149-193). Englewood Cliffs: Prentice Hall.

Porter, M.E., and Millar, V.E. (1985). How information gives you competitive advantage. *Harvard Business Review* (July-August), pp. 149-160.

Robson, W., (1994). *Strategic management and information systems.* London: Pitman Publishing.

Roschelle, J., and Teasley, S.D. (1995). The construction of shared knowledge in collaborative problem solving. In C. O'Malley (Ed.), *Computer supported collaborative learning* (pp. 69-97). Berlin: Springer.

Sterne, J. (1995). *World Wide Web marketing: integrating the Internet into your marketing strategy.* New York: Wiley.

Ter Hofte, G.H. (1998). *Working apart together. Foundations for component groupware.* Enschede: Telematica Instituut.

Vennix, J.A.M. (1996). *Group model building. Facilitating team learning using system dynamics.* New York: Wiley.

Chapter 7

World Wide Wait

Fui Hoon (Fiona) Nah
University of Nebraska-Lincoln

Kihyun Kim
University of Nebraska-Lincoln

Introduction

The explosive popularity of the World Wide Web (WWW) is the biggest event in the Internet era. Since its public introduction in 1991, WWW has become an important channel for electronic commerce, information access, and publication. With exponential growth in the WWW market, Internet connection speed has become a critical issue. The *long waiting time for accessing web pages* has always been a major problem for WWW users (Lightner, Bose and Salvendy, 1996), especially with the increasing use of multimedia technology and the doubling of Internet users every 18-24 months. A recent survey conducted by the GVU (Graphic, Visualization, & Usability) Center at the Georgia Institute of Technology also indicates long downloading time to be the biggest problem experienced by WWW users (GVU, October 1998). This problem is so noticeable that WWW users sometimes equate the "WWW" acronym with "World Wide Wait"! Although information technology for supporting the infrastructure of WWW is continually being updated and improved, it is still not able to satisfy industry requirements and demand.

In this chapter, we review the usage pattern of WWW as well as topics related to speed of Internet access such as bandwidth, Internet connection alternatives, and technology to speed up WWW access. In addition, we report an experimental research that measured and analyzed users' "tolerable" waiting time in accessing the WWW. Based on the results of the study, we provide guidelines for web designers regarding page size restrictions in web development.

Table 1. Frequency of Web Use

Usage Pattern	More than 9 times/day	5 to 8 times/day	1 to 4 times/day	A few times/week	Once a week	Once a month	Total
Frequency	1215	654	1177	217	18	10	3291
Percent (%)	36.9	19.9	35.8	6.6	.5	.3	100.0

Source: GVU's (October 1998) 10th WWW User Survey (http://www.gvu.gatech.edu/user_surveys)

Table 2. Hours of Web Used

Use Pattern	0–1hrs/week	2–4 hrs/week	5–6 hrs/week	7–9 hrs/week	10–20 hrs/week	21–40 hrs/week	Over 40 hrs/week	Total
Frequency	28	302	362	433	1119	697	350	3291
Percent (%)	0.8	9.2	11.0	13.2	34.0	21.2	10.6	100.0

Source: GVU's (October 1998) 10th WWW User Survey (http://www.gvu.gatech.edu/user_surveys)

Usage Pattern of WWW

As Internet usage pattern influences the speed of Internet access, we will highlight findings on WWW usage pattern from a recent survey administered by the GVU (Graphic, Visualization, & Usability) Center at the Georgia Institute of Technology in October 1998. Detailed information about the survey as well as the results of the survey are available at http://www.gvu.gatech.edu/user_surveys/survey-1998-10/.

Usage Pattern Survey

In 1994, the GVU Center at the Georgia Institute of Technology started administering surveys on WWW usage pattern on a biannual basis. The data collected not only provides basic understanding of the web population but also trends and patterns in WWW usage. The following are some of the findings from the most recent GVU's (October 1998) 10th WWW user survey.

Frequency of Web Use

The results for "frequency of web use" are: 36.9% use WWW browsers more than 9 times a day, 19.9% use them 5 to 8 times a day, 35.8% use them 1 to 4 times a day, and 7.4% use them less than once a day.

Hours of Web Used

How many hours a week does the web population use WWW browsers? The results of the survey indicate that 34.2% use WWW browser less than 10

Table 3. Current Connection Speed

Use Pattern	0 – 28.8 Kbps	33.6 Kbps	56 Kbps	More than 56 Kbps	Total
Frequency	468	481	852	909	2710
Percent (%)	17.3	17.7	31.4	33.6	100.0

Source: GVU's (October 1998) 10th WWW User Survey (http://www.gvu.gatech.edu/user_surveys)

Figure 1. Changes in Connection Speeds (in bps)

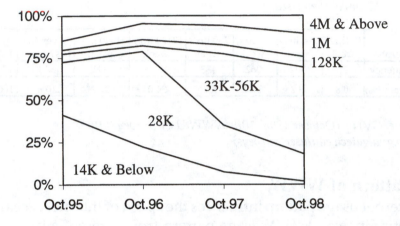

Source: Based on Findings from GVU's WWW User Surveys (http://www.gvu.gatech.edu/user_surveys)

hours a week, 34.0% use them 10 to 20 hours a week, 21.2% use them 21 to 40 hours a week, and 10.6% use them more than 40 hours a week. Note that 65.8% of the survey respondents spend more than 10 hours a week on surfing the web, signifying the popularity and increasing importance of the WWW.

Connection Speed

As for Internet connection speed, 17.3% connect to the Internet at less than or equal to 28.8 Kbps, 17.7% connect to the Internet at 33.6 Kbps, 31.4% connect at 56 Kbps, and 33.6% connect at more than 56 Kbps. Hence, *the majority of web users (66.4%) access the Internet at a speed of no more than 56 Kbps.*

Trend in Connection Speed for Internet Access

Based on results of the Georgia Tech GVU's WWW user surveys, we plotted the trend in Internet connection speeds employed by web users from 1995 to 1998 (see figure 1). The following observations were made. First, since 1996, the proportion of web users employing high-band Internet connection speeds (1Mbps and above) has *gradually* increased. Second, the proportion of mid-band (128 kbps) users remains small (less than 7%) over the years. Third, high-speed modems (33-56 kbps) were *rapidly* replacing low-speed modems (less than 33 kbps). Lastly, a large proportion (about 70%) of web users connect to the Internet using dial-up modems (56kps or less).

WWW Access and Acceleration Methods

This section explains the concept of bandwidth and its relationship with speed of Internet access and web response time, factors influencing the speed of WWW access, as well as the various WWW access methods and web acceleration techniques.

Problems with Bandwidth

The findings from the GVU's (October 1998) 10th WWW user survey indicate that the *top two* problems faced by web users are the long downloading time for web pages (61.4%) and for the long downloading time advertising banners (62.3%). What are the possible reasons for the slow WWW access, and what kinds of techniques can be used to overcome the problem?

According to Nielsen (1997), the following are the four main factors influencing web response time:

- *Throughput of server*

  The throughput of a server is related to its hardware capacity. If incoming traffic to the web server suppresses the server throughput or capacity, accesses to the web pages would fail. With constant exponential growth in the WWW market, it is critical to carry out server capacity analysis and planning activities on a regular basis to identify potential capacity problems in advance and to project and meet future needs. Companies may need to constantly upgrade their server to meet the exponentially increasing Internet traffic trend. Despite the low cost of hardware, some companies still do not invest enough in server capacity to cope with high incoming traffic.

- *Both server's and user's connection speeds*

  The Internet connection speed is largely determined by the connection methods used by both the user and the server. Connection to the Internet can be established using dial-up modem, ISDN, satellite, cable, DSL, and T1/T3. Each of these methods has different features and characteristics, which will be discussed later in the chapter.

- *Browser speed*

  There are many browsers available in the market and they generally achieve good performance. However, each browser offers different features and performs differently with different configurations. The latest browser is also not always the fastest because of newly added functions and security patches.

- *The Internet itself*

  The Internet itself can be a bottleneck. The development of a new infrastructure for the information superhighway, known as Internet2, is currently underway. The U.S. government has invested heavily in developing the Internet2 project. The Internet2 project will be discussed briefly later in the chapter.

Bandwidth and Internet Connection Alternatives

In this part, we will first introduce the concept of bandwidth after which we will discuss six common Internet connection methods and the benefits of each.

Bandwidth

Generally speaking, bandwidth is a measure of the rate at which data can be transmitted over the network and is usually measured in bits per second (bps). Since bandwidth is a measure of network capacity, it is often used as a synonym for 'throughput' or 'speed'.

Internet Access Alternatives

The six most commonly used Internet access methods are dial-up, ISDN (Integrated Services Digital Network), satellite, cable, DSL (Digital Subscriber Line), and T1/T3. Generally speaking, the Internet access services listed in Table 4 are ordered from the slowest (dial-up) to the fastest (T1/T3) and from the cheapest (dial-up) to the most expensive (T1/T3).

- *Dial-Up Modem*

  This is the most popular Internet connection method over the regular phone line. The modem handles conversion between digital data and analog signal. A modem contains both a modulator that it uses to send

Table 4. Comparison of Internet Connection Services

Service	Typical Monthly Cost	Typical Maximum Speed		Availability
		Downstream	Upstream	
Dial-up	$20	56 kbps	33.6 kbps	Universal
ISDN	$50-$130	128 kbps	128 kbps	Widespread
Satellite	$50 (for 100 hrs)	400 kbps	33.6 kbps	Widespread
Cable	$30-$65	1-5 mbps	33.6kbps-2.5mbps	Limited
DSL	$49-$1200	144 kbps-8 mbps	64 kbps-8 mbps	Very Limited
T1/T3	$300-$3000	56 kbps-45 mbps	56kbps-45 mbps	Widespread

Source: McCracken, H., "Bandwidth on Demand", PC World, March 1999, pp.109-118.

information and a demodulator that it uses for arriving information. The modulator converts digital data to the analog signal for data transmission over the phone line while the demodulator converts incoming analog signals to the digital format readable by the computer. The current speed of dial-up modems can reach 56 kbps for download and 33.6 kbps for upload.

- *ISDN*

  ISDN (Integrated Services Digital Network) is the digital communication service provided by telephone companies. The speed of ISDN can reach 128 kbps for both downloads and uploads. For frequent transmissions of small amounts of data, it can be more than two to four times as fast as an analog connection such as dial-up modems.

- *Satellite Connection*

  Satellite connection utilizes satellite network technology to connect to the Internet using a satellite dish. Satellite television providers such as DirecTV offer satellite Internet connection that is available anywhere in the continental U.S. The advantage of satellite connection is that the technology does not require telephony infrastructure such as the case of ISDN, but it requires a 21-inch satellite dish. In the case where users reside in a rural area, this technology is the only possible high-speed connection to the Internet. The current maximum bandwidth of satellite connection is 400 kbps for download and 33.6 kbps for upload transmission. What that means is that the dish can only be used for receiving data.

- *Cable Connection*

  Cable connection is the digital communication service provided by cable companies. It uses cable modems and is suited for residential use because most residential areas are already wired for cable. The performance of cable modem varies across the country depending on its type (*symmetrical* and *asymmetrical*) and the cable company providing the service. The current bandwidth of cable connection can reach as high as 5 Mbps for download.

Table 5: Estimate of Best Possible Download Time

File Size	50K	100K	500K	1MB	2MB
Dial-up Modem (28.8 kbps)	14 Sec.	28 Sec.	2.4 Min.	4.9 Min.	9.7 Min.
Dial-up Modem (56 kbps)	7 Sec.	14 Sec.	1.2 Min.	2.5 Min.	5.0 Min.
ISDN (64 kbps)	6 Sec.	12 Sec.	1.1 Min.	2.2 Min.	4.4 Min.
ISDN (128 kbps)	3 Sec.	6 Sec.	0.5 Min.	1.0 Min.	2.1 Min.

Source: Derived using Hairy® Calculator (http://www.hairynet.com/highsierra/netcalc.htm)

- *DSL*

  DSL (Digital Subscriber Line) is a recent technology that allows for high-speed data communications over ordinary phone lines. By directly transmitting digital data, a much wider bandwidth becomes available. The current maximum performance for these devices is around 144 Kbps-8 Mbps for downloads and 64 Kbps-8Mbps for uploads.

- *T1/T3*

  T1/T3 connection is a dedicated phone connection service to the Internet. Both are very popular options to business users who need high bandwidth. The current maximum performance for T1 and T3 are 1.54 Mbps and 45Mbps respectively for downloads and uploads. A T-1 line consists of 24 64-kbps channels; whereas, a T-3 line consists of 672 64-kbps channels. Although a T-1 line is often used to connect between business user and Internet Service Provider (ISP) and a T-3 line is often used to connect between ISPs and Internet backbone, the distinction between the two is getting vague.

WWW Download Time

Bandwidth has a direct effect on web response time. The higher the bandwidth, the quicker the WWW access. For example, it takes about 10 minutes to download a 2MB file using 28.8K modem and about 2 minutes to download a 2MB file using ISDN (128 kbps). While interactive visual web pages are fancy, they take longer time to download (see Table 5). Figure 2 shows the Hairy® calculator (http://www.hairynet.com/highsierra/netcalc.htm) that can be used by web designers and administrators to estimate the best possible download time for a particular file size. The Hairy® calculator can also be used to compute the maximum desirable size of web pages given the Internet connection speed and the maximum "tolerable" waiting time of WWW users (refer to Table 7 at the end of chapter).

Technology for Accelerating WWW Access

The current trend toward multimedia and interactive web sites causes issues on connection speed to be more critical and important than ever before. To better serve customers in Internet connection and to minimize waiting time of web users, ISPs (Internet Service Providers), hardware manufacturers and software developers in the Internet industry are constantly exploring new technology and techniques to accelerate WWW access. In this part, we introduce the caching and modem bonder methods to help speed up WWW access.

Figure 2. Hairy® Calculator

Input File Size Here 2 (MB)	KB	MB (selected)	GB
	Hours	Minutes	Seconds
9.6 Kb	0	29	7
14.4 Kb	0	19	25
28.8 Kb	0	9	42
56 Kb	0	4	59
ISDN (64 Kb)	0	4	22
ISDN (128 Kb)	0	2	3
T1 (1.54 Mb)	0	0	10
Cable Modem (10 Mb)	0	0	1
Cable Modem (27 Mb)	0	0	0
T3 (45 Mb)	0	0	0
ATM (155 Mb)	0	0	0

Source: http://www.hairynet.com/highsierra/netcalc.htm

Web Caching

What is caching? The concept of caching is well established in computer science. In the1960s, computer designers studied and understood the usefulness and efficiency of caching function when performing repetitive processing. Caching involves storing the repetitive portion of the program in a high-speed block of memory (called cache) that is tightly bound with CPU to speed up the process.

Introducing the caching feature to the Internet environment would lead to faster WWW access. Generally speaking, the caching technique can be used to reduce response time by reducing the load on the web server, using a caching proxy server or accelerating the web browser.

Caching Proxy Server

A proxy server receives a request for an Internet service (such as a web page request) from a user. It then looks at its local cache of previously downloaded web pages. If it finds the page, it returns it to the user without having to forward the request to the Internet. If the page is not in the cache, the proxy server, acting as a client on behalf of the user, requests the page from the server out on the Internet. When the page is returned, the proxy server relates it to the original request and forwards it on to the user. In short, the proxy server caches web pages (and possibly ftp and other files) so that successive requests for these pages (or files) can be satisfied without going through the Internet.

- Microsoft's Proxy Server (http://www.microsoft.com/proxy/) can also serve as a firewall while Squid (http://squid.nlanr.net/Squid/) is available on the Unix systems.

Web Server Accelerator

With the rapid growth and popularity of the WWW, web servers are frequently the bottleneck. The effect of introducing caching as a web server accelerator (also known as reverse proxy caching) can be large if we consider the repetitive patterns of Internet access and the benefits of caching.

- For example, Novell's new web server, called BorderManager (Lee, 1997), could decrease the workload on web server because it uses web server accelerator, called Fast Cache function. Michelle Arden, vice president of Novell's Border Service Group, said "Instead of purchasing more expensive hardware or upgrading costly bandwidth, BorderManager Fast Cache provides a high performance, scalable caching solution for businesses to deliver web based content to their employees."

Web Browser Accelerator

Web browsers can be accelerated using one of two technologies: smart caching or read-ahead browsing. Smart caching replaces your browser's existing cache and pulls elements from your hard drive, the Internet, or both to accelerate web surfing. It logs the pages you frequent and keeps them cached on your hard drive. Read-ahead browsing, as its name implies, works by prefetching text links (and sometimes graphics) while you're still reading a page.

- For example, Net Sonic Internet Accelerator program (http://www.web3000.com) employs the smart caching technique. When you first visit a web site, this program will save the page in the cache of your

PC. The next time you visit that web page, Net Sonic Internet Accelerator will check whether there is any change to that web page. If there is no change, this program will pop up the stored page that was saved the last time. But if the page is updated since your last visit, Net Sonic will download only the part that has changed. If you visit the same web page frequently, you will find significant improvement in download time (Gilster, 1998).

Other examples of accelerator programs that employ the smart caching and read-ahead browsing methods include: Connectix Surf Express Deluxe (http://www.connectix.com), Kiss Software Speed Surfer Internet Toolbox (http://www.kissco.com), Bevoni TurboExplorer (http://www.bevoni.com/turboexplorer/), PeakSoft PeakJet (http://www.peak.com) and IMSI NetAccelerator (http://www.imsisoft.com/netaccelerator/).

Another way to accelerate web access time is to change Registry settings that affect transfer and throughput speeds.

- For example, the MTU-Speed Pro (http://www.personal.u-net.com/~mjs/download.htm) shareware helps you fine-tune settings for TCP/IP connections to increase connection speeds and stability while PPP Boost (http://www.c3sys.demon.co.uk/ppp.htm) changes default settings from one suited for local area network to that for a typical dial-up session.

A review of top 10 web-acceleration tools can be found at http://www.cnn.com/TECH/computing/9810/26/topaccel.idg/ (Neuman, 1998).

Modem Bonders

Unlike browser accelerators, modem bonders harness modem capacity. They're pricier than browser accelerators because they require two modems, two phone lines, and two separate ISP accounts.

- Examples of modem bonders include: Amquest Modem Comsuite (http://www. amquestmodem.com), Diamond Multimedia Systems SupraSonic (http://www.diamondmm.com), Microsoft Windows 98 Dial-up Networking (http://www.microsoft.com), MidCore Software MidPoint Teamer (http://www.midcore.com) and Ragula FatPipe Internet Home (http://www.ragula.com).

Internet2 Project

One of the key solutions to minimizing *world wide wait* is to upgrade the capacity of the current Internet, which is very often the main reason or bottleneck for slow WWW access. In other words, we are referring to the next version of Internet called Internet2 (http://www.internet2.edu). The Internet2 project started in October, 1996 with participation from 34 research universities in the United States to create a faster, more powerful network for academic purposes. To date, over 140 universities have joined the Internet2 project and established Internet2 working groups to explore specific technical challenges related to enabling advanced broadband network applications, IPv6, and multicasting. The working group members include representatives from universities, as well as affiliate and corporate members. With the higher bandwidth of Internet2, richer content (e.g., video, audio, virtual reality) can be transmitted and more interactivity can take place over the Internet. It is unclear if the bandwidth provided by Internet2 will suffice in meeting the rising demands for interactivity and virtual reality on the Internet. Until it is so, WWW waiting or access time will remain a major concern among web users. In the next section, we will introduce the concept of tolerable waiting time for accessing web pages and a related research.

Users' Tolerable Waiting Time for Accessing Web Pages

Research on computer response time has yielded the following results (Miller, 1968; Nielsen, 1993):

1) **0.1 second** is about the limit for having the user feel that the system is reacting instantaneously, meaning that no special feedback is necessary except to display the result.
2) **1.0 second** is about the limit for the user's flow of thought to stay uninterrupted, even though the user will notice the delay. Normally, no

Table 6. Statistics on Waiting Time for WWW Access

	Subjects' Average Waiting Time for First Access to Non-Working Hyperlinks		
	1st non-working hyperlink	2nd non-working hyperlink	3rd non-working hyperlink
Control (36 subjects)	**13 Sec.** (8 out [or 22%] of 36 accesses > 15 Sec.)	**4 Sec.** (0 out of 36 accesses > 15 Sec.)	**3.3 Sec.** (0 out of 36 accesses > 15 Sec.)
Treatment (34 subjects)	**37.6 Sec.** (27 out [or 79%] of 34 accesses > 15 Sec.)	**17 Sec.** (7 out [or 21%] of 34 accesses > 15 Sec.)	**6.7 Sec.** (2 out [or 6%] of 34 accesses > 15 Sec.)
Mann-Whitney Test	p<.000	p<.002	p<.004

special feedback is necessary during delays of more than 0.1 but less than 1.0 second, but the user does lose the feeling of operating directly on the data.

3) **10 seconds** is about the limit for keeping the user's attention focused on the dialogue. For longer delays, users will want to perform other tasks while waiting for the computer to finish, so they should be given feedback indicating when the computer expects to be done.

Even though the traditional human factors guideline suggests 10 seconds to be the limit in response time before computer users lose interest (Miller, 1968; Nielsen, 1993), Nielsen (1995, 1996) estimates it to be 15 seconds in the case of WWW access. According to Nielsen, web users have been trained or conditioned to endure longer "suffering" from past experience accessing the web. Is 15 seconds the tolerable waiting time for accessing the web? Unfortunately, there is no empirical evidence indicating that 15 seconds is the "magic number" for users' tolerable waiting time for web access. The question needs to be investigated empirically.

Exploratory Study on WWW Waiting Time

An exploratory experimental study was conducted to assess users' tolerable waiting time in accessing the WWW. Two scenarios were studied – with and without feedback provided to users in the form of a status bar, which refers to a *moving* bar that signifies to the users that the system is processing the request. The bar moves in a bidirectional manner (left to right, right to left, left to right, and so on) until the user request is satisfied (i.e., the web page is downloaded). It does not provide waiting duration information.

Seventy subjects participated in the experiment. The subjects were undergraduate students enrolled in an introductory MIS class. They were randomly assigned into two groups for the experiment. The first group (i.e., control group) was provided with a browser that did not have a status bar. The second group (i.e., experimental group) was provided with the same browser that included a status bar. The experiment was given to the students as a class assignment that required them to look up specific information on the web. The subjects were proficient users of the WWW. All subjects used the same browser and interface, and they accessed exactly the same web pages. All subjects began their browsing task from a standard web page that was designed specifically for the experiment. This standard web page provided links to the information needed to complete the assignment.

The subjects were asked to look up the names of 10 web acceleration tools using the standard web page provided. Of the 10 hyperlinks provided on the standard web page, only 7 of them were working. Upon clicking on any of these 7 working hyperlinks, their corresponding web page would appear almost instantaneously (i.e., negligible access time). The fourth, seventh, and ninth hyperlinks triggered an *infinite* waiting time. For these 3 nonworking hyperlinks, the subjects would have to click the "STOP" icon to terminate the wait. The subjects' waiting times for accessing each of these 3 hyperlinks (from the time they clicked on the hyperlink to the time they clicked the "STOP" icon) were captured automatically by the computer log and used for data analysis.

The results of data analysis support our hypothesis that the inclusion of status bar prolongs users' waiting time (see Table 6). The average waiting time for the *first* access to a *nonworking hyperlink* was 13 seconds for the control group (no status bar) and 38 seconds for the experimental group (with status bar). The Mann-Whitney test indicates that this difference is significant at $p=.000$. As subjects proceeded with the task, their average waiting time for accessing the nonworking hyperlinks declined. This was probably because subjects became more confident that these web pages, having come from the same server, would not be successfully downloaded. The average waiting time for the first access to the next different *nonworking hyperlink* was 4 seconds for the control group (no status bar) and 17 seconds for the experimental group (with status bar). The average waiting time for the first access to the last *nonworking hyperlink* was 3.3 seconds for the control group (no status bar) and 6.7 seconds for the experimental group (with status bar). The Mann-Whitney test indicates that both of these differences are significant ($p<.002$ for the former and $p<.004$ for the latter). Although subjects' waiting times declined with the number of nonworking hyperlinks observed, their waiting times may not decline if these nonworking hyperlinks are associated with web pages that reside on *different* servers. This hypothesis will be tested in future research.

In the data analysis that follows, we will look *only* at the "best case" scenario where subjects were surprised to encounter the *first nonworking hyperlink* and were, therefore, relatively *more patient* in waiting to access that web page. Thus, the results that follow will have to be interpreted from the perspective of a "best case" scenario.

This study attempts to verify Nielsen's (1995, 1996) hypothesis that a 15-second guideline be used for WWW access. Nielsen's hypothesis is *not* well supported in the control setting (web browsing with no status bar), where only 8 [or 22%] of the 36 accesses for the first nonworking hyperlink exceeded waiting time of 15 seconds. As discussed earlier and presented in Table 6, users' tolerable waiting time was prolonged significantly in the more popular setting where a status bar was provided, with 27 [or 79%] of the 34 accesses for the first nonworking hyperlink exceeding waiting time of 15 seconds. Hence, Nielsen's proposal for a 15-second guideline is better supported in the case where a status bar is provided on the web browser.

This exploratory study is a pilot for a series of experimental studies on WWW waiting time (Nah et al., 1998). To the best of our knowledge, no *experimental* study has been carried out to assess the degree to which web users are able to tolerate long access time on the WWW. Given that long waiting time for web access has always been one of the leading concerns for web users (GVU, 1998; Lightner et al., 1996), it is important for researchers and practitioners to: 1) understand users' waiting behavior in accessing the WWW, 2) propose and evaluate techniques to reduce users' perception of waiting time, and 3) recommend a trade-off between aestheticism of web page and download/access time. The flow theory proposed by Csikszentmihalyi (1990) can be used as the theoretical foundation for future research.

We intend to use the results of this pilot and the experience gained from this research to develop the foundation for future research on WWW waiting time. We also hope that this exploratory research will arouse the interest of other researchers to examine user-related issues and problems in this important research area.

Summary, Recommendations and Conclusions

In this chapter, we present: 1) the usage patterns of WWW, 2) trends in WWW connection speeds, 3) factors influencing WWW access time, 4) the different ways to connect to the WWW as well as the characteristics of each, 5) estimation of WWW download time for various connection speeds, 6) technology to accelerate WWW access, and 7) the Internet2 project which is the next version of Internet. We also report on an exploratory study to assess users' tolerable waiting time in accessing web pages and to better understand users' waiting behavior when accessing the WWW. The results of our study indicate that the 15-second guideline proposed by Nielsen (1995, 1996) for web access is too large if the web browser does not provide a status bar. However, in the scenario where a status bar is provided, the 15-second guideline can be used if it is considered reasonable and acceptable to miss approximately 21% of visitors to the web site (i.e., according to Table 6, only about 79% of visitors wait up to 15 seconds). In the case where a 15-second guideline is considered acceptable, Table 7 can be used as a guideline for size limits of web pages at various connection speeds, computed using the Hairy® calculator. As indicated by Nielsen (1997), "web pages have to be designed with the speed in mind – SPEED MUST BE THE OVERRIDING DESIGN CRITERION." We, therefore, suggest that web designers and

Table 7. Estimated Size Limit for 15-second Download

Internet Connection Service	Maximum Size of Web Page
Dial-up Modem (28.8 kbps)	55K
Dial-up Modem (56 kbps)	105K
ISDN (64 kbps)	120K
ISDN (128 kbps)	250K
T1 (1.54 Mbps)	2.9MB
Cable Modem (10 Mbps)	19MB
Cable Modem (27 Mbps)	50MB
T3 (45 Mbps)	85MB

developers utilize data captured from their users' waiting behavior to derive an acceptable limit for access time, and apply the Hairy® calculator to determine the size limit for their web pages. It should be noted that the guideline presented in Table 7 does not take into account other factors such as network traffic, server capacity, and browser speed. In general, the size of web pages may need to be adjusted downward based on other factors.

With the emergence of the e-commerce business paradigm, Internet access time will be one of the most important factors leading to success in e-commerce. The America Online (AOL) incident that occurred in 1997 (known as America *Offline* during the crisis) also demonstrates the importance of access time for Internet users. The crisis occurred when AOL introduced a fixed monthly rate for Internet access, which prompted many subscribers to stay on-line. As a result, the network was not able to handle the load, forcing the six million AOL subscribers to have to tolerate the network's glacial pace response to access the Internet. Although such an extreme Internet access incident is unusual, especially with the increase in network bandwidth over the years, the AOL incident signifies the importance of web access time. It also demonstrates the need to study issues relating to web users' waiting behavior, and the trade-off between web aestheticism and web access time, especially from the marketing perspective.

We hope this chapter spurs research interest in human factor issues relating to waiting behavior of WWW users, particularly the relationship between web response time and users' waiting behavior. From a practitioner's perspective, this chapter provides information that helps users assess the various WWW access alternatives as well as speed up WWW access using web acceleration tools. It also provides guidelines and suggestions for web masters and designers involved in web-based (or e-commerce) project design and development.

References

Czikszentmihalyi, M. (1990). *Flow: The Psychology of Optimal Experience.* Harper & Row, New York.

Graphics, Visualization & Usability (GVU) Center (1998). *GVU's WWW User Surveys.* Georgia Tech Research Corporation, April 1995-October 1998 [Online]. Available: http://WWW.cc.gatech.edu/gvu/user_ surveys/ [1999, April 30].

Gilster P. (1998, November 15). For Online Speed, Hit NetSonic's Accelerator. *The News and Observer* [Online]. Available: http://www.news-observer.com/daily/1998/11/15/biz04.html [1999, April 30].

Lee, R. (1997, August). *Web Server Acceleration with Novell® BorderManager: A Case Study of www.novell.com* [Online]. Available: http://www.novell.com/bordermanager/casestudy.html [1999, April 30].

Lightner, N.J., Bose, I., and Salvendy, G. (1996). What is Wrong with the World-Wide Web?: A Diagnosis of Some Problems and Prescriptions of Some Remedies. *Ergonomics, 39*(8), pp. 995-1004.

McCracken, H. (1999, March). Bandwidth on Demand. *PC World,* pp.109-118.

McDonald, G. (1999, March). Do Web Accelerators Work? *PC World,* pp.145-154.

Miller, R.B. (1968). Response Time in Man-computer Conversational Transaction. *Proceedings of AFIPS Fall Joint Computer Conference, 33,* pp. 267-277.

Modzelewski, P. (1998, January). Internet Connection Alternatives. *PC Magazine* [Online]. Available: http://www.zdnet.com/pcmag/pctech/content/17/01/it1701.001.html [1999, April 30].

Nah, F.H., Siau, K.L., Kim, I., Zhang, W. (1998, May). WWW: World-Wide Wait. *Proceedings of the Information Resources Management Association (IRMA) International Conference,* Boston, USA, pp. 603-609.

Neuman, S. (1998, October 26). Top 10 Web-acceleration Tools. *PC World Online* [Online]. Available: http://www.cnn.com/TECH/computing/9810/26/topaccel.idg/ [1999, April 30].

Nielsen, J. (1993). *Response Times: the Three Important Limits* [Online]. Excerpt from Chapter 5 of Usability Engineering by Jakob Nielsen, Academic Press, 1993. Available: http://www.useit.com/papers/responsetime.html [1999, April 30].

Nielsen, J. (1995, December). *Guidelines for Multimedia on the Web* [Online]. Available: http://www.useit.com/alertbox/9512.html [1999, April 30].

Nielsen, J. (1996, May). *Top Ten Mistakes in Web Design* [Online]. Available: http://www.useit.com/alertbox/9605.html [1999, April 30].

Nielsen, J. (1997, March). *The Need for Speed* [Online]. Available: http://WWW.useit.com/alertbox/9703a.html [1999, April 30].

Chapter 8

A Matter of Necessity: Implementing Web-Based Subject Administration

Paul Darbyshire
Victoria University of Technology, Australia

Andrew Wenn
Victoria University of Technology, Australia

Introduction

The WWW is a resource of enormous potential for education. The use of this resource for presentation of learning materials is well documented (Alexander 1996; Darbyshire and Wenn 1996; Freeman 1997), but the Web can also provide versatility and be of great benefit to subject administrators. By exploiting the Web's distributed nature and platform independence, a subject administrator can provide better service to students and at the same time increase the flexibility and efficiency with which some of the more mundane administration tasks are performed.

In this chapter, we describe the design and development of a Web Based Learning Administration (WBLA) system initially developed to complement work we began on Web Based Learning (Darbyshire and Wenn 1996a). This project became a matter of necessity because of the multi-campus nature of our university. In the background section, information is given on subject management, Web based administration, Victoria University of Technology and a survey of similar work undertaken by others. A development framework and a model are then discussed. The details of the architecture of the of the WBLA system project we are building and security are discussed in the next section. A detailed description of the system is given and related to the model previously presented. Some responses to a trial of the system are given and future enhancements we envisage are presented in the final section.

Background

Computers have been used in education for some time now. Indeed, even prior to the widespread introduction of personal computers into the classroom in the early 1980s, academics have been using computers in a variety of ways to complement teaching. Traditionally, delivery of a university subject involves two components, *teaching* and *management*.

The teaching component of a subject includes all matters related to the preparation and delivery of the educational material, while the management component includes all other nonteaching aspects. These include: maintaining records, preparing exams and assignments, collecting assignment for marking, marking assignments and communicating with students. Efforts to use computers to supplement/ replace teaching have been labelled with terms including: Computer Aided Instruction (CAI); Computer Managed Instruction (CMI); Computer Aided Learning (CAL); on-line teaching and learning and more recently Web Based Learning (WBL) (Darbyshire and Wenn, 1998). The use of computers to aid in the management tasks associated with subjects has been termed Computer Managed Learning (CML).

Subject Management

Computer Managed Learning is "the application where the computer does not have an instructional role and where the function of the computer is in the control, administration and testing of the learning process" (Stanford and Cook, 1987). Computer Mediated Communication (CMC) is the term used to denote those computer functions responsible for the facilitation of communication between instructor and student(s), or student and student(s). Some of the management functions mentioned above such as assignment submission cross the boundaries between CML and CMC (Byrnes and Lo, 1994). Computer Mediated Communication can incorporate assignment submission (Kaye, 1989), but when combined with other elements such as maintaining records, then the system is in the domain of both CML and CMC (Byrnes and Lo, 1994).

Since all aspects of managing a subject mentioned above are important, we use the term *Subject Management* to represent the functions belonging to both CML and CMC. Subject management tasks are normally transparent to the student and it is essential that they be performed in as an efficient manner as possible for the smooth functioning of a subject. If these functions are performed inefficiently, the inefficiencies become immediately obvious to the students and can detract from the learning process.

A number of factors can impact the efficiency of subject management. What would normally be acceptable when coordinating a subject on a single campus can become unacceptable when new dimensions such as distance learning or multiple campuses are added. Many of the subject management tasks above have been implemented in CML/ CMC systems. Byrnes and Lo (1994) describe a number of these including:

- *Submit* at Wollongong University, New South Wales, Australia
- *NetFace* at Monash University, Victoria, Australia
- *TRIX* at Athabasca University, Canada
- *TeleEducation* at Mount Allison University, Canada

These systems rely on specific hardware and software infrastructure. Thus, while the systems perform well in their specific tasks, their operation is limited to the infrastructure upon which they were developed. There is an increase in flexibility gained, but that flexibility is limited. For instance, if one department within a university develops the system, then other departments lacking the same infrastructure cannot make use of the system. If the system is developed by a central IT department on a university wide infrastructure, the flexibility may still be limited across the university because familiarity with the technology is limited to particular sectors.

Web-based Subject Administration

With the development of the Web in the early 1990s, and the first World Wide Web (WWW) conference in 1994 (Cailliau, 1995), the use and development of systems on the Web gained momentum and a new paradigm became available for developers of CAL and CML/ CMC systems. Regardless of the infrastructure, systems supporting Web protocols are now able to provide uniform and seamless access to all such systems connected to the Internet.

The advantages of using Web-based techniques to deliver and manage a subject are many. The Web is an excellent instructional tool and using the web to manage that instruction is a natural extension. The Web is now controlled by standards (W3C, 1997; W3C, 1998) and by using only these standardized aspects in the software developed, we can address concerns that arise due to the disparity of software and equipment owned by students. This does not of course address the question of student access to the Web. There are advantages for students even if the only access they have is through a university's computer laboratories. These include the versatility of access to notes, bulletin boards, marks and electronic assignment submission. The familiarity people have with Web technology is a subtle and often overlooked advantage of using the Web for these applications. This familiarity produced by the use of the Web for entertainment, communication, business and research, reduces learning curves associated with use of such systems. This also results in less apprehension about working with these systems.

The conversion of an existing LAN based system to a Web based one has been described by Hart (1996). A number of reasons were cited for the conversion. First was the incompatibility between the computers used at the university (Macintosh's) and those used by the majority of students at home (PC's). The Web was seen as a means of creating platform independent course materials. Second was that the LAN based system was limited to on-campus students, while using the Web made the material far more accessible to part-time and off-campus students.

If aspects of a subject can be managed from a series of standardized Web pages from one computer connected to the Web, then these same functions can be performed from any computer that has a web connection and browser. This includes access from home via a standard modem and Internet connection. Thus, differing machines with different capabilities, software requirements and access do not restrain a subject coordinator. Web based subject management becomes platform independent and accessible from virtually anywhere.

VUT Context

The project being described was initiated by the authors to address problems that arose due to the structure of their department and subsequent teaching patterns, imposed by university amalgamations. The Department of Information Systems is part of the Faculty of Business of Victoria University of Technology based in Melbourne, Australia. The university is one of the country's youngest universities having been formed in the early 1990s as a result of amalgamations due to recommendations of a Parliamentary Review of Higher Education. It has 14 campuses located in and around the Melbourne metropolitan area and a student population of approximately 50,000.

The Information Systems Department has a teaching presence on six of the fourteen campuses, and although recently our personal teaching activities have been confined to two campuses, in some circumstances in the past it has peaked at 4 campuses in one day. We teach subjects ranging from Operating Systems and Programming to Information Management. Subject enrollments range from 130 to 18 students per subject each semester. The WBLA system we describe in this chapter has been developed in response to the demands placed on us as the university has grown during a time when tertiary sector funding has become scarce. Also, the student profile has altered over the years since the formation of the university.

The university has long been committed to education quality and access. A Personalized Access and Study policy that guarantees a place to anyone who is over 21 years or who has passed the Victorian Certificate of Education

(VCE) has recently been implemented. As a result of this policy and other factors, the student population is intellectually and ethnically diverse and geographically dispersed.

Similar projects

It is important to realize that the system described here is the result of our ongoing efforts over a period of three years. During this time a number of commercial products such as *TopClass, Learning Space, Lotus Domino* and others have become available but we considered that the cost of these was too high to warrant applying for funding to purchase one of them. This not to say that commercial software is unsuitable. We were too far advanced in the development of the system to abandon it. Indeed Freeman's research has shown that a TopClass based system has had a very positive reception from a large group of students (Freeman, 1997). As will be outlined later, the expenditure on this project (in terms of hardware, software and cost of labor) has been kept to a minimum. In fact the whole project could be seen as an effort in utilizing what was already available in the department.

In Hart's (1996) description of a Web based system for CMI incorporating some aspects of subject management, he notes the positive attitudes of students using the system, with most criticism being levelled at the lack of access to the Web itself. Hart also notes that the reception from part-time students was very supportive as this allowed them to complete most of their work in distance mode. The major limitation according to Hart, was the lack of communications facility offered by the Web, with most communication being one-way. In the system described below, the authors make use of threaded discussion groups to overcome this limitation.

Bodendorf and Langenbach (1998) in discussing their approach to WWW-based courses describe a system based around the concept of building blocks with reusable core components implemented in HTML, Java, JavaScript and other compatible formats. Their system includes many similar functions to the one described below, but would appear to have gone further down the track of setting up a framework for the creation of "WWW-based teachware" (p. 626). The system as described appears to be mainly oriented towards student access to teaching materials with little emphasis placed on work submission or administrative tasks.

One system that does allow students to submit their work and teaching staff to mark it via Web access, is the *Hypertest* system. Hypertest is a Web-based group e-mail/blackboard system with a simple, single text entry window. However, because it does not allow students to attach files or to format the text in the document window it has not met with a great deal of user acceptance. Despite encouragement to do otherwise, "student[s] prefer to use e-mail, telephone and fax instead of Hypertest for group meetings and discussions" (Maheshwari, 1998, pp 1073).

Becker *et al* (1998 pp. 596), have been studying the use of software such as *CU-See-Me* for videoconferencing and whiteboard based activities for students who "are geographically dispersed and have access to Web technology at the office or at home." The effective use of electronic communications in a synchronous mode is seen as important to Becker. Brooks (1997) discusses such issues as cooperative learning, videoconferencing and whiteboarding, as well as ways of promoting self-regulated learning but does not consider the benefits that the Web could bring to subject administration practices.

Framework and Model for Subject Management

As with other development efforts in this area, there has been no overall path to follow apart from the need for flexibility. Available technology, experience, student feedback and current work practices have guided development to this point. However in late 1998, a working group of the IEEE, Learning Technology Standards Committee (LTSC), Architecture and Reference Model Working Group (IEEE 1484.1) accepted the Learning Technology Systems Architecture specification (IEEE, 1998) as a 'Base Document'. In the following subsection, this document is briefly discussed. Following the discussion on the new IEEE developments, the model upon which our work is based is presented. This is a modified version of a model proposed by Byrnes et.al (Byrnes, 1995).

Development Framework

In late 1998, the IEEE LTSC working group accepted the Learning Technology Systems Architecture (LTSA) Specification (IEEE 1998) as a base document, to be worked into a draft standard. Although our development efforts began before the knowledge of the specification was available, it is worthwhile briefly discussing the specification and its implications for future development.

The aim of the LTSA specification is to provide a framework for understanding existing and future systems, to promote interoperability and portability by identifying critical system interfaces, and to provide a technical horizon of at least 5-10 years while remaining adaptable to new technologies (IEEE 1998). The LTSA specification is pedagogy neutral and represents the Information Technology issues of Learning Technology systems. A full description of the specification is beyond the scope of this chapter. The specification describes five layers of refinement and the third layer (Component Layer) is of interest to us as it provides an abstraction of the Information

Figure 1: LTSA System Component Layer

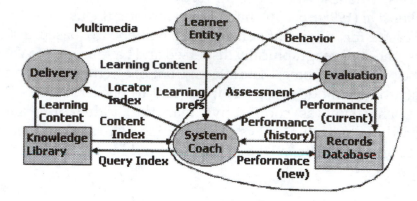

System components present in a Learning Technology System.

Figure 1 shows the elements of the third layer of the LTSA specification. Components are shown using standard System Analysis and Design constructs. The *Learner, Instructor* (shown as *System Coach*), *Delivery* and *Evaluation* are represented as system processes. The *Records Database* and *Knowledge Library* are shown as data stores, and the interaction between the instructor and learner are represented as directed data-flows. The instructor and learner may traditionally be thought of as entities, however, as both learning and instruction can be regarded as a process it makes sense to represent them as such in the above diagram.

Figure 1 represents an abstraction, for which there would exist a mapping onto any real implementation conforming to this standard. The section of Figure 1 circled above, containing the *Evaluation* and *System Coach* processes, *Records Database*, and the *behavior* and *learning preferences* data-flows represents the elements of the component layer that would be mapped onto a real implementation of a subject management system. For example, the abstraction in Figure 1 can be mapped onto the real implementation of the traditional classroom. The teacher takes on the role of all processes except the *learner entity*, the *records database* maps onto the traditional report card and transcripts and the knowledge library maps onto school library. This mapping is shown in Figure 2, with the data-flow labels of Figure 1 removed to reduce diagram complexity.

Figure 3 shows a mapping of elements from the layer-3 abstraction onto a Web-based learning system using a browser for presentation. The processes of *delivery, system coach* and *evaluation* are mapped onto the browser. The records database is mapped onto a suitable server-resident database and the knowledge library is mapped onto a courseware database. There are specific mapping's of interaction (data-flows) onto the human interface component.

Figure 2: Mapping of layer-3 components onto traditional classroom

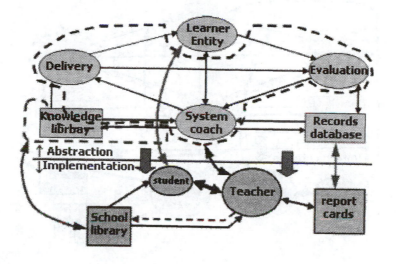

This system displays a tight integration of components, and further detail would be needed for a complete mapping.

The LTSA specification has just become a base document of the IEEE working group, which means it will now be developed into a draft standard. Developers have been asked not to show conformance of their products to the specification at this stage. While this is not yet a standard, it is encouraging to see this document being prepared as such. The subject management system we have been developing over the last three years does loosely conform to the LTSA specification, as shown in Figure 3. However, with a more detailed breakdown, additional work would be needed enable a more complex conformance mapping. Given that the current base document will in all likelihood evolve into an IEEE standard, the current specification does provide a theoretical framework in which to develop further work.

Model

There has been no universal model to which prior CML/ CMC systems have been constructed. Much of this is due to the specialized infrastructure used by different systems and lack of a standardized platform. With the work on an international standard briefly discussed in the previous section and the continued development of the Web as a standard platform, the groundwork for such a model has been set.

Byrnes *et al* (1995) proposed a model that incorporated both CML and CMC functions. We have adopted and slightly modified this model for use

Figure 3: Mapping of layer-3 components onto Web-based learning system

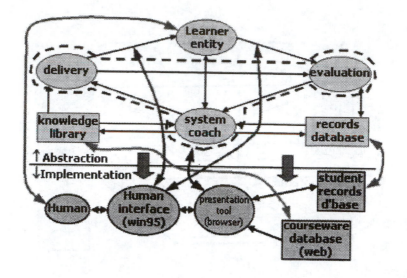

with the Web based system to be discussed in the following sections. The model identifies a number of components associated with subject management:

- Web based testing and marking.
- Web based Administration tasks, e.g. record keeping, student management.
- Web based facilities for managing Web Based Learning materials.
- Web based Assignment management.
- Web facilitated instructor /student communication.

These are standard subject related tasks, whether or not the subject is taught or managed by electronic means. Managing a subject via the Internet requires shifting from manual or manual/software based techniques to methods employing web-based techniques. At this stage, we have implemented Web-based components to help with the latter four, and we are currently designing a database and web scripts to help with the first. This is described in the section on further work. The model above does loosely map onto the layer-3 components of the LTSA specification in the previous section. However, the model was adopted before the specification was released. In the following sections we discuss our WBLA system in the context of the modified Byrnes *et.al* model.

Architecture of WBLA System

Before discussing the functionality of our WBLA system the current architecture is described. The architecture of the system has evolved over time as the authors' expertise in Web programming developed, new tools became available, and the need for increased flexibility and functionality arose. A cyclic relationship has evolved between the development effort to add functionality and the architecture of the system.

The structure of the WBLA system in its current form is shown in Figure 4. All pages containing learning material and subject information are considered as distributed, and hence reside on the Web. No attempt is made to centralize these pages, thus maintaining versatility of the learning material and placing responsibility for this material in the hands of the subject coordinators.

In the system structure shown in Figure 4, there is a bifurcation of the Web pages that allow access to the WBLA system. Those Web pages allowing student access to the system are housed in a separate directory to the staff pages. The staff pages are housed in a directory requiring password access, discussed in the section on security below. There are three databases comprising the system, each which stores different types of data. The separation of data is discussed in further detail later, but to the user of the system no distinction is made. Assignment files submitted by students are physically stored in a directory structure representing subject/ assignment breakdown

Figure 4: Structure of the Web Based subject management system

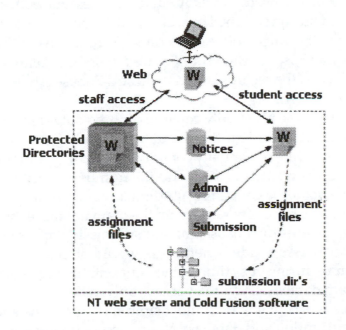

and are accessible to authorized staff via the Web.

Originally, the WBLA system was located on two separate servers. Web pages for student functions such as assignment submission, marks retrieval and bulletin board access were located on a Unix server. The functions directly accessible by staff were located on a 486 PC acting as a Web server. This PC was set up using the *O'Reilly* Web server software, *Microsoft Access* and *Cold Fusion*. Following a semester trial, we obtained some funding that enabled us to purchase *Windows NT*. After appropriating a *Pentium* PC with two gigabytes of disk space we replaced the 486 PC with an NT server.

Recently, the reliability and management of the Unix server which housed part of the WBLA system has come under question, forcing a rethink of our *'split system'* policy. Part of the initial reason for the policy was security, keeping as many student functions as possible separate from staff functions. As our experience with NT grew and our confidence with its security increased we relocated the entire WBLA Web site to the NT server. We have recently obtained more funding for hardware, and the current hardware and software configuration is an Intel Pentium 200 MHz machine with 128Mb RAM, Windows NT Server 4.0, Internet Information Server (IIS) 4 and Cold Fusion 3.1. Cold Fusion is a product that allows special scripts to be constructed which can contain normal HTML statements and special commands to facilitate access to Open Data Base Connectivity (ODBC) complaint databases.

The underlying databases are constructed using Microsoft Access. They are configured and accessed as ODBC data sources via SQL commands embedded in Cold Fusion scripts. Thus, any ODBC compliant databases can be substituted for the Microsoft Access ones currently used. The current structure of the databases is shown in Figure 5 below. Explanations of the importance and use of the records stored in these database tables are detailed in the following sections.

The WBLA database physically consists of three databases loosely connected via key fields. Although these databases could be folded into one central database, we were continually conscious of security and performance on the Web. Thus, we wanted to minimize the number of write accesses via Web pages to the database containing student assignment marks and passwords. To this end we have separated from the main database the tables that are updated by students during assignment submission and posting to the on-line notice board. As a side benefit, this would actually help database access performance during busy times. Once students are registered, all other access to the main database is by read access only.

Performance is acceptable with most simple transactions such as message posting, registration and database record access taking approximately

Figure 5: Structure of the WBLA Databases

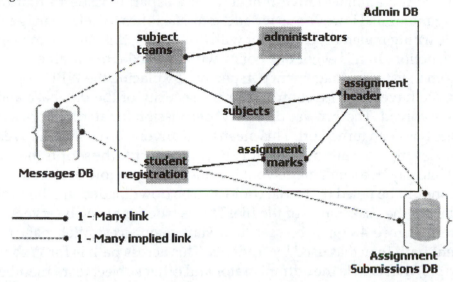

one to two seconds from on-campus locations. Assignment submission times depend on Web traffic and file size, which are beyond our control. There are approximately 250 students currently registered in the database. When the user base expands, as is expected in the near future when more staff come "on-line", the database may need to be upgraded.

Security Issues

When making use of a system such as the WBLA, security and privacy issues take on a new dimension, from both staff and student perspectives. From feedback obtained (discussed in a later section), we found that students were concerned by both these factors. For their part, this led to some trepidation about using the system. Most of the concern raised was for the safety of submitted assignments and their reliable delivery to the subject administrators. From the subject administrator's perspective, security of the WBLA database is important as all details of student marks and assignment submission dates are stored in the databases. While security was one of our major priorities, students raised concerns about privacy at an early stage. There was no concern from them about receiving marks and feedback online from the web, but they were concerned that only they should have access to this material. To this end we have implemented a registration and password mechanism which is tied into most functions of the WBLA system. This is discussed in the WBLA description section.

Initially in order to address the issue of security, we decided to physically split the learning and administration functions, thereby exploiting the distributed nature of the web. This duality to the system does allow us to focus on the administrative issues of subject management via the Web, and to treat security of the administrative functions as a separate issue to that of the learning material. However, as we add more facilities to help manage Web-based learning materials, consistent with our model, this duality may prove an obstruction. In this event our policy will have to be reexamined.

From a system management perspective, by placing the WBLA on an NT server, we have far more control over the security of the database and the scripts involved. The 'browse directory' permission for all directories in the Web site has been turned off. This means that anyone browsing the Web site cannot view the contents of a directory but only execute the scripts they know exist. This may be a small matter, but it is one more step towards securing the site. It should be noted that a file could also be downloaded via the Web if a user knows the exact name of the file. This is true for all Web servers.

From Figure 4, it can be seen that staff may access Web pages via a different path than that used by students. This access path is for Web pages (or scripts) that enable the administrator and other subject team members to manage aspects of the subject. These scripts are physically located in a separate subdirectory from the normal student scripts, and have general Web access removed. As a consequence, anyone trying to access this area is automatically prompted by the operating system for a valid user name and password of a user who has access to this subdirectory. By giving only relevant staff members an NT user/password combination, we can provide a first level security barrier to unauthorized access.

As a second level of security, every staff member authorized to use the system has an entry in the administrators' table shown in Figure 5. This entry contains a WBLA username and password. Once through the NT directory security, the WBLA system displays its own logon screen, and compares a user's response to the administrators table in the database. If the response represents a valid administrator username/ password combination, a security cookie is created and stored in the user's browser for the lifetime of the browser session only. With this cookie, the staff member is then given access to a variety of administration functions, to be discussed in the following section. A logout function on the main menu page disposes of this security cookie.

The main reason for the second password is that if a lecturer executes an administration script in the classroom, and hence supplies their NT username and password, the Web browser remembers it. Thus, if the lecturer does not close the browser afterwards, a student clicking on the appropriate link will not be prompted for the username and password a second time. By using a security cookie generated by the subject management system and providing a specific logout function, existence of the cookie can be checked for to allow or prevent further access to the subject management functions. This is not a guarantee of security, however, since a lecturer typing in a URL and not executing the logout function will leave the cookie active in the browser. The logout function destroys the cookie, and any further check for its existence will fail.

Assuming that lecturing staff follow all precautionary procedures, the WBLA system is still open to 'hacking'. As the system under question is not immune to such attempts, other precautions have also been taken. Passwords stored by the subject management system in its databases are one-way encrypted upon storage, and on any attempted access, the password supplied is also encrypted and compared to the original one stored. Thus, if the database is accessed somehow, the stored passwords are not easily identifiable.

The databases are password protected so the appropriate passwords are needed for access. This means that the database passwords must be used in the Cold Fusion scripts that access them. However, the Cold Fusion scripts have been encrypted using the encryption utility supplied with the product. At this stage all appropriate steps have been taken, but further security under Windows NT is being investigated.

Each student using the system is also given a registration consisting of their student ID number and a password. The students do not need this ID and password combination to access the Web pages containing course material, but they are necessary to perform certain functions that are discussed in the following section.

WBLA System Description

The WBLA system was designed to operate in a multi-campus environment, and as such will involve a good many staff and students dispersed over a wide geographical area. In order to meet one of its design criteria, "to alleviate pressure on the subject administrator", the WBLA system was designed to be user driven as much as possible. That is, apart from some initial setup of basic data such as administrators, subjects, campus locations, etc., the users of the system enter most other data. This includes both the subject lecturers and students.

The WBLA system is not integrated into the university's student record system, and at this stage there is no desire for this to eventuate. The only drawback to this is that a student registration (ID, password and other information) must be created for each student wishing to use the system. In order to alleviate the workload of the subject administrator, we have made this process user driven, getting the students to register themselves during the first tutorial of the subject each semester. This does require the students to be able to make an entry into the student registration table, creating a situation where bogus registrations may appear.

To resolve this problem, each lecturer/ tutor has a '*maintenance word*' as well as their WBLA password. The maintenance word is given by the lecturer/ tutor to students in the first tutorial for registration purposes and then changed, possibly during the tutorial itself via a Web page, after all students have registered. This maintenance word cannot be changed except with the use of the lecturer's/ tutor's personal password. By only temporarily granting access to the maintenance word, we reduce the incidence of possible bogus registrations. Any lecturer/ tutor using the WBLA system can register students that miss the registration in the first tutorial. The registration process is independent of the subject they are studying. This process seems to work efficiently, and the numbers of registrations that are missed in the first sessions are minimal.

During the registration process, the student supplies their desired password to the system. This is then used by the WBLA system to verify identity for all functions concerned with assignment submission and obtaining access to results. Once registered, the student has control of assignment submission, marks viewing, and checking the assignment submission database. Initially a subject enrollment function was included where registered students could create an enrollment record for a particular subject. This was used as a final check to ensure students were not submitting assignments to subjects in which they were not enrolled. However, this seemed to introduce an undesirable level of complexity, so the subject enrollment functions were removed. All checking is now performed through the student registration table only.

The use of a registration system was necessary in order to address security and privacy concerns of students. Without the use of an ID/ password combination, a system cannot distinguish between users, making it impossible to implement privacy and security measures. In the remainder of this section, the functions of the WBLA system are described. Each subsection will describe our efforts in providing functionality for each of the elements of the underlying model.

Web-Based Testing and Marking

While Web-based testing and marking would naturally form part of any Web based subject management system, this functionality has not yet been incorporated into the system. However, this is an area currently under consideration with some groundwork having been performed. This is discussed in the section on further work.

Web-Based Record Keeping

There are four types of electronic records currently kept by the WBLA system. These are the student registration records, the administrator's record, the student marks, and the assignment submission records. The registration process was described at the beginning of this section.

Students' marks are stored in a table governed by their registration, and assignment-header records in the WBLA database as depicted in Figure 5. An assignment-header record is created for each assignment in each subject and is discussed in detail in the next section. Students may view their assignment marks at any time from any computer with a Web browser. To successfully view a mark for a particular assignment, the student's correct ID and password must be supplied. Thus, no one can query a student's mark except the student in question. By using password protected viewing we are able to provide the degree of privacy requested by students.

When a result inquiry is successful, students are presented with the mark they achieved, what the assignment was marked out of, what the assignment is worth in terms of overall percentage and a list of comments on their work. In response to frequent student requests, the highest, lowest and average mark for that particular assignment are also displayed. It is envisaged that a future development of the system will include the storage of final exam marks in this database.

Assignment marks and comments can be placed on the Web for student access by any subject team member. As assignments may be completed by groups of students, the data entry form contains a field for a space-separated list of ID numbers representing members of the group, a field for the mark obtained and a text area field for comments. This form is shown in Figure 6. When submitted, a script creates an entry in the assignment marks table shown in Figure 5 for every student whose registration appears in the list. The mark achieved and comments are stored in each of these entries.

This method of recording comments to provide feedback to students is cumbersome and has caused some debate amongst staff members. It does not model the way lecturing staff work in practice, and consequently has become a weak point in the system. Subject lecturers / tutors usually annotate written work at the required point as they read it, and then return it to students. By working this way, the marking process, and subsequent reading of annotations by students is made easier.

Using the form in Figure 6 does require a change of habit from the usual practice. The entire assignment would have to be read, and either comments on the form added during this process or after a thorough reading. Where this method has been tried, there have been no complaints or comments from the students. The concern stems from staff members who do not see this method as a viable alternative. As the purpose of the WBLA system is to provide flexibility for staff, this concern must be addressed. This method of feedback

Figure 6: Entry screen for assignment marks

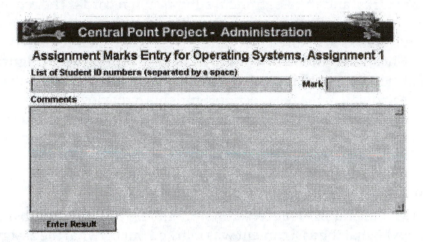

was easy to implement, and is a beginning to what will be a slow evolutionary process. This has been marked as an area for improvement, and a possible solution is discussed in the final section.

By being able to enter marks into the WBLA database via a set of standard Web pages, flexibility is introduced. The subject administrator and other lecturers/tutors can move from one campus to another, or be at home, and have full access to the record keeping facility of the WBLA system. This eliminates the need for transporting personal spreadsheets or database tables from one computer to another. Only access to a standard Web browser is required. Also, since the underlying database is Microsoft Access, reports can easily be prepared to help with final subject mark collation and campus breakdowns.

Another record stored by the WBLA system is the assignment submission record. These records enable staff members to track the submission date and time of assignment work by students. As the submission process generates the records for submitted assignment work, they are discussed in the following section.

Web Based Assignment Management

Assignment collection, marking and redistribution is one of the most onerous tasks associated with subject coordination, particularly in a multiple campus situation when trying to maintain common due dates. This is the where we hoped the WBLA system would aid subject coordination the most. If we look at all the specific activities involved in preparing, distributing and collecting assignments, there are quite a number of activities where a WBLA system could alleviate the pressure on the subject administrators. The list below shows the major activities of the assignment life cycle, identified by Byrnes et al (1995). Those activities with a tick beside them are the ones where we specifically use the WBL/WBLA system.

- Prepare assignment
- Distribute assignment and guides √
- Prepare assignment answers
- Arrange for multiple point collection noting date and time √
- Mark assignments
- Remove penalty and late marks √
- Record marks √
- Distribute marked assignments √
- Provide and distribute a sample solution √
- Answer queries on assignment marks √
- Collect resubmitted assignments √
- Remark assignment
- Distribute remarked assignment and comments √
- Collate all assignment results for final submission √

One of the things that the WBLA system is able to do well is collect assignments from students and record the submission dates and times. Using this system we can set common dates and times for assignment collection. This is usually not an issue when a subject is delivered at a single campus. When a subject is delivered on multiple campuses with different lecture and tutorial times, the issue becomes magnified. Common assignment delivery and collection times become problematic, and staff must not be perceived as giving undue advantage to one group or another.

By implementing a Web-based assignment collection facility in the WBLA system, a single person on one campus can administer this process. Students must have registered first, and they must supply their ID and password before they can submit an assignment using this facility. The Web form used for submission is shown in Figure 7. The form allows the student to specify their ID/ password combination, name, campus, assignment partners and the file they wish to submit for the assignment. The subject and assignment number of the submission are selected from drop down lists, automatically populated from entries in the *subject* and *assignment header* tables represented in Figure 5.

In order to be able to submit an assignment, the subject administrator must first create an assignment header record. These headers were briefly discussed under record keeping, and the purpose of this record is to describe the assignment. It contains information about the particular assignment such as its number, the marks allocated to it, and what it is marked out of. This data

Figure 7: Web assignment submission form

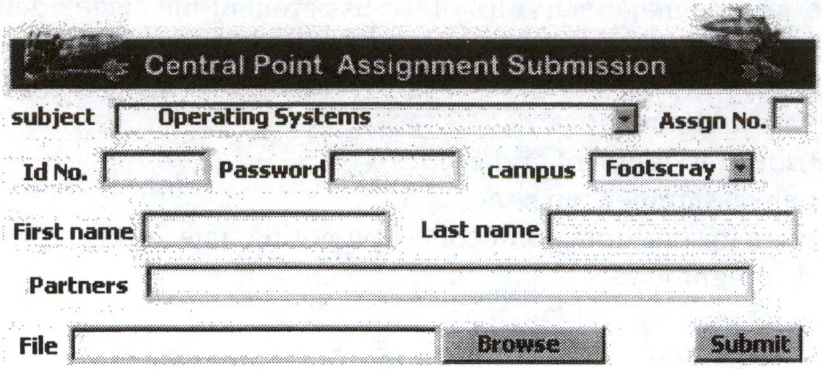

is used by the WBLA system when reporting results to students. The script that creates this assignment header also creates an assignment specific subdirectory where the student file submissions will be directed. Only the WBLA administrator designated as the subject coordinator can add assignment headers. Marks for assignments are linked to the student registration and assignment header tables on a one-to-many relationship.

Students can only submit assignments when an appropriate assignment header has been created. This record contains a field designating whether the assignment results can be released to students or not. Consequently, students cannot view marks for an assignment until the results have been released. This enables administrators to ensure all assignments have been marked before any student can access their marks. Otherwise the displayed maximum, minimum and average marks would not be a true representation, thus possibly causing consternation amongst the students.

Since recommendations concerning forms based uploading of files have not been implemented in the HTML standard as yet, (Nebel and Masinter, 1995), it is at this point that special scripts need to be written to accept non-text-based files. By designing the system to cater for binary files, we give the student the ability to submit, and the subject coordinator to receive files of any type. Typically these will be in *Microsoft Word* format. Where multiple files are involved such as with programming projects, the students can use a compression package such as *WinZip* to effectively create a single file for submission over the Web.

There is one problem concerning assignment submission and the Microsoft Internet Explorer browser that needs to be discussed. The Web page shown in Figure 7 that students fill out in order to submit an assignment contains a standard HTML form field of type *File*. A field of this type causes a button to be displayed by the browser, which the users can click. This allows them to choose their file for submission via the standard operating system file selection dialog box. In some versions of Internet Explorer, this does not operate as described by the HTML standard without first downloading and installing an extra add-on utility. This causes unnecessary confusion, and we recommend to students not wishing to go to the extra trouble of obtaining the add-on, that Netscape Navigator be used.

Once submitted, the student details are recorded along with the submission time and date in an assignment submission record. The name of the submitted file is also saved in the submission record of the WBLA database. The submitted assignment file is stored in a designated directory. This process is depicted in Figure 4. Multiple submissions are easily facilitated by the WBLA system because it automatically chooses a unique file name for the assignment should a previous submission with the same name be detected. The submission records are physically stored in a separate database to the rest of the WBLA data. The main reason for this separation was to aid in security and performance.

After successful submission, the student is given immediate feedback on assignment submission success in the form of a list of students who have submitted assignments for the subject, with dates and times. It is this immediate feedback that has helped the WBLA system gain student acceptance. When working with partners, the WBLA database can also be interrogated at any time to check that the partner has made a successful submission.

Another option that was considered in place of Web based assignment submission was the use of attachments using e-mail. However, this has been used for a number of years on an *ad-hoc* basis at Victoria University and submission by e-mail attachment has been difficult at best. Problems arising from the use of e-mail include incompatible e-mail systems (even within the university), recognition of different mime types by different forwarding mail servers and students lack of knowledge on the use of attachments. Also, there was often a significant delay before students were informed that submission was successful, often causing worry.

One of the most convenient functions provided is the ability to access the assignments submitted via the assignment submission facility from any Web browser. To access assignments for a particular subject and assignment number, an administrator must be a member of that subject's designated team. When the appropriate subject and assignment number is selected, the administrator is presented with a dynamically populated Web page containing a list of submitted assignments, with the surname displayed as a link to the assignment file. A portion of such a page is shown in Figure 8.

By clicking on the surname link, the submitted file can either be opened or downloaded to the local system for viewing at a later stage. We find this particularly useful in our multi-campus situation as any subject team member can access their assignments from any location without having to physically pick up the assignments. All that is required is a Web browser and Internet access.

Web Facilitated Instructor/ Student Communication

Maintaining reasonable communication channels between our students has become a matter of some concern. There are two aspects to communication we see as important. Firstly, being able to communicate to all groups over all campuses while not being perceived to favor one group over another (Darbyshire and Wenn, 1996a). Secondly, students invariably reach a point where they need to see someone and we need to maintain an avenue of help even when a lecturer is not available on that particular campus. To highlight the importance of the second point, students may travel from many campuses to attend lectures at another campus. Apart from that small window of opportunity per week, students do not have direct access to teaching staff. Lecturing staff may also have sole responsibility for a subject on multiple campuses, and when not teaching there, are physically based on one campus, again isolating particular groups of students. We have implemented several measures to help cope with these situations.

Firstly, for personal communication, all students are encouraged to use the phone or e-mail to contact us. The use of e-mail does have some problems associated with it, but they are being addressed by teaching e-mail usage in earlier semesters. Next, we have also implemented, as part of the WBLA system, two bulletin boards (shown as one database called *messages* in Figure 5). The first bulletin board is used solely by the subject coordinator to post announcements, links to web sites, hints for assignments, and files to download.

This subject notice bulletin board is introduced in the first lecture and

Figure 8: Dynamically populated Web-page of submitted assignments

Administrator Assignment Access

Assignment Access for Operating Systems, Assignment 1

Id	First Name	Surname	Date Submitted	Partners
9508732	Samantha	Bayliss	28-Aug-1988	N/A
9710094	Salvatore	Coiro	28-Aug-1988	
9707176	Sergiu	Cota	28-Aug-1988	Woosuk Chang
9508264	Fady	Esber	26-Aug-1988	no-one
9401598	Renee	Jolley	28-Aug-1988	NONE

tutorial, and its frequent use is encouraged. By posting announcements to this bulletin board, we can effectively reach all students on all campuses within a short time period. This helps avoid costly delays that cannot be tolerated in a 13-week semester, and will be further exacerbated by the proposed introduction of a 10-week trimester.

One thing we try to make clear to students is that they should make use of all resources at their disposal. One of the greatest resources the university has is its own students. Where one student has a problem, another may have a solution. At one campus, former students in a subject using the WBLA system for another, may be able to help a student who is currently doing that subject at another campus, and vice versa. To help foster this interaction, we have implemented a bulletin board, designed for student use, for each subject that is part of the WBLA system.

Using this bulletin board, students who have not necessarily met, can post messages to each other, across different campuses. To avoid the obvious problem of the odd student leaving abusive and bogus messages the students must supply their registration ID and password along with the text of the message. When posting a message the registration database is checked for a valid ID and password combination. In this system, the student's ID is stored along with the message, thus students posting inappropriate messages can be dealt with. When another student displays the message, the first name of the student who posted the message is displayed along with the text of the message.

Both of these notice boards are implemented as threaded message systems using Cold Fusion and Microsoft Access. The student notice board is an example of asynchronous communication. Other possibilities have been considered such as the use of synchronous communication in the form of a chat facility. While chat programs are available and can be integrated with our WBLA system, at this stage we have not gone down this path. Before a chat forum is introduced, we wish set in place a formal arrangement; whereby, common Web meeting times can be introduced as part of the subject curriculum.

To date, the use of the student bulletin board system has been disappointing. Similar experiences have also been encountered by others using asynchronous communication facilities (Maor 1997; Lund 1997). To address the problem, in Semester 2, 1998 a more proactive role was taken by the subject coordinator in one subject using the WBLA system. Notices were posted to the subject notice board, and also other messages were posted to the student notice board containing information not in the official notice. Hints on assignments, links to appropriate sites and questions were posted. As a result, activity on the student notice board increased markedly. However, activity became subdued when the proactive role was ceased approximately midway through semester.

Web-Based Facilities for Managing Web Based Learning Materials

At this point in time, little work has been done in this area. As a precursor to further development, the point of access to the system is now a dynamically generated Web page. Thus, the links on the first Web page (*Central Point Project*; Darbyshire and Wenn, 1998), to the Web based learning materials are generated from an Access database containing the subject code, the subject administrator and the URL to the home page for the subject.

Feedback

To gauge the student response to and acceptance of the WBLA system, a mini-survey was taken of students over the two campuses where this system was tried in semester two 1997. The survey was given to students in a subject delivered on two campuses by a single lecturer. The subject comprised a total of 57 part-time and full-time students.

The survey consisted of six Lickert style questions concerning the use and security of the WBLA system. Students could respond by circling a number from one to five, one being the worst negative response and five being the best positive result, three being the median result. This survey was not designed to gather empirical data or statistics on system use. The success of any system depends on user acceptance. The purpose of the survey was to judge this and set the stage for further development.

The Questions asked were:
1. Being able to submit assignments via the Web pages was a good idea.
2. I liked the idea of looking up marks via the Web pages.
3. I felt confidence in the security of my marks on the Web pages.
4. Getting immediate feedback on assignment submission acceptance was a good idea.
5. I felt confidence in using the Web facility to submit my assignments.
6. I felt confidence in the security of my assignment submission on the Web

A total of 46 surveys were returned to the subject lecturer representing 80% of the student population for the subject. This represents responses from all the students present in the lecture at the time the survey was distributed. No attempt was made to contact the missing students as the response rate was deemed both representative and adequate for our purpose. The quantitative mean of the forty-six responses for each of the questions is shown in Figure 9.

As can be seen, the overall response and acceptance of the WBLA system from the students' perspective was excellent. However, we believe the smaller figures for Questions 3 (4.13), 5 (4.07) and 6 (4.11) highlight student concern over the security of their assignments and marks on the Web. The response to Question 5 indicates that there was some concern about using the Web to submit assignments in a timely manner. Some of this concern probably resulted from the excessive downtime experienced during the semester due to the change of internet carriers. The response to Question 4 indicates that students need to obtain immediate feedback from the system as to whether their assignments had been successfully received. This is one of the advantages we believe the WBLA system provides over the use of e-mail attachments for assignment submission.

Further Development

We have had many requests and suggestions for increasing the functionality of our evolving system, as well as many ideas of our own. One of our major goals is to develop the system to the point where it is self-contained. That is, the functionality is increased to a point where no behind-the-scenes manipulation is required and all functions can be transparently performed using menu options offered by Web pages. To this end, the following enhancements are planned:

Web Based Testing and Marking

It was originally perceived that Web based testing would be integrated with facilities for managing Web Based Learning materials. In this way it

Figure 9: Mean responses to mini survey questions

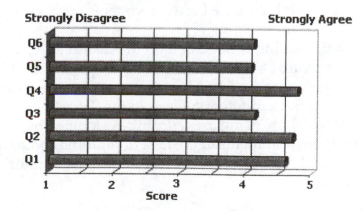

Figure 10: Preliminary architecture for Web based testing and marking

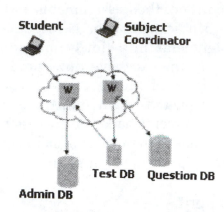

could be used as a set of evaluation exercises at the end of a body of educational material to test understanding. Further research by the authors has indicated it would be better to integrate Web based testing and marking fully into the subject management system.

Preliminary design work for this has been undertaken. Although Web based systems can be used in many types of testing environments, unless the system is used for the presentation and subsequent automatic marking of multiple choice type questions, the system will merely act as a delivery mechanism for answers to traditional type questions. In this case, there is little to gain in the use of the technology for such a purpose. If a Web based system is used to present multiple choice type questions to the user, then these are readily marked by such a system and computer based analysis is straight forward. This type of system is already used commercially by industry based training providers, such as the Microsoft professional certifi-cation program, and a similar certification program offered by Banyan Systems Inc. Other Web based education systems such as TopClass also provide this functionality.

Multiple choice testing is not common in Australia. As a precursor to development in this area a trial was run in the Department of Information Systems during semester two 1998. This trial used multiple choice questions in the final exam for three different subjects in the department. The purpose of the trial was threefold: to gain experience in developing a bank of questions for testing, to introduce students to the idea of multiple choice questions in their final exam, and to compare the results to previous traditional testing methods.

The results of the trial are not reported here. The preliminary architecture of the testing and marking subsystem to be incorporated into the subject management system is shown in Figure 10. We envisage the subject coordinator being able to supply a set of criteria from a Web page that will build an exam to be completed by students at a later date.

Managing Web-Based Learning materials

There are plans to extend the facilities for managing Web Based Learning Materials. At this stage the WBLA system does not do this and relies on the expertise of the subject administrator for placing learning material on the Web and maintaining links. More flexibility is needed for those staff members who do not have such expertise and further integration of the administration system with the learning component will be required. The ultimate aim is to provide a transparent interface to the underlying architecture of the Web to aid subject administrators in publishing materials.

The first step, a dynamically populated initial page, where the Web addresses of subject home pages are found from the Subjects table in the WBLA database has already been taken.

Web Based Assignment Management

In order to model the way teaching staff work when marking assignments, it is planned to investigate the use of software such as *Microsoft Word* for annotating submitted work at the point of reference. In this way, teaching staff can insert comments at particular points in submitted work as per usual. We then plan to investigate a Web based facility for teaching staff to resubmit the marked work to the same submission point where the student submitted the original work. Students can then be given access to the annotated assignments in much the same way as teaching staff can download submitted assignments from the Web. This will need to be controlled by ID and password to maintain privacy.

Housekeeping

Administrator access levels are to be implemented within the existing database. With the use of access levels more functions can be provided to some users on a restricted basis. This will include some superuser type functions such as creating new subjects, new users and setting initial system configurations. User access levels would also enable subject coordinators to formulate subject teams without the intervention of a system administrator.

One of the more annoying routine tasks is the constant request by students to find out their passwords. A scheme where a student can request their passwords be e-mailed to them is currently under development. This will require students to supply an e-mail address when registering. This is a relatively simple matter, as all students in the university are now granted an e-mail address upon enrolment. This would enable students to request and receive their password by e-mail in a matter of minutes without the intervention of the subject coordinator or one of the tutors.

Conclusion

The potential of the WWW for use in teaching is still largely untapped. We believe that students also benefit when the Web is used for subject administration, as well as for the placement of learning materials. Both students and subject administrators benefit from the increased versatility and platform independent access the Web offers.

The system described in this paper implements many of the features found in *TopClass* and other similar commercial systems. It does have support for asynchronous discussions but does not have videoconferencing, whiteboarding or similar synchronous collaborative-learning support mechanisms. We see the main strengths of the system lying in the fact that it was economical to develop, has good support mechanisms for subject coordinators, and because it has been developed incrementally with feedback from both students and lecturing staff, it has been shaped to our requirements.

What began as a seemingly simple exercise in improving productivity and flexibility has blossomed rapidly. The scope for improvement and future enhancements is enormous. One criticism often leveled at us runs along the lines of, "why waste time doing this when you can buy a package that already does this"? Our answer is relatively short. Minimal funds were available, and we did not initially set out to reinvent the wheel.

Progress on the system is slow. However, we are heartened by the encouragement of both students and staff members. One of the largest groups to utilize the versatility such a system can offer is the part-time students. To them, being able to submit assignments from work, and collect their results via the Web is a major benefit. The integration of on-line teaching material with Web based subject administration can only help to maximize their learning experience.

The exercise has been worthwhile. Problems encountered during the construction of our system have provided many insights into both the technology available, and its application to education. Before undertaking such a task today, the effort and expenditure must be weighed against the availability of similar available products. Experiences with other products and our own development efforts lead us to believe that what we have developed suits our need and is possibly more adaptable by us for future expansion. Similar commercial products can be expensive to license, but probably not more so than staff time involved in developing such a system. However, the benefits gained are not all tangible. The valuable experience, insights and expertise gained have been passed on to our students in the form of practical instruction and involvement.

Acknowledgments

The authors would like to gratefully acknowledge: Frank Farance of Farance Inc., Vice Chair of the Learning Technology Standards Committee, Architecture and Reference Model Working Group (IEEE 1484.1), for his kind help and advice on the LTSA Specification and provision of extra materials, and Professor Glenn Lowry for proof reading the final draft and his valuable advice.

References

Alexander, S. (1996), Teaching and Learning on the World Wide Web, HREF *http://www.scu.edu.au/sponsored/ausweb/ausweb95/papers/education2/ alexander/*.

Becker, S. Duggin, T. Keyes, K (1998). "The Use of Web Technology to Support Student Collaboration in and Information Systems Cohort program" in Koshrowpour, M. *Effective Utilization and Management of Emerging Information Technologies*, Idea Group Publishing, Hershey, USA pages 596-602.

Bodendorf F. and Langenbach C. (1998). "Requirements and Software Support of Multimedia-Based Distance Learning" in Koshrowpour, M. *Effective Utilization and Management of Emerging Information Technologies*, Idea Group Publishing, Hershey, USA pages 626- 628.

Brooks D. W. (1997), *Web-teaching: a guide to designing interactive teaching for the World Wide Web*. Plenum Press, New York.

Byrnes, R. and Lo, B. (1994), "A Computer-Aided Assignment Management System: Improving the Teaching-Learning Feedback Cycle," *http:// www.opennet.net.au/cmluga/byrnesw2.htm*.

Byrnes, R., Lo, B., and Dimbleby, J., (1995), "Flexible Assignment Submission in Distance learning," WCCE'95.

Cailliau, R. (1995), "About WWW," *Journal UCS*, Vol 1 No. 4, http:// www.iicm.edu/jucs

Darbyshire, P. and Wenn, A. (1996), "Using the WWW as a MultiCampus Instructional Aid: some experiences and guidelines." Work in Progress Paper presented at EdTech'96, University of Melbourne, 7-10 July, 1996.

Darbyshire, P. and Wenn, A., (1996a). "Experiences with using the WWW as a multi-campus instructional aid," *Proceedings of the Teaching Matters*

Symposium 1996, Victoria University of Technology.

Darbyshire, P. and Wenn, A., (1998), "Central Point Cyber Classroom," *http://busfa.vut.edu.au/cpoint/cp.htm.*

Freeman, M., (1997), "Flexibility in access, interaction and assessment: the case for web-based teaching programs," *Australian Journal of Educational Technology*, 13(1).

Hart, G., (1996), "Creating an Online Teaching Space," *Australian Journal of Educational Technology*, 12(2).

IEEE (1998), "LTSA Specification Version 4.00," Learning Technology Standards Committee, *Architecture and Reference Model Working Group* (IEEE 1484.1) – base document, *http://www.edutool.com/ltsa/ltsa-400.html*

Kaye, A. 1989, "Computer-Mediated Communication and Distance Education," In R. Mason and A. Kaye (Eds.), *Mindweave*, Oxford, Pergamon Press, 3-21.

Maheshwari A. K. (1998). "Web-based System for Assisting Education: An Empirical Assessment," in *Association for Information Systems 1998 Americas Conference Proceedings* http://www.isworld.org/ais.ac.98/proceedings/track26/maheshwari.pdf accessed.

Maor, D., (1997). "Discourses with Teachers via the World Wide Web," *Proceedings ASCILITE '97*, Curtain University, Western Australia

Nebel, E. and Masinter, L., (1995), "RFC 1867 Form-based File Upload in HTML," *http://sunsite.auc.dk/RFC/rfc/rfc1867.html.*

Stanford, J.D. and Cook, H.P. 1987, "Computer Managed Learning - Its application to increase student achievement sing formative self-assessment," *Proceedings CALITE 87 Conference*, University of New South Wales, Sydney, 367-378.

W3C (1997), "HTTP/1.1 - Proposed Standard RFC 2068," World Wide Web Consortium, *http://w3c.org/Protocols/rfc2068/rfc2068.*

W3C (1998), "HTML 4.0 Specification: W3C Recommendation," World Wide Web Consortium, *http://www.w3.org/TR/REC-html40/.*

Chapter 9

Web-Based Competency and Training Management Systems for Distance Learning

Tammy Whalen
University of Ottawa, Canada

David Wright
University of Ottawa, Canada

Abstract

The Web has had a major impact on how corporate training departments manage employee training. The evolution of computers and networks allows companies to implement a precise customer-focused approach. Through the use of competency and training management systems such as the SIGAL system used by Bell Canada, organizational training plans can be efficiently communicated throughout the organization, training needs can be linked to the performance evaluations of individual employees, and online training materials can be conveniently delivered to employees at their desktops. In the future, we predict that training management systems will evolve to incorporate analytic tools that can calculate the return on training investment, evaluate the impact of training on job performance, and determine the impact of training on corporate profits. This chapter discusses the value to companies of using a Web-based system for competency and training management, using the case of Bell Canada as an example of how companies are implementing these tools today.

Introduction

Web-based technologies have created an opportunity for companies to revolutionize the management and delivery of employee training and development. The interest that corporate training departments have in effectively meeting the needs of the end user is nothing new. Trainers have always been committed to delivering high-quality training that has a positive impact on company performance. What is new is the precision with which high-powered computers and high-bandwidth networks allow training departments to implement their customer-focused approach. Through the use of competency and training management systems such as the SIGAL system now being piloted at Bell Canada, organizational training plans can be efficiently communicated throughout the organization, training needs can be linked to the performance evaluations of individual employees, and online training materials can be conveniently delivered to employees at their desktops. This chapter discusses the value to companies of using a Web-based system for competency and training management, using Bell Canada as a case study.

Background

Distance learning has its origins in computer-based training, or CBT. Large companies with a high need for alternative methods of training employees were the first to adopt CBT. IBM, for example, started using CBT to train employees in the late 1960s. Computer technicians, typically working almost exclusively at client sites maintaining IBM mainframe computers, took training related to their jobs using the computers they serviced. The use of distance learning has become more widespread as computers become more powerful, and high-bandwidth networks extend their reach throughout the corporation. Today, many companies are implementing Web-based training that is delivered to desktops, computers in employees' homes, and laptops in any location through corporate intranets, extranets, or the Internet. As the use of distance learning has increased, organizations are realizing there is also a need for online training management systems to provide access to training materials and track their use.

Benefits of Web-Based Training Delivery

Web-based training has several advantages that have encouraged companies such as Bell Canada to explore the possibilities of its use for employee training. Asynchronous courses, comprised of HTML pages and in some cases, multimedia elements such as graphics, animation, video, or recorded audio offer great flexibility in how course materials are both accessed and used. Since asynchronous courses do not have a live instructor, they can be completed by employees at their convenience, at any geographic location with access to a network connection, and at a pace that is set by each individual. Primary consumers of distance learning are sales people who, more than most workers, spend their time away from normal office settings. For example, IBM's sales and marketing force are equipped with mobile computing equipment and use Lotus Notes on a regular basis to take training from hotel rooms and other locations anywhere in the world they happen to be working (Whalen and Wright, 1998).

Another important benefit is the cost savings over classroom training, primarily realized through a reduction in the time it takes employees to complete courses which results in a reduction of salary costs away from the job, and an elimination of travel expenses. Reports illustrating the cost benefits of distance learning over classroom training are appearing more frequently in the literature. The July/August 1998 issue of *Educational Technology* was devoted to return on investment (ROI) studies, and the American Society for Training and Development (1998) has compiled a bibliography of the literature on ROI. Phillips (1998) notes that ROI analysis for training investment is a hot topic because overall training budgets are increasing, and the amount spent on educational technologies is also growing very rapidly. The problem that trainers have in applying ROI is that the process can be very complex due to the many data elements that must be collected and analyzed and costly in terms of staff time required.

The use of Web-based training was initiated in Bell Canada after a thorough investigation of the viability of Web-based training for the company. The Bell Online Institute (BOLI) was established in 1997 to serve as a focal point for distance learning initiatives in Bell Canada. A cost-benefit analysis of Web-based training was undertaken for Bell Canada by Whalen and Wright (1998). This study was undertaken to evaluate the cost-effectiveness of a pilot project to evaluate three Web-based courses on telecommunications topics delivered on four different software systems, known as learning platforms, to 200 Bell Canada engineers in the Fall of 1998.

One of the results of this study was the finding that Bell Canada would save between $3 and $33 for each dollar spent on Web-based training when results were projected over a five-year period. Although the costs of course development are significantly higher than those of traditional classroom training, reduced delivery costs per student mean that overall savings are greater than the development costs, with payback occurring in less than one year. Table 1 illustrates the variability in the ROI for each of the courses produced for the pilot. All of the courses cost considerably less to deliver than classroom-based courses, and the most significant factor in producing a favorable ROI turns out to be the extent of the inclusion of multimedia

Table 1: Return on Investment for Web-Based Training Delivery at Bell Canada Projected Over a 5-Year Period

Course	ROI	Dollars Saved for Every $1 Spent
Routing (synchronous)	3283%	$33
Frame Relay (asynchronous)	697%	$7
TCP/IP (asynchronous using WebCT)	228%	$3
TCP/IP (asynchronous using Mentys)	283%	$3

Source: Whalen and Wright (1999)

elements in the course. For example, the TCP/IP course included a 10-minute video that illustrated sections of the course content, and ROI was notably lower for this course because of the high cost of video production.

Issues, Controversies, Problems

Many organizations, including those in the telecommunications industry, have had to become increasingly competitive in order to survive. Higher levels of competition have resulted in many challenges that must be addressed through training. A "map" of the competencies required by an organization, including the existing competencies, is the first step in providing training that makes a real impact on organizational performance.

The determination of which specific competencies are required by individual employees is generally developed through continuous communication between employees and managers, keeping in mind the strategic direction of the organization. Dove (1998) identifies the need for an organization's competency sets to evolve over time, based on the constantly changing business environment. After competency assessments are complete, appropriate training is required to fill the identified gaps. To be effective, training must be relevant to current needs, readily available to employees, interfere as little as possible with daily work, and result in real improvements in overall productivity.

Managing Employee Training to Support Organizational Goals

Competency modeling, increasingly used by companies to build performance management strategies, is essentially a detailed description of the skills and knowledge required to perform a specific job. Competency profiles form the basis for both employee evaluations and the creation of individual training plans. On a company-wide basis, competency models map out the relationship between the company's business plan and the aggregate employee skill sets required to implement those business plans.

In their article entitled "Putting Competencies to Work," Zemke and Zemke (1999) describe how companies are using competency profiles to achieve mission-critical goals as a:

- vehicle to communicate to employees the behavior required to succeed in their jobs
- part of the process to create a training and development plan for each employee
- method of helping select employees for new roles in the organization.

First, competency profiles provide a clear description of what good performance looks like, e.g., "recognizes when it is important to act even when there is a degree of uncertainty." Communication of management expectations is particularly important in companies experiencing downsizing or reorganization, where a large number of employees are expected to adapt quickly to new roles in the organization.

Second, a training and development plan must be created to address each employee's identified needs. Gaps in skills and knowledge are often identified through the use of what are known as 360 degree assessments. In a 360 degree assessment, each employee is given feedback from their supervisors and several co-workers which they have chosen to evaluate their performance. The criteria for evaluation are based on a specific competency profile for the employee's job.

Apart from the need for clear performance standards, companies must also have policies and practices in place that support the efforts of employees. Ensuring that reward systems are in place will encourage the acquisition of new skills and peak performance. A properly designed and supported training management system gives all employees the opportunity to succeed. To be successful, competency-based training must be accompanied by appropriate employee incentives to complete the training. Rubino (1997) lists five criteria that must be satisfied for reward systems to be successfully implemented:

- successful fit with the organizational environment
- a system that is fair to employees
- a system that yields financial returns to employees
- a system that involves employees and managers
- goals are made clear through communication.

Tracking training results means that those who have the highest levels of success will have the best chance at promotions, performance bonuses, or other rewards, for example, the opportunity to attend conferences.

Training management systems also function as a course catalog and front end for delivering available courses. The gaps that are identified by the 360 degree assessments form the basis for the employee's training plan. Ideally, an employee can access the recommended courses listed in his or her training profile simply by using a computer mouse to click on a course title and the training management system will then load the course material ready for use.

Delivery of courses to the desktop falls into a category of distance learning known as electronic performance support systems (EPSS). EPSS is a term often used to describe "just-in-time" training that supports a specific job requirement. As Malcolm (1998) points out, EPSS' real breakthrough is not so much in the use of technology but in new thinking on the part of training managers. Trainers have now come to realize that increasing employee productivity flows from providing training relevant to specific job tasks at an employee's desktop in an electronic format.

By communicating the criteria for promotion to all employees, Zemke and Zemke point to examples where companies have decreased employee turnover. Essentially, employees perceive that companies are using fair criteria when assessing employees for promotion, and this knowledge gives each employee the opportunity to prepare him or herself for promotion through training and development activities. The flip side of 360 degree assessment is that the company is able to obtain valuable feedback on overall company performance, which amounts to an aggregation of the behavior of all employees.

Organizations who manage training are making strategic decisions about their training investments. These organizations operate with more complete information and can make better decisions about how training dollars are invested, as well as ensure that their demand for particular employee skills matches supply. At a local management level, managers are better informed about the competencies of their employees and better able to match employees to the work that needs to be done on a daily basis.

Knowledge of organizational competencies can equally lead to a decision to reduce the level of particular skills that are no longer required or available in overabundance. Although downsizing has earned a poor reputation through ill-considered and indiscriminate implementations, the regular adjustment of staffing levels is essential for companies to remain competitive. Managing training is the first step in reducing layoffs by proactively retraining employees who possess skills no longer required and redeploying employees into new positions.

The third use of competency profiles is to improve the process of filling job vacancies. This is done by developing profiles to be used as job descriptions when hiring to fill job vacancies, using the profiles to tailor interview questions for job applicants, and to describe the skills of employees already working in the company to identify potential internal candidates for job vacancies. Employers are able to improve the supply of required employee skills by offering training to increase certain skills in the organization, and employees reap rewards through increasing their job opportunities and earnings.

Pay for Performance

Directly linking pay to competencies is a rising trend in organizations. Glaxo Wellcome and Guinness both use generic competence profiles to establish pay ranges (Brown and Armstrong, 1997). While ensuring that employees attain required levels of knowledge is the first step in measuring the success of training, improving job performance is the ultimate goal. Increases in competence are rewarded only when they lead to higher levels of contribution.

Crew (1998) argues that a performance-driven system promotes competition, maintains quality, and emphasizes a consistently high level of achievement. The goal of a performance-driven system is to set clear standards and to align resources, policies and practices with the support that students need to meet the goals that have been set for them. Management principles such as defining clear standards, setting training strategies designed to enable all students to meet the standards, and tracking results are required at all levels of the organization to make performance-driven systems a success.

As Davis, Lucas, and Marcotte (1998) put it, the goal of competency-based profiling and assessment is to make a positive impact on the goals, often financial, of the organization through making the best use of human resources. In other words, training is an investment in human resources, and if well-managed, should give a positive return. General Motors is another example of a corporation that is using a combined approach to competency assessment and training management to achieve corporate business goals. General Motors has assessed the desired personal leadership characteristics, business direction, communication, and program implementation needed by managers and linked these outcomes to specific training. To measure the success of the training initiative, that company simultaneously measures changes both in organizational culture and individual performance. Owens-Corning Fiberglass Corp. has taken a similar approach using the Web for training delivery (Gordon, 1998). Employees at Owens-Corning are able to access Web-based training materials that have been identified as key to their career development from training providers such as the American Management Association.

Improvements in performance can be measured in various ways. For example, higher productivity, higher quality output, fewer errors, faster product delivery to customers, or increased sales all would indicate an improvement in employee performance. Performance appraisal systems are the method typically used to identify training requirements and assess training results. Goals are often set both for individual employees and for group effort. For example, an individual may be required to increase his or her level of productivity during a particular period, and a productivity goal will also be set for the work group as a whole.

While some companies choose to link training and performance to direct financial rewards, other organizations simply rely on the power of the performance appraisal system itself to provide incentives for employees to successfully complete required training. If an organization requires that recent performance appraisals be reviewed before employees can receive promotions, there is an indirect link between the successful completion of training and financial compensation. Furthermore, depending on the nature of the organization and the job an employee performs, unsatisfactory performance appraisals may ultimately result in an employee losing his or her job.

Many companies are now using a performance-based pay structure under the theory that employees work harder when their paychecks are at risk. Under this type of system, pay may be:

- entirely based on performance, e.g., salespeople who get paid on commission
- partially based on performance, e.g., the top 10-30 percent of salary is paid only if certain performance criteria are met
- nominally based on performance, e.g., base salary is guaranteed, but a bonus is paid if performance meets or exceeds set criteria.

Will employees be able to withstand the pressures that pay for performance brings on a long-term basis? While there are companies which reward above-average performers with pay increases, some pay for performance programs are more oriented toward punishing below-average performers. Although the question cannot yet be answered with any accuracy, it seems likely that constant threats to withhold salary or lay off personnel are not sustainable strategies for companies in the long term. Apart from causing employees to continuously seek out more stable employment that then results in costly turnover, inspiring fear in employees seems an unlikely plan for increasing corporate profits.

Solutions and Recommendations

Enterprise-Wide Competency and Training Management Systems

Competency and training management systems are a key part of managing a company's human resources. Systems such as SIGAL can be viewed as management support systems that help manage organizational knowledge and the skills of individuals through training. Web-based learning platforms, the software systems that house and deliver distance training courses over the Web, are becoming increasingly sophisticated in features and functionality. Until recently, most of these systems offered little in the way of student administration and training management. However, developers are now paying more attention to the elements that are required to effectively deliver training over the Web such as:

- administration and management of company training objectives
- online employee competency assessment tools
- searchable database of collective competencies within the organization
- tracking employee requirements for specific courses through user profiles
- online course registration
- user interface for employees to access recommended Web-based courses
- online testing and database of test scores available to students, managers, and administrators
- tracking training budget commitments and expenditures
- gateway to broader human resource management systems such as PeopleSoft for linking HR records to employee training requirements and test scores.

The software systems that house and deliver Web-based training content have only recently begun to offer training management and student administration features. In his article "Enterprise Training: This Changes Everything," Stamps (1999) points out that there are two aspects to enterprise-wide training systems. The first is the ability to deliver training content over networks to employees throughout the organization. The second feature is the ability to manage the training for the entire organization through the use of a central training management system. While organizations have been adopting the use of Web-based and other distributed modes of training in increasing numbers in the past five years, enterprise training management systems are still an emerging area with numerous vendors entering the marketplace with new products.

Phillips and Pulliam (1997) identify the seven most important trends in the training and development field as:

1. measuring the effectiveness and efficiency of training and development in a systematic way
2. linking organizational and performance needs to program delivery
3. shifting the function from traditional training to a performance improvement role
4. integrating training into the strategic and operational framework of the organization
5. building partnerships with key clients and management groups
6. positioning training closer to the work site
7. using technology efficiently and effectively.

Vendors have responded to these needs by incorporating student management and course administration features into online course delivery platforms such as WebCT (www.webc.com), Asymetrix' ToolBook II (www.asymetrix.com), the Desktop Trainer from MicroVideo Learning Systems (www.microvideo.com), and many others.

We have identified seven primary features of enterprise-wide competency and training management systems:

- they house profiles of the skills required by the organization which form the benchmarks of the key knowledge and skills required for each position
- they are a user interface for the competency assessments of each employee that identify the gaps between current competencies and the ideal competency set
- they are the front-end for employees to access training that will bridge knowledge gaps, either through direct access to online courses or through providing information in the form of course catalogs for classroom-based training
- tracking of whether employees have taken recommended training and whether their post-training skill levels are sufficient to do their jobs
- through communicating to employees their expected competencies, competency gaps, the means of acquiring needed training, and reporting whether employees have successfully completed required training to supervisors, these systems help manage organizational knowledge
- provide a vehicle for the ongoing reassessment of the competencies required by the organization.

Organizational Requirement for Competency and Training Management Systems

While competency management can be done without the use of an online system, the number of details that must be tracked make online systems very effective for that purpose, especially in companies with large numbers of employees. Jones (1998) lists distance learning, performance support systems, and training management software among the leading new virtual human resource applications in the knowledge-based organization. Strategies must also be in place to collect, store, analyze, and distribute information and knowledge. As well, a technology infrastructure needs to be in place, change management programs must be implemented to help users adapt to a competency-based learning organization, and the training techniques employed must be results oriented.

Jones cites Duracell as an example of a company using an enterprise-wide training management system to manage training for its 9,000 employees worldwide. Some of the key features of the chosen system are information management for all training activities, training expense tracking, and an interface to other human resource applications. Duracell evaluated several training management systems on the market against a specific set of needs before choosing a system. Online training management systems are similar to other software products in that each has a unique set of features. Selecting an appropriate system, especially in an emerging area, can present a challenge. To help organizations choose a system that best serves their needs, Brandon Hall (1998) has recently published a report that evaluates the features of a wide variety of online training management products, providing organizations with invaluable information before choosing a system.

While delivering Web-based courses can provide organizations with clear financial benefits, the use of a training management system to deliver courses does not intrinsically either increase or decrease the costs of training delivery. The real value of using a competency assessment and training management system is less in decreasing the costs of training than in increasing the precision with which training investment can be managed.

Case Description: Use of the SIGAL System at Bell Canada

Competency Management at Bell Canada

At Bell Canada, all managers undergo an annual evaluation known as the Internal Contribution Assessment (ICA). Employees are evaluated on their performance of the accountabilities for the review period (ACAT) that had been set at the beginning of the year, their leadership capabilities (LCAT) and their technical capabilities (TCAT). Capabilities used for the evaluations are included in 18 broad categories ranging from those that span all jobs, e.g., "General Management Capabilities" to the job-specific, e.g., "Sales and Sales Support." These categories are each broken down into subcategories such as "Manage Projects" or "Build and Manage Customer Loyalty."

The subcategories are then even more minutely defined so that a clear picture of each job requirement emerges. For example, under "Manage Projects" one of the capabilities listed is "understand project management skills and concepts." Altogether, over 500 specific capabilities are defined for potential employee assessment. The next step is for supervisors and peers to rate employees on their performance of each capability using a 360 degree assessment process. Annual employee appraisals for nonmanagement staff are less often done, a problem that the company hopes will be improved with full implementation of the SIGAL system.

The aggregate capabilities of all managers form a picture of Bell Canada's "organizational knowledge" and the resulting database of capabilities serves to help the company understand strengths and weaknesses of the company's management resources. In situations where the company wants to change business direction, this assessment helps senior management make decisions about the skills that need to be acquired through hiring practices, or the converse, which employee skill sets are held in abundance in times of downsizing. The database is also used by human resource professionals for the practical purpose of helping to identify potential job candidates to fill vacant positions within the company.

SIGAL

The SIGAL system from Technomedia, Inc. (www.technomedia.ca) is presently being piloted at Bell Canada for enterprise-wide competency and training management and online training delivery to 200 managers in the Network Management Services (NMS) group described in the case study below. The system integrates existing Web-based course content in HTML format, online training delivery through its virtual classroom feature, course management tools, training management data for each employee, and employee records residing within the Peoplesoft human resource management system. SIGAL also does budget tracking for training expenditures.

To use this system, the overall skill set required for the organization is first established by senior management. Training and line managers then translate this information into competency profiles that are the benchmarks for the skill sets required for specific job positions. The next step is to assess how well each individual meets the benchmarks for his or her position. This may be done through employee testing or by asking the line manager to make that assessment.

After employees are assessed, appropriate courses that will fill identified gaps in knowledge or skills are recommended to employees. Web-based courses may be launched directly from the SIGAL system through the virtual classroom features. Post-course testing determines how well the knowledge has been digested, and when an employee has successfully completed a course, the system then sends an e-mail message with this information to the employee's supervisor.

Web-based training gained the interest of management because of the competitive advantages that just-in-time training to the desktop bring, and for the cost savings over classroom training. Employees involved in various Web-based training initiatives have felt that this mode of training meets their job needs. They have consistently reported that the flexibility of being able to take the courses on their desktops or on their laptops from other locations, flexibility on the time that the course can be taken, as well as the self-paced aspects of the courses are all valued features of Web-based training.

Post-course testing establishes how well an employee has learned the course material and testing results are stored in the system. Managers may also be asked to assess improvements in job performance. Links with human resources (HR) systems such as PeopleSoft enhance SIGAL by providing background information about each employee. For example, the employee's first language can be determined for presentation of the bilingual user interface in the employee's preferred language. Integration with HR systems allows the management of training to be an integral part of the overall human resources management for the organization. In the future, additional information sharing and reporting between the two systems is likely to occur. Table 2 summarizes the features of SIGAL with respect to training management functions and processes.

Broadband Training Initiative: Case Study

The broadband training initiative at Bell Canada is an example of how the company is using the SIGAL system for enterprise-wide Web-based competency and training management. The pilot project consists of 200 Bell Canada managers in the Network Management Services (NMS) group (Mcallen, 1999). The goal of the project is to improve skills in areas critical to job performance, with the added bonus of providing an opportunity for career development. The expected result is highly motivated leaders who will be capable of implementing the company's new strategies in an emerging technological field.

The process begins with employees, supervisors, and co-workers logging-on to the system either to complete the 360 degree assessment questionnaire, or to access the ICA form itself. All information, including co-workers' 360 degree assessment, supervisor assessments, and recommendations for training is input online. The result is an efficient and well managed employee evaluation system.

Part of the pilot includes making ten new asynchronous courses on the topic of broadband telecommunications available to employees. The courses were identified as "high need" for the NMS group because the ability to support broadband networks is a new requirement for their jobs. While designing new courses was one of the options considered, existing asynchronous Web-based courses from third parties were found and used in the trial.

Benchmarks for the levels of broadband communications knowledge were set by company training managers, working with line managers in the NMS group. Competency gaps for each employee were also similarly established. After a discussion between the employee and supervisor, the recommended courses are included in the employee's ICA and formally identified as a goal for the next review period. The identified courses are mandatory, and successful completion within a 1-year period is required and noted on the ICA for the next review period.

Employees access the courses from their desktops using the SIGAL system as a front-end user interface via the corporate intranet. Two servers are used to deliver the training: one server to house the SIGAL system and the other the training content. During the formal training period, employees start by taking a pre-course test to evaluate which, if any, of ten Web-based courses are required to fill gaps in their knowledge of the subject area. As employees complete the courses, their supervisors are notified by the system via e-mail, although post-course test scores are only given to the employees themselves.

Other competency assessment and training management projects are anticipated in the near future with other employee groups. Eventually, Bell expects to use the system to manage competencies and all training, both Web- and classroom-based, for all employees in the company.

Barriers to the Use of Web-based Competency Assessment and Training Management

Although related, online competency management and Web-based training delivery are essentially two different functions, each with its own set of problems.

Online Training Development and Delivery

The cost of developing Web-based training courses can be prohibitive. In the BOLI study, total fixed costs (in Canadian dollars) for developing Web-based courses were as high as $160,049 (Whalen and Wright, 1998). Although delivery costs per student are less than those for classroom courses – at Bell Canada, roughly 90 percent less – organizations need to train a minimum number of students in order to break even. This calculation needs to be made by training departments on a case by case basis to ensure that resources are

Table 2: Training Management Functions, Processes, and SIGAL Features

Training Management Functions	Processes	SIGAL Features
Competency Management of Organization	• strategic analysis of competency profiles for each business unit and for each position	• searchable database of collective competencies within the organization • user interface to external systems
Competency Management of Employees	• individual competency testing and training plan	• online assessment tools • tracking employee requirements for specific courses • user interface to external systems
Course Management	• integration with course delivery systems	• user interface to access online course catalog • user interface to access online courses (i.e., virtual classroom) • online discussion groups for students and instructors • online access to electronic library • scheduling of online and classroom courses including equipment and instructor resources
Student Management	• registration, evaluation, tracking test results	• online course registration • database of test scores • gateway to broader human resource management systems
Financial Management	• financial tracking of training commitments and expenditures	• financial tracking of training commitments and expenditures
Performance Evaluation and Economic Return	• online student testing • online student course evaluations • tracking test scores and course evaluations • performance appraisals by managers	• integrated online knowledge and application testing • online student course evaluations • reporting features for training management functions • links to human resource management systems such as PeopleSoft

well-spent.

Another issue is the availability of adequate computer hardware for employees. More than one organization, including Bell Canada, has investigated the benefits of Web-based training only to find that a large number of the employees need substantial upgrades to the current equipment on their desktops. A related problem is the availability of bandwidth. Even organizations with state of the art intranets may find that existing applications running over the network occupy most of the bandwidth available, leaving expensive upgrades to the network the only option if Web-based training is to be implemented.

Some complex subjects are also difficult for employees to internalize if asynchronous courses are not supplemented with access to a person who can answer student questions. Training departments need to use their considerable expertise in instructional design in order to judge which courses are the best candidates for asynchronous Web-based delivery.

Competency Assessment

As Stamps (1999) points out, considerable time and effort must go into building the competency models that guide the learning processes in order to maximize the potential of these new products. Like SAP, BAAN, PeopleSoft and other systems that are leaders in enterprise-wide systems development, training management systems represent fundamental changes to the way companies conduct their internal training businesses. With the use of training management systems comes the need to overhaul and standardize all training practices, equip and training all training staff in the use of the system, migrate employee training information from current records to the new training management database. And this is just the beginning of the costs of using a total training management system that involves competency assessment and tracking features, as information needs to be added to the system at least annually for each employee. Even after a company has decided to create and manage competency profiles for its employees, the choice of whether to use a paper-based or a Web-based system for this purpose may well depend on how many employees need to be managed, and whether the variety or complexity of their jobs necessitate the tracking of a large number of competencies.

Future Trends

Many organizations are presently at the stage of evaluating different types of distance learning and the focus tends to be on which Web-based course delivery platform best meets the needs of the organization. As more courses are delivered via the Web, an increasing number of companies will find that a training management system is required to ensure that employees have easy access to online courses. Web-based courses make it much easier to track whether students have taken courses and track the results of online testing. Online courses even make it possible to see when employees took courses, where they left off, and which test questions employees found the most difficult. During the next few years, many organizations will adopt the Web as a core mode of training delivery, and training management systems will be the next area where interest will be concentrated.

To a great extent the increased use of competency assessment and training management systems will simply be the result of the availability of these systems in the marketplace. The need to manage competencies and training is not a new idea. Back in the early 1990s the Canadian Department of National Defence purchased a custom-made competency assessment and training management system because of the high need that organization had for managing training related to the many occupational trades in the military. As similar systems become available off-the-shelf, organizations without the monetary resources to commission custom software will also be able to take advantage of the benefits of competency and training management systems.

With time, competency and training management systems will become even more sophisticated in features and functionality. Better links to human resource management systems such as PeopleSoft will allow for more financial analysis on training and performance. As well, analytic tools will likely be incorporated that can evaluate return on investment and the impact of training on job performance and corporate profits. The result will be a more accurate picture of organizational performance and job performance, and perhaps closer ties between training, job performance, and financial compensation.

Conclusion

Enterprise-wide systems function as a user interface to both internal and external online training delivery systems and manage user and course information for online and classroom training. As a user interface, these systems allow employees to go directly from individual training profiles that contain management recommendations for Web-based courses, to a virtual learning center where competency assessment testing is done and the courses themselves may be accessed. The system keeps an online record for each employee and data residing in broader HR systems such as PeopleSoft can also be linked to the training management system.

For investments in training to be most effective, information management is key. Training is one element of the performance management of individual employees and the organization as a whole. Competency and training management systems allow for the sophisticated management of information related to training. Systems such as SIGAL effectively manage information related to individual and organizational competencies, training delivery, financial management of training, and performance tracking.

Appendix: Glossary

Asynchronous: network communication which is not done in real time; for example, e-mail or the use of HTML pages.

Client: an end-user computer using a browser program (such as Netscape) to receive multimedia documents from a Web server.

HTML (Hypertext Markup Language): the standard document format used on the Web.

Internet: an international network linking millions of computers via telephone lines using the TCP/IP protocol.

Intranet: an internal network linking corporate computers using the TCP/IP protocol.

Return on Investment (ROI): the financial gain (or loss) resulting from the use of Web-based training. ROI = (Present Value of Savings From Web-Based Training / Present Value of Costs of Web-Based Training) * 100.

Server: an Internet host computer using a program (such as NCSA's HTTPD) to store and transmit multimedia documents for an information service (such as the World Wide Web).

Synchronous Communication: real-time network communication such as video conferencing.

Web: a network of multimedia documents stored on Internet or intranet servers, which can be seen by using a browser. Documents are formatted with the HTML standard and transmitted with the HTTP standard

Acknowledgment

The research for this chapter was supported in part by Industry Canada's Network of Centers of Excellence in Telelearning.

References

Bibliography: Return-on-Investment – ASTD Publications (1998). Alexandria, VA: American Society for Training and Development, http://www.astd.org/

Brown, Duncan and Michael Armstrong (1997, September 11). Terms of enrichment. *People Management 3(18)*, 36-38.

Crew, Rudy (1998, March). Creating a performance-driven system. *Economic Policy Review 4(1)*, 7-9.

Davis, Steven R, Jay H. Lucas, and Donald R. Marcotte (1998, April). GM links better leaders to better business. *Workforce 77(4)*, 62-68.

Dove, Rick (1998, January). A knowledge management framework. *Automotive Manufacturing & Production 110(1)*, 18-20.

Gordon, Jack (1998, June). Outsourcing to the Web. *Training 35(6)*, 98, 99.

Hall, Brandon (1998). Online training management software: How to choose a system your company can live with. Brandon Hall Resources.

Jones, John W. (1998). Virtual HR: Human resources management in the information age. Menlo Park: Crisp Publications.

Malcolm, Stanley E. (1998, March). Where EPSS will go from here. *Training 35(3)*, 64-69.

Mcallen, Alwyn (1999, March 9). Associate Director, Human Resources, Bell Canada. Personal communication.

Phillips, Jack J. and Patti F. Pulliam (1997, December). The seven key challenges facing training and development. *Journal of Lending & Credit Risk Management 80(4)*, 25-30.

Phillips, Jack J. (1998, July-August). The Return-on-Investment (ROI) process: issues and trends. Educational Technology 38(4), 7-14.

Rubino, John A. (1997, Summer). A guide to successfully managing employee performance: Linking performance management, reward systems, and management training. *Employment Relations Today 24(2)*, 45-53.

Stamps, David (1999, January). Enterprise training: this changes everything. *Training 36(1)*, 41-48.

Tammy Whalen and David Wright (1998). "Distance Training in the Virtual Workplace," in The Virtual Workplace. Harrisburg, PA: Idea Group Publishing.

Whalen, Tammy and David Wright (1999, Spring). Methodology for cost-benefit analysis of Web-based telelearning: Case study of the Bell Online Institute. *American Journal of Distance Education ()* (in press).

Zemke, Ron and Susan Zemke (1999, January). Putting competencies to work. *Training 36(1)*, 70-76.

Chapter 10

Electronic Commerce in Egypt

Sherif Kamel
American University in Cairo

Abstract

The information and communication technologies have had remarkable impacts worldwide on the emergence of a number of trends and applications affecting business, the industry and the economy. One of the vastly growing waves in today's changing environment is electronic commerce. It is directly affecting the way people communicate, interact and do business. Electronic commerce currently represents 2% of the global business transactions but promises to dominate the business environment in the 21st century. The successful presence of electronic commerce through the Internet has helped create low cost and more efficient channels for product and service sales through a more dynamic and interactive venue of opportunities where the world becomes the market place.

This chapter reflects on the ways business will be developed and formulated in the 21st century. As the world is converging into a global village where supply and demand interacts across nations and continents, electronic commerce represents an opportunity for many countries around the world. Egypt, one of the rapidly growing economies among the developing world has thoroughly invested in transforming its society to deal with the information-based global market economy of the coming century. Respectively, one of the associated technologies in business development and trading has been electronic commerce. With the introduction of the Internet since 1993 in Egypt, today there are around 250,000 Internet subscribers served by 50 Internet service providers and representing the starting point for a potential electronic commerce community.

As the Internet grows in magnitude and capacity, electronic commerce will flourish and will have direct implications on the socioeconomic and business development process in Egypt. This chapter demonstrates Egypt's vision with regard to electronic commerce and its possible utilization in its developmental and planning processes. Moreover, the chapter will demonstrate the roles of the government, the public and the private sector facing the challenges and opportunities enabled by electronic commerce, and how Egypt places the new enabled information and communication technologies as tools that can help in the nation's development process.

Introduction

Information and communication technology, information highways, and globalization are some of the driving forces of change in today's market place (Kamel 1995). The Internet promises to improve people's daily lives in the way they work, study, and are entertained with diverse implications affecting many aspects and sectors of life. The economy, the industry and the business society are among the beneficiaries. The growth of the Internet, the numbers of users and the applications introduced have been remarkable over the last decade. Projections show that the growth rate will continue to rise in the years to come, as the world becomes more aware of the opportunities enabled by the Internet as vital source of information and knowledge at the individual and organizational levels (Kamel 1997).

This chapter provides an overview of one of the rising stars and applications of the Internet: "electronic commerce" that is perceived to become the way to do business in the 21st century. Thus, firms worldwide are starting to invest in cyberspace as their gateway to the business world in the next millennium whereas those who stick to the traditional ways will lag behind and lose out with regard to business opportunities for development, expansion and growth. The chapter demonstrates the concept of electronic commerce globally and proposes ideas and suggestions for a developing country such as Egypt that has chosen to leap frog by investing in information and communication technologies to keep pace with the developments taking place worldwide. The trade-off has been vital and the factors involved have economical and social implications. The first option was to develop the country horizontally in traditional sectors, however, risking lagging behind further in technology and innovation. The second option was to push the high-tech industry and develop the country vertically through heavy investment in sectors such as high-tech, communications and information technology with ultimate implications and benefits on all other sectors (GOE Report 1997).

Since 1985, the decision made at the highest level of policy making was to build Egypt's national information infrastructure to become the platform for the development of all sectors and industries through better allocation of resources and rationalization of the decision making process by using timely, relevant and accurate information. During the period 1985-1995, a public-private sector partnership for growth and development had a remarkable impact on the buildup of Egypt's information infrastructure "infostructure" (Kamel 1995), with over 600 information and decision support systems and centers established across Egypt's 26 governorates (provinces) targeting Egypt's socioeconomic and development planning (Kamel 1993).

The introduction of the Internet and the formulation of many informatics projects across the country coupled with a massive national plan for training and professional development in the related areas to information technology have had also an invaluable input in building an information technology literate society. The components of the information technology industry including people, training, information, technology and the partnership between the public and the private sector represented the building blocks required to prepare Egypt for the 21st century from an information perspective. The next millennium promises to bring to the world, especially the developing world, more challenges across different sectors of the society. From that perspective, it is up to the nations of the world, including Egypt, to prepare itself and its society for a more aggressive and competitive global market place that promises to be information-driven.

The objective of this chapter is to present Egypt's vision of electronic commerce. Egypt has chosen to be among the first countries of the developing world to penetrate this new window of opportunities for development and growth. Therefore, the government and the private sector united their resources to pave the way for an Egyptian presence on the cyber world of business to establish bridges and vehicles for cooperation between Egyptian and international business organizations. Electronic commerce is perceived to have the potential to support Egypt's business and socioeconomic development. Currently, efforts are underway to prepare the infrastructure with its human, technology and information components for a strong, dynamic and continuous presence on the electronic commerce platform. The chapter will demonstrate what has been done globally, as well as in Egypt, the current status, and the action plan currently being implemented and what is expected in the future and its implications with the related challenges and opportunities.

Background

The Internet is the largest network of computers in the world providing a wealth of information and knowledge. As it grew over the years since the

1960s, many businesses became interested in the Internet as a medium for conducting business transactions. In 1992, the National Science Foundation in the United States relaxed its Acceptable Use Policy enabling the conduct of business transactions over the Internet. Hence, commercial networks started to join the Internet becoming more open to the business community. However, it was not until the World Wide Web was conceived by CERN "the European Particle Physics Laboratory" in Geneva Switzerland that electronic commerce applications began to prevail and establish a presence (EU Report 1997).

The World Wide Web links computer networks globally and allows users to access information on the Internet using a visual interface that includes multimedia such as sound, image and motion pictures (Hammond 1996). Respectively, the increased global outreach of the web with its decreasing cost for setup and maintenance as opposed to the traditional marketing and sales techniques have induced firms globally to set up web sites and use electronic methods for disseminating information about their products and services (Tapscott 1996).

Electronic commerce is one of the most important topics in today's global business environment. Therefore, understanding the degree to which the Internet will change business and society is the issue under discussion in the business community. Money has become increasingly abstract over the years and it will shortly exist without any physical reality (Kosiur 1997). The concept was invented 5,000 years ago with the introduction of the first coin in the Temples of Sumer (EU Report 1997). Since then, the ratio of paper money to gold reserves has remained amazingly constant where money as a unit of wealth representation was exchanged for a specific value of goods or a set amount of gold. Recently, many other forms of money were introduced better known as "plastic money". However, with the Internet evolution, additional forms are being introduced capitalizing on the cyber innovation of the information and communication technologies. The new trend is "digital cash", sometimes referred to as electronic money or electronic cash (Kosiur 1997). Digital cash is becoming increasingly vital especially in an electronic commerce environment where all transactions, business development operations and interaction will be electronic and via information networks (Lynch and Lundquist 1996).

The global society is currently witnessing a phase of transition from an information age that was physical to an information age that is digital (Lynch and Lundquist 1996). This transition promises to cut costs, save time, increase revenue and provide a general digital sense of the world as one global digital village where people can communicate anytime, anywhere, where time and distance barriers are removed and/or decreased (Kamel 1995).

Today, it costs only a small amount to use the Internet. In the near future, it will cost virtually nothing (Tapscott 1996). While the underlying costs of telecommunications are collapsing, Internet usage is experiencing an unprecedented exponential growth (Kalakota and Whinston 1996). At the policy level, national and regional plans are being formulated as part of a global consensus to deregulate national networks, to open up nations and territories to competition, to forge alliances between former competitors and to wire up the three-quarters of the world that is still unconnected. This is being perceived as an integral part of the global information society (EU Report 1997). From that perspective, one could claim that "getting-wired" is the key to business development and economic growth in the years to come (Chase 1998).

Electronic commerce represents a new evolution of trading, offering a border-less global marketplace (Kalakota and Whinston 1996). For Egypt, electronic commerce represents a tremendous challenge, but also a great opportunity for growth and development (Hashem and Ismail 1998). Business on the Internet is booming and many retailers, brokers and suppliers around the world are actually changing habits in the way they do business by introducing new methods and creating new opportunities through cyberspace. Without a doubt, the Internet is ushering in an era of sweeping change that will leave no business or industry unaffected. In that respect, in three years, the Internet has gone from a playground for nerds into a vast communications and trading center where some 100 million users/organizations swap information or do deals around the globe (Business Week 1998).

The Internet facts show that business to business electronic commerce accounted for 78% of the total spent on cyber transactions in 1998. For the travel industry the impact will account for 35% of all on-line sales by the year 2002 up from 11% in 1998 according to a Datamonitor study. Also by the year 2002, book sales and software will each be 10%, insurance 9%, music 8%, clothes 7% and hardware 5%. Moreover, it is expected that U.S. businesses will exchange an estimated 17 billion U.S. dollars in 1998 over the Internet that is more than double the figure in 1997. By the year 2002 this figure is expected to hit the 327 billion US dollars mark (*Business Week* 1998). This is caused by the fact that the Internet is re-engineering the fundamental nature of business transactions as every link in the supply chain is wired; the traditional roles of manufacturers, distributors and suppliers are blurring and buyers will be the ultimate winners (EU Report 1997).

The benefits to the economy of electronic commerce are boundless (Kamel 1995). Electronic commerce is not a product; it is a force. It is a powerful agent that will transform the way many products and services are developed and sold. It will change many rules of the business game. With the growing and continuous changes in information and communication technologies, many aspects of life have been greatly affected; one of which is commerce and trading (Chase 1998).

E-commerce: "The Concept"

Electronic commerce as a concept and as an application is developing rapidly because of the unprecedented growth rate of the World Wide Web. Electronic commerce is about doing business electronically (Kosiur 1997). It is defined as "the performance of business transactions and buying and selling of information, products, and services digitally" (Tapscott 1996). It is based on the digital processing and data transmission including text, sound and video (Lynch and Lundquist 1996). It covers different forms of business interactions, between business-to-business and business-to-consumers, using information and communication technologies (Silverstein 1999). This encompasses many activities such as on-line marketing and advertising, on-line catalogs, electronic payment, fund transfers as well as consumer goods and services such as information, financial, legal services, healthcare and newly introduced virtual malls (Kamel 1995).

E-commerce: "The Internet Revolution"

Electronic commerce is not a new phenomenon. For many years firms have exchanged business data over a variety of communication networks (Kalakota and Whiston 1996). But there are now an accelerated expansion and radical changes, driven by the exponential growth of the Internet. Until recently, there were only business-to-business activities on closed proprietary networks. However, today electronic commerce is rapidly expanding into a complex web of commercial activities transacted on a global scale between an ever-increasing number of participants, corporate and individual on the Internet. Table 1 demonstrates the changes in electronic commerce that occurred in recent years (EU Report 1997).

However, electronic commerce is not limited to the Internet. It includes a wide number of applications in the narrow-band (videotex), broadcast (teleshopping), and off-line environment (catalog sales on CD-ROM), as well as proprietary corporate networks (banking). However, the Internet with its robust and network-independent protocols is rapidly federating innovative hybrid forms of electronic commerce (Silverstein 1999). Electronic commerce is creating a virtual market with innovative virtual businesses and trading communities where firms are outsourcing, distribution services are becoming virtual, and buyers, sellers and intermediaries in fields such as computing, automobile and aerospace are actively integrating their supply chains creating interactive value-added services to businesses and consumers.

The Case of Egypt: "Internet, Electronic Commerce and the Future"

Evolution of the Internet in Egypt

Egypt's telecommunications sector has improved significantly since the early 1980s. In 1997, it reached more than 4.5 million wire lines with a teledensity rate of more than 7.4. Internationally, the number of channels expanded substantially to 8,066 in 1997 compared to 820 in 1977. Microwave links, along with satellite earth stations and submarine cable systems, also helped connect Egypt with the rest of the world. The quality of services has improved with fiber optic technology and automatic and digital exchanges (Mintz 1998). In 1996, the Global System for Mobile Communications (GSM) and Very Small Aperture Terminal (VSAT) networks were added (Kamel 1998). Egypt Telecom is the predominant provider of telecommunications services in Egypt (Kamel 1996). In 1998, Egypt Telecom was transformed into a joint stock company to establish and operate local telecommunication networks including those with international links (Mintz 1998).

Internet services in Egypt started in October 1993 through a 9.6K link between by the Egyptian Universities Network (EUN) and France that carried the Bitnet and Internet traffic. In 1993, 2,000 people used the Internet; in 1994, the Egyptian domain was divided into four major areas (*http://www.ise.org.eg*). The academic subdomain (eun.eg) gets bandwidth via a gateway at the Supreme Council of Universities and provides services for universities and schools. The (sci.eg) subdomain served the scientific research institutes at the Academy of Scientific Research and other research centers like the National Telecommunications Institute. In 1994, a commercial subdomain (com.eg) and a government subdomain (gov.eg) were estab-

Table 1: For traditional electronic commerce the network is a means to move data, for Internet electronic commerce, the network is the market.

TRADITIONAL E-COMMERCE	INTERNET E-COMMERCE
Business-to-business only	Business-to-consumers Business-to-business Business-to-public administration User-to-user
Closed "clubs", often industry specific	Open marketplace, global scale
Limited number of corporate partners	Unlimited number of partners
Closed proprietary networks	Open, unprotected networks
Known and trusted partners	Known and unknown partners
Security part of network design	Security and authentication needed
THE MARKET IS A CLUB	**THE NETWORK IS THE MARKET**

lished through a partnership between the Egyptian Cabinet Information and Decision Support Center (IDSC) *http://www.idsc.gov.eg* and the Regional Information Technology and Software Engineering Center (RITSEC) *http://www.ritsec.com.eg.*

Interconnectivity was improved in 1994 by establishing 64K digital access to France in cooperation with IDSC, EUN and Egypt Telecom (Kamel 1996). To promote the popularity of the Internet, IDSC and RITSEC provided free Internet access for Egyptian public and private corporations, government agencies, non-governmental organizations, and professionals from 1994 until 1996. The free access formula was credited with helping to boost the rate of growth of Internet users during that time within small and medium sized enterprises, professionals from a wide range of sectors such as trade, manufacturing, tourism, health care, and social services.

In 1996, the government decided to replace its free Internet access policy by an open access policy, where Internet services for the commercial domain were privatized, and more 12 Internet service providers elected to start operation at that time. By early 1997, more than 50,000 Egyptians were using the Internet, representing a much broader spectrum of society than the academic and scientific community served by 20 ISPs. In April 1999, there were more than 250,000 Egyptians using the Internet served by 50 Internet service providers all across the country (Kamel 1998).

In 1996, a project to deploy VSAT services for Internet connectivity was initiated to provide rural areas with data communications infrastructure. VSAT complements the terrestrial solutions and has the potential to help reduce the gap in services between relatively well connected regions, such as greater Cairo, and remote and rural locations, such as in Upper Egypt. In 1997, asymmetric communication was introduced to speed up Internet data downloading by relying on a hybrid connectivity solution involving satellites and terrestrial links "Zaknet" (Kamel 1997).

In order to develop Egyptian content on the Internet, IDSC and RITSEC began implementing the Egyptian Information Highway Project in late 1995. The project seeks to accelerate growth by promoting electronic dissemination of information, establishing information highways in key sectors of the economy, contributing towards a wide access to information, supporting the development of secure on-line databases, and training people to establish the national information highway (Hashem and Ismail 1998).

Pilot information networks have been launched covering culture, tourism, health care, environment, education, public services and local government administration (Kamel 1995). Beneficiaries have been investors, developers, health care professionals, environmentalists, government officials and the general public. Internet service providers also started to add content.

Moreover, some ISPs began to differentiate themselves by their target clients, and developed information materials of interest to their market segments (such as financial markets). Leading magazine and newspapers also began to offer virtual editions. Some leading nonprofit organizations, ranging from business associations to economic research institutions, also developed content for Egypt. Professional associations, such as the Internet Society of Egypt, launched in 1996, have naturally developed rich web sites. The government of Egypt has also begun to provide information on the Internet (Kamel 1996).

Putting the Internet in Egypt in perspective, one should say that while the Internet has clearly grown in the past four years in Egypt, it would be useful to place Egypt in the context of the Middle East region and the rest of the world. Egypt has approximately 17,000 host computers, by far more than the rest of the Arab nations combined. However, on a host computers/capita basis, Egypt is in the bottom 12.5-50% segment of the world in terms of computer host density when compared with population. Although Internet users in Egypt double once every 10-12 months, which is somewhat above the region's average, this is only 50-60% of the global rate which is doubling every six months. The ratio of Internet subscribers to population is 1: 1,500 in Egypt and 1:5 in the United States (Mintz 1998).

The Internet in Egypt Today

The explosion in the number of companies rushing in to offer Internet services is a reflection of the market's judgement as to the demand for Internet services in Egypt today. Competition is intense at the retail level. This has resulted in a downward trend in prices to Egyptian Internet users, but they are still paying a great deal more than their international counterparts. Egyptian Internet users also face frustrations with the quality of Internet services, a reflection of the limitations in the telecommunications infrastructure (Mintz 1998).

Egypt Telecom, in cooperation with IDSC-RITSEC, has installed a set of digital multiplexors as the first digital backbone in Egypt for Internet services. The International connectivity to and from Egypt is provided via satellite links using Intelsat and fiber connectivity using SEMWE-2 to Europe and via TAD-12 to the United States. Rural areas are now provided with data communication services via VSAT terminals with hub-based and hubless communications (Mintz 1998). There are several Internet gateways in Egypt. There are two gateways with IDSC-RITSEC serving the public sector and provide Internet connectivity for the great majority of ISPs in Egypt, which primarily serve the private sector and households. There are other gateways serving the academic establishment at the Egyptian Universities Network serving all 12 Egyptian universities and research centers and providing connectivity for plans to wire hundreds of secondary schools to the Internet. There is another gateway at the American University in Cairo, and additional gateways are being established for private sector Internet service providers such as Internet Egypt and GegaNet (Mintz 1998).

There are currently 50 Internet service providers in Egypt where service is concentrated in Cairo with 7 Internet service providers in Alexandria and more limited service offered in Upper Egypt, Red Sea and Sinai. Egyptian ISPs have been competing primarily on the basis of price, with end-user costs diminishing as competition heats up. Some ISPs have targeted specific markets, such as financial markets or offering corporate solutions. Some have opened Internet cafes in conjunction with their Internet services. Ninety percent of the Internet service providers obtain bandwidth through RITSEC which itself handles approximately 70% of the Internet traffic in Egypt. The Egyptian University Network and two private ISPs (GegaNet and Internet Egypt) have their own private gateways outside of Egypt.

Internet Users can be divided into three categories: academic, government and commercial, 50% are from the business community, 30% are academic and 20% are from the public sector. Sixteen of Egypt's 26 governorates have at least some limited Internet usage. The services offered by the ISPs in Egypt can be described as follows: most of them offer electronic mail, 95% offer Telnet and FTP, 98% offer WWW access, 85% offer hosting of home pages, 25% offer training and 50% offer services such as web design, and hosting news groups (Mintz 1998).

The information content from Egypt on the Internet is aggressively booming. This is being formulated with an objective to make the Internet more relevant and appealing to Egyptians (*http://www.idsc.gov.eg*). There are many efforts that are exerted and examples that can be drawn for the Egyptian information content on the Internet. These efforts could be characterized as: efforts by the government to develop awareness and utilization of the Internet, efforts by non government organizations to disseminate economic information, applications developed by the private sector as information providers, and commercial efforts to market and provide electronic commerce over the Internet. Following are some examples to demonstrate these efforts.

The government, through IDSC-RITSEC, has championed Internet use with its Egyptian Information Highway Project since 1995. Some of its projects included TourismNet (*http://163.19.101/index1f.htm*) that promotes Egypt's tourism services through information and by providing a wealth of information on its history. CultureNet (*http://www.idsc.gov.eg/culture*) seeks to promote awareness of Egypt's culture and heritage and acts as a central resource for Egypt's cultural community; connecting to major Egyptian museums, libraries, and cultural institutions. GovernoratesNet (*http:// www.idsc.gobve.eg/govern*) seeks to encourage and support socioeconomic and development planning in Egypt's governorates. Egypt Government Online (*http://www.misrnet.idsc.gov.eg*) seeks to provide online information with respect to government services, profiles and news. These are just samples of the information content that is growing every month from different perspective and sector including the government, the industry, the business community and the society at large. They also include nonprofit organizations, research centers, business associations and educational institutions.

Electronic Commerce in Egypt

The role of information and communication technology is increasingly affecting socioeconomic and business development plans in Egypt (Kamel 1995). Therefore, in its strive to lift-up its developmental process, Egypt has formulated a national plan demonstrating its vision to prepare itself for a more competitive and global market environment that is enabled by the information age. The plan attempts to capitalize on the cutting-edge information and communication technology that could help rationalize the decision making process and optimize the allocation of resources (EECI 1999).

The objective of formulating and implementing electronic commerce technologies has a strategic objective in leveraging the nation's business development and socioeconomic status. However, to realize such a long-term objective the following needs to be realized:

- To formulate a framework for electronic commerce coherent with the national political, social and legislative environment and compatible with the global electronic commerce environment.
- To develop the national information infrastructure required for electronic commerce.
- To promote the use of electronic commerce through the implementation of pilot projects focusing on hi-tech industries.
- To improve awareness and stimulate cooperation among all concerned parties including the government, industry, the private sector and the general public.
- To promote and develop Egypt's know-how and skills required for successfully implementing electronic commerce.

Electronic commerce promises to offer enormous opportunities for the global market place leading to profound structural changes and impacts on the labor market where new employment potential will focus on information-based and added-value services. In that respect, electronic commerce is potentially a vital factor for business and industry growth in Egypt. The Global Information Infrastructure Commission announced in 1997 that the overall movement to on-line commerce will bring network generated revenues to over 1 trillion US dollars during the first decade of the next millennium illustrating the trend towards a growing importance of electronic commerce (GIIC Report 1996). This represents a window of opportunities for Egypt. It is believed that failure to adapt to the growing electronic trends will result in negative implications with respect to the business development world in the years to come. Egypt, as a developing country, could capitalize on the possible opportunities presented by electronic commerce.

Among the community of Internet services and information providers in Egypt, there is a clear interest in applying the Internet to commerce. There is a growing community of Internet users that are moving to the Internet to market and promote for their ideas, products and services. For example, the ABC supermarket chain (*http://abcsupermarkets.com*) started its web-based electronic commerce in 1998 allowing customers to order groceries over the Internet. ABC Supermarkets had the first electronic web site in Egypt and the region, with its entire focus being local grocery shopping. However, there are greater opportunities for electronic commerce dissemination in Egypt with a focus on business-to-business as opposed to business-to-customers opportunities. From that perspective, many several Internet service providers have targeted Egypt's banking and capital markets area as most deserving of electronic commerce applications (Mintz 1998). Banks are starting to initiate online credit card approval systems to facilitate transactions and multinationals are using the Internet to improve their internal operations.

Moreover, the government of Egypt has invested time and effort in making national economic information available on the Internet. For example, Egypt's State Information Service (SIS) (*http://www.sis.gov.eg*) includes information on investing in Egypt, its economic growth, foreign trade, agriculture and irrigation, industry, energy, transportation and tourism among others. Additionally, IDSC publishes its monthly economic bulletin online (*http://www.sis.gov.eg/online/html/index.htm*). The bulletin includes key economic indicators reflecting the performance of the Egyptian economy and state of the global economy. The Egyptian Center for Economic Studies, an independent organization, (*http://www.eces.org.eg*) web site describes its activities, its research reports and findings, and publishes on-line series of articles to contribute to the discussion of ideas and policy options for enhancing economic development in Egypt. The Economic Research Forum (*http://www.erf.org.og*) is a non-governmental organization whose mission is to provide an institutional mechanism to initiate and fund policy-relevant research, to disseminate research results, and to function as a resource base for researchers. It is the first research networking institution of its kind in the region. The web site describes the forum's organization, structure, research agenda, activities and membership in the network. The Forum's web page has searchable databases with working papers, conference proceedings, and other publications.

On the business side, one of the Internet service providers, Misr Information Services and Trading (MIST), a local company, produces online information with respect to foreign exchange fluctuation (*http://www.moneyvan.com*) and stock prices (*http://www.egyptianstocks.com*). Moneyvan allows monitoring of real time trading in the money markets. It is connected with the Central Bank of Egypt to continuously monitor the development of the money market in Egypt. Beneficiaries are foreign exchange dealers and international trading companies. Egyptianstocks tracks stocks and mutual funds. Beneficiaries are small investors and brokers wanting to track the market from their homes. The web site contains a description of Egypt's capital markets and a comprehensive list of Egyptian stockbrokers with hyperlinks to these brokerage houses. This service has over 650 subscribers such as banks and stockbrokers, where 55% are online, and a large number of investors are in Cairo and Alexandria.

Another information provider is Kompass providing a comprehensive wealth of information on 22,000 Egyptian firms. The database is currently available on the Internet where browsers can find the contacts of each company listed for free but need to pay for the actual company information. Egyptian International Trade Point (*http://www.tradepoint.cs.tut.fi*) is Egypt's electronic linkage with UNCTAD's Global Trade Points Network, composed of more than 116 trade points located in 80 countries. The web site, managed by the Ministry of Trade and Supply in Egypt targets listing of trade opportunities for Egyptian businesses, providing information on international customs, banks and packaging requirements, and establishing a database for Egyptian exporters and importers.

E-Commerce: "An IT-Based Development Tool"

Electronic commerce represents a dynamic model for the information society. However, neither the people nor the firms in many countries are prepared for the new technology. There is a need for more and better training and education in the use of the new technology, as well as other issues such as awareness creation and readiness by governments and public authorities to assume their responsibilities. Electronic commerce requires new skills for network literacy. Consumers will need to become familiar with information technology for communicating and ordering goods and services electronically. Moreover, from a socioeconomic perspective there is a need for public and widespread participation in the evolving information society, to avoid the risk of creating classes of information haves and have-nots.

Electronic commerce will have a profound impact on businesses, institutions and upon the lives of consumers and employees, it is not self-evident how exactly electronic commerce will and should develop in a country like Egypt. Therefore, a broad and continued societal dialog about these issues is essential to overcome the hurdles and reap the benefits. As we approach the 21st century, strong internationalization of markets, globalization of corporate strategies, and the increasing mobility of capital and know-how characterize the economic process worldwide (Kamel 1995). The prime movers and shakers behind this development are the new possibilities of global information and communication technology and the processing of graphical and audiovisual data in worldwide information networks.

Electronic commerce has a wide range of implications for international trade and business. With the promise of a cashless society, more facilitated and closer communication, border-less marketing and trade, as well as a more and transparent business environment, the opportunities are extensive and the potential is yet untapped. With issues of security of financial transactions being addressed and where standards are today being set, to overcome these obstacles, the reality of electronic commerce is becoming more tangible.

With the dawn of the 21st century, one needs to address the opportunities that electronic commerce holds for Egypt. Such an issue compares with one that occurred more than a hundred years ago, when the world's economy evolved from an agricultural society to an industrial society. Had it not made this shift, Egypt would have been left behind, unable to survive in the New World order. Similarly, electronic commerce brings about the same type of decision, where it provides unprecedented opportunities for increasing trade, promoting investment, facilitating business transactions, providing a larger and more varied market and supplying an unparalleled marketing tool.

Electronic commerce as a medium for foreign trade is a catalyst for export implying an increase in Egypt's exports and a better formula for its balance of trade that will eventually have positive impacts on its economy. Electronic commerce could also enable Egypt to experience a more open economy and increase its comparative advantage worldwide. The volume of transactions of electronic commerce is expected to reach the 1 trillion U.S. dollars mark by the beginning of the next century. Such an opportunity holds a lot of promise for the economic development of Egypt, providing it with new opportunities for penetrating international markets. This is especially true for small and medium sized enterprises, which lack the resources enabling them to promote themselves globally. The advent of the Internet and electronic commerce has contributed in reducing costs such as that of traveling, marketing and advertising, as well as reducing time and space requirements to perform transactions. This is due to the ability to communicate remotely, as well as advertise and promote at a distance.

Moreover, electronic commerce is not limited to boosting trade. Many other sectors can benefit from electronic commerce including: the financial services (insurance, banking, trading); tourism; entertainment and music; advertising and marketing; information services, education and training, the media (electronic books, newspapers, journals, news services) as well as other services such as medicine, and real estate. Electronic commerce carries strong socioeconomic implications for the Egyptian citizen. On an individual level, Egyptian citizens will be able to perform transactions worldwide and trade products across national borders and elevate their own standard of living. Electronic commerce will create many job opportunities where Egyptians will have the chance to venture and establish small and medium enterprises with global market access. Software developer will be able to work for international customers.

E-Commerce Challenges and Opportunities in Egypt

There are a number of challenges and opportunities that face the full-fledged implementation of electronic commerce in Egypt. There are many issues that need to be resolved and questions that need to be answered if Egypt wants to realize the desired objectives from electronic commerce and transform the challenges into opportunities. Following is a description of some of the challenges faced, the opportunities developed, what is required to be done and some of the efforts that were exerted in Egypt to transform a number of these challenges into opportunities to help realize business and socioeconomic development.

E-Commerce: "The Opportunity"
Global Competition

Electronic commerce represents a vehicle for global competition for Egyptian firms. It could help in sustaining and leveraging their position in the global market place. Electronic commerce provides a dynamic approach to business development and trading focusing on the use of information technology in integrating developing countries in the multilateral trading system. Moreover, the World Trade Organization, as a supporting arm to electronic commerce activities, is cooperating in enhancing trade and investment opportunities of developing countries through electronic commerce.

Government Transparency

Electronic commerce offers tax, fiscal, labor, social, and economic administrations, many possibilities to simplify, accelerate, and reduce the cost of business transactions between firms. It also provides an opportunity to slim down the structures of the government itself by reducing the distance between government administration and the individual leading to government transparency. The government of Egypt, in that respect, has been investing time and effort in providing the optimal environment and support from its organizations for electronic commerce.

Informatics Industry

Electronic commerce and the Internet infrastructure including people, information and technology are formulating an environment encouraging the creation of a hi-tech industry. Currently, surveys in the United States estimate that there are 190,000 job vacancies in the information technology field in the private sector and it is expected to reach around 1.5 million in the coming 10 years representing an example of the worldwide shortage of information technology professionals. This shortage represents an opportunity for Egypt. With the right infrastructure in place, the global software shortage can be transformed from a threat of a brain drain to an opportunity, to create a local informatics industry that is capable of competing in the global market.

Economic Research and Analysis

The accumulation of timely and reliable information is essential for sound economic policy analysis and formulation that is enabled by the Internet tools. The Internet provides raw economic data permitting researchers to download data and statistical packages and to draw conclusions regarding the economy. It provides a body of knowledge in agriculture information, which is a critical sector for Egypt, for researchers such as worldwide weather patterns, international agricultural trade statistics, commodity prices, and particular markets. These elements are of high relevance to Egyptian policy analysts both from the perspective of researching worldwide policies and conditions, and developing comparative analysis with the local conditions.

Professional & Institutional Networking

Economists, businessmen and policy analysts need to continuously exchange information and collaborate in joint projects within a dynamic global economy. The Internet, for that purpose represents an ideal platform for such professional networking. Virtual conferences and Internet newsgroups offer other opportunities for networking. Professional networking can perfectly work in Egypt. It can aid policy analysts to work more collaboratively with colleagues in the region and worldwide, it can also open channels for discussions to get wider perspectives on key policy matters.

Institutions need to remain current on global economic and market conditions. Economic policy institutions such as business associations, think tanks or universities can grow stronger by having international partnerships. Institutional networking works best when organizations have a common agenda and mutual interest. In such circumstances, the Internet is a great tool. Egyptian research institutions can benefit from joining by having access to research findings, international experience, and viewpoints from leading economic researchers from around the world.

Making Information Publicly Available

Transparency is still an issue. Making information publicly available is not yet well received in Egypt. There is definitely progress than before but not yet enough to establish a solid presence on the World Wide Web. Transparency is important for an informed public and advocacy is important to lobby for change. Respectively, the governments worldwide use the Internet to publish policies, laws and regulations so that they are clear for both citizens and concerned international partners. Non-governmental organizations use the Internet to push for policy reforms and change. These applications of the Internet are relevant to Egypt permitting the government to clarify policies, and permitting non-government organizations to work together towards change.

Business Services

The attempts to use the Internet to facilitate international trade and investment are proof of the importance of information in the emerging global economy. The business-oriented Internet programs offer opportunities to influence economic policies, comparing policies across national boundaries and using the Internet transparency as an agent for change. The Internet's web-based business services also help users to research and identify business opportunities and conduct transactions and trading opportunities across borders irrespective of time and distance. In 1998, business-to-business electronic commerce amounted to 17 billion U.S. dollars and it is expected that in 4 years, this figure might reach 327 billion US dollars. The opportunities for Egypt to benefit from this new digital age of commerce are substantial, particularly as Egypt seeks to promote exports of its agricultural and industrial production.

E-Commerce: "The Challenge"
Internet Quality and Cost of Services

The telecommunications infrastructure in Egypt has improved significantly over the past decade. However, there is still a lot to be done to survive in the digital age. Moreover, the fact that Egypt Telecom has a monopoly for domestic and international telecommunication services became a barrier to the introduction of more bandwidth and high speed integrated networks that the private sector could supply. Another problem is the cost structure of the Internet services with the majority of users not capable of affording the cost of the Internet, especially since all ISPs have reported that Internet users are very price sensitive. Therefore unless costs can be substantially reduced, the potential market and application of the Internet in Egypt will remain constrained.

Respectively, the role of the government becomes vital in setting the policies and encouraging the private sector investment by privatizing government controlled telecommunications firms and by promoting and preserving competition within the industry. The objective is to avoid the inflation of prices, better service, the elimination of the telecommunications monopoly and to ensure that on-line service providers can reach end-users on reasonable and nondiscriminatory terms and conditions. Moreover, with per capita income in Egypt at 1,460 U.S. dollars, purchases of computers, telephone lines, and use of Internet services is beyond the reach of the majority of Egyptians, hence hindering the diffusion of the Internet in Egypt at large.

Training and Awareness

The Internet was only introduced to Egypt in 1993. Thus, there is still a lack of appreciation for its capacities among businesses, government, nonprofit organizations and professionals across sectors. Few have been trained in the use of the Internet. Private Egyptian universities are well equipped with computing and networking facilities and literate Internet instructors. However, few of the large public university professors are incorporating knowledge of the Internet in their instruction. To date, the Regional IT Institute (RITI) located in Cairo *http://www.riti.ritsec.com.eg* that is a subsidiary of RITSEC is the main training institute in Egypt with respect to Internet applications. RITI has trained over 2,000 government and private sector employees through 160 training courses since April 1994. RITI is also the cofounder of the Cairo Internet Conference and Exhibition (Cainet) *http://www.cainet.org.eg*, since its inception in 1996, becoming today the main Internet event for the community in the region (Kamel 1999). The conference had an average attendance of 1,200 per annum in its first 4 years from different private, public and government sector organizations contributing comprehensively to the awareness of the Internet in Egypt.

Moreover, the Egyptian government is implementing a massive awareness plan for electronic commerce demonstrating its potential commercial use. The plan covers small and medium enterprises but also consumers, government entities and children. The focus on children is to prepare a young generation with a business sense Little Shopper is an electronic commerce web site for children. It is a government initiative initiated by the ministry of education to provide Internet connectivity to two thousand Egyptian schools.

Language Barriers

The majority of Internet material is in English, and little content is in Arabic. This creates barriers to using the Internet in Egypt. Currently, there are efforts exerted by a number of software vendors to develop software applications to translate the English content into Arabic. Moreover, individuals and organizations wishing to publish materials on the web are faced with problems due to the limited web development tools in Arabic.

Financial & Regulatory Issues

The Internet is truly a global medium. Therefore, tariffs on goods and services delivered over the Internet should not be introduced. The World Trade Organization advocates that the Internet be declared a "free-trade zone." The Internet lacks the clear and fixed geographic lines of transit that historically have characterized the physical trade of goods. Thus, while it remains possible to administer tariffs for products ordered over the Internet, but ultimately delivered via surface or air transport, the structure of the Internet makes it difficult to do so when the product or service is delivered electronically. Therefore, Egypt advocates that the Internet be declared a tariff-free environment with regard to electronic commerce.

From that perspective, the financial and regulatory issues are among the most important to resolve. It is important therefore, to realize that moving from a highly regulated government such as Egypt into electronic commerce will not be an easy step to take. The highly paper dependent work cycles are deeply engraved in the government's corporate culture. Thus, the newly digital format will be highly resisted from middle and senior management levels. The amount of bureaucracy tied into the working environment is very high on the government level and moving into an electronic environment will need awareness, training and cultural adaptation. That is the challenge that the Egyptian government in cooperation with the private sector is currently undertaking (EECI 1999).

Legal Issues

The Egyptian government supports the development of a global uniform commercial legal code that recognizes, facilitates, and enforces electronic transactions worldwide. Electronic commerce is heavily relying on distance selling where parties conclude their agreements without meeting physically reflecting an element of risk for purchasers of goods and recipients of services. Consequently, the government of Egypt advocates the establishment of a legal environment based on a decentralized, contractual model of law agreed electronically. This would help develop a model providing uniform fundamental principles designed to eliminate administrative and regulatory barriers and to facilitate electronic commerce by encouraging government recognition, acceptance and facilitation of electronic communications.

With respect to privacy, Egypt is encouraging the development of a voluntary market-driven key management infrastructure that will support authentication, integrity and confidentiality. As for intellectual property rights, it constitutes one of the main challenges facing Egypt in its effort to revitalize economic and social development as it enters an age where information and knowledge make up and empower the economy. Therefore, in recent years, Egypt has embarked on a full-fledged program to combat intellectual property infringement by improving the legislative framework through issuing and amending copyright laws, and promoting awareness on the national, institutional and individual levels as to the importance of protecting intellectual property rights (EEIC 1999).

The government plays a crucial role in all phases of electronic commerce penetration in Egypt. It tries to balance its regulatory and controlled roles with the ability to let the market determine the business environment. It encourages industry self-regulation with minimal government intervention with respect to imposing bureaucratic procedures. A nontraditional policy of bottom-up governance plans to be instituted and the existing regulatory framework is currently amended to reflect the needs of the new electronic age. The government's task is to create a flexible legal framework for electronic commerce that matches its development pace and permits optimal flow of information.

In Egypt, the success achieved through government-private sector partnership in commercialization of the Internet services will push the deregulation of other value-added services in the country where the communication infrastructure deployment is one of the promising areas for private sector participation. Coherence, transparency and coordination should be the government's guiding principles in the information age. Organizations and institutions involved in determining regulations and policies are encouraged to coordinate together to formulate a coherent electronic commerce framework. Currently, a government entity is being formed to protect the Internet consumer from possible electronic commerce crimes. The goals of the association "Internet Consumer Protection Organization" are to protect and guide Egyptian consumers, promote electronic commerce among Egyptian merchants on national and international levels, and diffuse awareness and trust in electronic commerce in Egypt (El Kassas 1998).

The Egyptian government is continuously interacting with representatives of the industry and the business community in an attempt to gradually give the private sector the liberty to be the driving force of electronic commerce in the country. It should be the private sector's role to lead Egypt towards being "electronic commerce ready". In the Internet commercialization via the model of cooperation between the public and private sectors, the government has played a catalytic role in raising awareness as well as deploying the infrastructure; while the private sector carried value-added services to the end user. This success will be replicated in electronic commerce.

Conclusion

Born global, electronic commerce encompasses a wide spectrum of activities, some well established, most of them very new. Driven by the Internet revolution, electronic commerce is dramatically expanding and undergoing radical changes engendering a wide array of innovative businesses, markets and trading communities creating new functions and new revenue streams. Electronic commerce presents enormous potential opportunities for consumers and businesses worldwide. Its rapid implementation is an urgent challenge for commerce, industry and governments. Electronic commerce makes it possible to trade at low cost across regions and national frontiers. To reap its full benefits the development of efficient distribution channels and a cross-border network is necessary for the physical delivery of goods ordered electronically.

Considering the essentially cross-border nature of electronic commerce, global consensus needs to be achieved. Therefore, it is important to pursue international dialogs, involving government and industry, in the appropriate multilateral fora, as well as bilaterally among different trading partners. This includes international cooperation to fight against organized cross-border crime on new communication networks. Promoting a favorable business environment will involve reinforcing awareness and confidence in electronic commerce for customers, as well as encouraging best practice among businesses. In parallel, public administrations will have a key role to play through their procurement power and their early implementation of key electronic commerce technologies. In the future, strong synergies between "electronic commerce" and "electronic administration" should be actively encouraged to develop, for the benefit of all involved (El Kassas 1998).

In light of these issues, this chapter presented the concept of electronic commerce worldwide with reflections on the Egyptian experience with a set of proposals for action to promote and diffuse the electronic commerce culture in Egypt. These issues address access to the global marketplace, legal and regulatory issues, and promoting a favorable business environment that could help boost the business and socioeconomic development plans of the country.

References

ABC Supermarkets [WWW site] URL *http://www.abcsupermarkets.com.*

Business Week Report Doing Business in the Internet Age. (1998, June 22). Annual Report on Information Technology.

Chase, L. (1998). *Internet World: Essential Business Tactics for the Net.* John Wiley and Sons, Inc. New York, USA.

CultureNet [WWW site] URL *http://www.idsc.gov.eg/culture*

Economic Research Forum [WWW site] URL *http://www.erf.org.og*

Egypt Electronic Commerce Initiative–EECI. (1999, March)

Egyptian Center for Economic Studies-ECES. [WWW site] URL *http://www.eces.org.eg*

Egyptian International Trade Point. [WWW site] URL *http://www.tradepoint.cs.tut.fi*

El Kassas, S. (1998, March). *Towards Electronic Commerce in Egypt Certificate Authority for Egypt.* Proceedings of the Cairo Internet Conference and Exhibition: Cainet 98. Cairo, Egypt.

European Union (1997, April). *European Initiative in Electronic Commerce.* Communication to the European Parliament, the Council, the Economic and Social Committee and the Committee of the Regions.

GovernoratesNet [WWW site] URL *http://www.idsc.gov.eg/govern.*

Government of Egypt Online [WWW site] URL *HTTP://WWW.MISRNET.IDSC.GOV.EG*

Hammond, R. (1996). Digital Business. Coronet Books. London, UK.

Hashem, S and M. Ismail (1998, November). *The Evolution of Internet Services in Egypt: Towards Empowering Electronic Commerce.* Proceedings of the

Global Marketplace for SMEs Conference, Manchester, UK.

Information and Decision Support Center Monthly Economic Bulletin. [WWW document] URL *http://www.sis.gov.eg/online/html/index.htm.*

Information and Decision Support Center–IDSC. [WWW site] URL *http://www.idsc.gov.eg*

Internet Society of Egypt-ISE. [WWW site] URL *http://www.ise.org.eg.*

Investing in Egypt (1997) Government of Egypt Report.

Kamel, S. (1997). *DSS for Strategic Decision-Making.* Cases on Information Technology Management in Modern Organizations. Hershey: Idea Group Publishing.

Kamel, S. (1995, May 21-24). *Information Superhighways, a potential for socio-economic and cultural development.* Proceedings of the 6th International IRMA Conference on Managing Information and Communications in a Changing Global Environment, Atlanta, Georgia, USA.

Kamel, S. (1995). *IT Diffusion & Socio Economic Change in Egypt.* Journal of Global Information Management, Vol. 3, No.2.

Kamel, S. (1993, May). *Decision Support in the Governorates Level in Egypt.* Proceedings of the 4th International IRMA Conference on Challenges for Information Management in a World Economy, Salt Lake City, Utah, USA.

Kamel, T. (1999, March). *Evolution of the Internet in Egypt.* Proceedings of the 4th Cairo Internet Conference-CAINET'99, Cairo, Egypt.

Kamel, T. (1998, May). *Internet Commercialization in Egypt: A Model from Africa.* Africa Telecom Conference Proceedings, Johannesberg, South Africa.

Kosiur, D. (1997). *Understanding Electronic Commerce.* Microsoft Press. Redmond, USA.

Kalakota, R and, A. Whinston. (1996). *Frontiers of Electronic Commerce.* Addison Wesley, USA.

Lynch D.C. and L. Lundquist. (1996) *Digital Money: the New Era of Internet Commerce.* John Wiley and Sons, Inc. New York, USA.

Mintz, S. (1998, October). *The Internet as a Tool for Egypt's Economic Growth.* An International Development Professionals Inc. Report.

Tapscott, D. (1996) *The Digital Economy Promise and Peril in the Age of Networked Intelligence.* MacGraw Hill, USA.

Regional Information Technology and Software Engineering Center-RITSEC. [WWW site]URL *http://www.ritsec.com.eg*

Regional IT Institute-Regional Information Technology Institute [WWW site] URL *http://www.riti.ritsec.com.eg*

Silverstein, B. (1999) *Business-to-Business Internet Marketing.* Gulf Breeze Maximum Press, USA.

State Information Service-SIS. [WWW site] URL *http://www.sis.gov.eg.*

TourismNet. [WWW site] URL *http://163.121.19.101/index1f.htm.*

Chapter 11

Managing the Business of Web-Enabled Education and Training: A Framework and Case Studies for Replacing Blackboards with Browsers for Distance Learning

Mahesh S. Raisinghani
University of Dallas, USA

David Baker
Digital Think, Inc., USA

Very few men are wise by their own counsel; or learned by their own teaching. For he that was only taught by himself, had a fool for his master.

— Ben Johnson

Abstract

Studies have shown that people remember 20 percent of what they see, 40 percent of what they see and hear, and 70 percent of what they see, hear, and do. Interactive learning applications provide a multi-sensory learning environment that maximizes the way people retain information. This accelerates learning and permits novices to perform like experts while they learn new skills. Powerful authoring systems enable vast amounts of information to be compiled quickly and presented in compelling and meaningful ways. In addition, these applications are easy and inexpensive to update. With interactive multimedia, everyone sees the same information and is exposed to identical learning environments. The reliability of instruction, quality of information, and presentation of material is consistent from user to user and from session to session. This chapter discusses a framework for distance learning and distributed learning and two case studies of a web-based synchronous learning environment in two organizations with different corporate cultures. Current challenges and implications for management are discussed.

Introduction

With the Web-based training market in U.S. growing at 150 percent a year, it is expected to expand from $92 million in 1996 to more than $1.75 billion by the year 2000, according to recently completed research from International Data Corporation. According to Montgomery Securities analyst Ellen Julian, the $16 billion world market for technical training will hit $28 billion in the year 2001. Web-based training is growing rapidly, fueled by the emergence of the intranet as a major training medium, the increase in Internet and intranet access, advancements in Web technology, and an increasing demand for technical skills in everything from Web design to Enterprise Resource Planning (ERP) implementation. From the student/learner standpoint, the web-based training offers convenience, flexibility and savings in dollars and in time. This has led to an enormous amount of confidence in the growth of web-based training. A case in point is the CBT Group; an Irish company with sales of $118 million that trades at a price so speculative it makes private school tuition look cheap—13 times sales.

The worldwide information technology training market is large and growing as illustrated in table 1. Although classroom-based training continued to be the delivery medium of choice, it lost significant ground in 1997 to high technology-based delivery vehicles such as CD-ROM, the Internet, and corporate intranets (IDC, 1997).

The purpose of this chapter is to move beyond hypertext/multimedia documents that are archives of an instructor's course notes or supporting

Table 1: *Worldwide Information Technology Training Market Revenues*

	1996	2001	1996-2001 CAGR
World Total	$16.4 billion	$27.9 billion	11.2%
United States	$7.1 billion	12.9 billion	12.7%
U.S. Web-based	74.0 million	3.4 billion	109.7%

Source: International Data Corporation, 1997.

materials. Its focus is on the interaction between the instructor and the student instead of the one-way transfer of information from author to reader or server to client. Unlike the first academy of higher learning in Greece, established approximately 2,300 years ago, where the students spent most of their time in the company of great thinkers, today our students spend less than 5 percent of their time with individual instructors over the course of a semester (Kelly, 1998). This is primarily due to the economic pressures on the students who have to balance their time between education, family, and work. Since higher education is the compass for the advancement of society, it is critical to meet the demand for greater access to higher education with a focus on learning rather than teaching and based on research that has shown that multisensory delivery of data can be effective in the learning process.

According to Peter Drucker, "Universities won't survive. The future is outside the traditional campus, outside the traditional classroom. Distance learning is coming on fast." (Gibson and Herrera, 1999). The first qualification for the Internet as instructor is its global reach. With Internet access options growing faster than college tuition fees, a company can virtually be assured that remote training will be available to nearly 100 percent of the work force, regardless of a remote worker's location.

Another credential making the Web a more qualified teaching medium than CD-ROMs is the Web's adherence to standards, such as the HyperText Markup Language (HTML) and the emerging Extensible Markup Language (XML). In addition to the centralized nature of content on the Web, which enables course materials to be updated instantly, corporate training materials composed in HTML/XML are accessible to all students, regardless of the computer they use or the operating system running on that computer.

Collaborative technologies such as messaging, document conferencing, chat and multipoint audio- and videoconferencing help create an interactive learning environment between students and teachers. After the introduction section, the market for continuing education is evaluated. This is followed by a discussion of the distance learning and distributed learning frameworks. The next section discusses the enabling technologies and the pros and cons of the instructor-led, computer-based, and web-based training. The training methodology and the key differentiators of a web-based synchronous learning environment are discussed in the following section. Real world emphasis is provided by two case studies from Motorola and Texas Instruments with a discussion of the experiences from the field. At the end of the chapter are the current challenges, conclusion and questions for discussion. An appendix is provided to address the economic issues of distance learning.

The Market of Continuing Education

According to the United States Department of Commerce, university education spending reached an estimated $198 billion, while corporate training and education reached roughly $52 billion or 0.7% of the gross domestic product. With an average annual growth rate of between 5% and 6%, spending on company-sponsored training and education alone has easily outpaced the 2% to 2.5% overall growth in GDP. The percentage of people currently using information technology directly in their jobs has tripled since 1970 (Carnevale, 1996). According to a United States Department of Commerce study, 93% of all organizations in the United States allocated some percentage of their training and education budget to basic computer skills training (http://www.lotus.com/products/learningsp, June 9, 1998).

Changes in technology have spawned new ways of working, new business processes and new ways of delivering education. Within this context of rapid technology change, training and education is seen as an ongoing necessity, enabling workers to remain current with required skills and knowledge. Technological forces such as the convergence of data, voice, and video to a single platform and the wider Internet access which makes web-based training more affordable and convenient than conventional methods; social forces such as the "baby boom echo" where the baby boomers and their kids need education and training; and economic forces such as the intensified global competition are coming together to drive demand for continuing education and training. Current estimates indicate that the training workers receive will become obsolete within three to five years.

The need for life-long learning is also reinforced by the frequency with which people change careers. It has now been estimated that the average person entering the labor market can anticipate six to seven career changes. Whether to remain employable in their current organizations or to prepare for future opportunities, employees at all levels of organization value the opportunity to develop their skills and increase their marketability. According to a *Computer World* survey titled "What Makes a Company a Great Place to Work," the opportunity for training and development was cited as an important criterion. Forty of the 100 companies selected as the "best place to work" provide between 7 and 10 days of formal training per employee year.

Thomas Davenport, Peter Drucker, Peter Senge, N Venkatraman and other thought-leaders in knowledge management and organizational learning have identified that attracting a well-educated and highly skilled workforce and providing individuals with ongoing training creates the foundation for organizational learning, an organization's only sustainable long-term competitive advantage. While workers and their employers value ongoing education and training, people are working more hours and report having less free time to pursue other non-work activities. In her 1991 book *The Over-worked American*, Harvard University economist Juliet B. Schor used government census and labor data to calculate that the average employee now works approximately 163 more hours, or an extra month per year, than in 1969.

The convergence of these various forces has created a situation in which corporations require employees to learn new skills and acquire new knowledge quickly and continuously. While individuals are motivated to learn for personal and professional development, the logistics of attending classroom education are increasingly difficult to manage. To respond to this situation, corporations, higher education institutions, and training businesses are looking to:

- increase speed and flexibility
- reduce costs associated with offering classroom training as the only delivery vehicle
- leverage instructors' expertise to a broader population of participants
- leverage team learning and collaboration for performance and productivity.

The Current State of Corporate Education

The American Society for Training and Development has defined learning technologies as the use of electronic technologies to deliver information and facilitate the development of skills and knowledge. Delivery is one area in which the distinctions between leading-edge firms and the industry as a whole are quite pronounced.

Leading-edge firms have shifted more of their training delivery to learning technologies and are most concerned with the impact such technologies will have on their training practices. Yet, even among those firms, learning technologies still have a long way to go before they become a viable delivery mechanism for most of the training that companies provide.

The Human Performance Practices Survey (HPPS) was administered by the American Society for Training & Development in the first 6 months of 1998 and indicates that, though certain learning technologies have made some inroads and new technologies are being introduced almost daily, most training (i.e., 83.8 percent of all training time) is still classroom-based and instructor-led (Bassi and Van Buren, 1998). Training delivered by learning technologies and self-paced methods account for only 5.8 percent and 7.3 percent of all training time respectively. Other delivery methods account for about 3 percent. In leading-edge firms, more training (i.e., 8.4 percent) is delivered via learning technologies, though instructor-led training is still the most common (i.e., 80.9 percent).

Unlike other aspects of training such as training frequency, the industry group is not a primary determinant of the use of delivery methods. Instead, company size, and training and work practices, appear to be shaping which delivery methods are used. Large companies use learning technologies to deliver training more than small companies and are more likely to use a given learning technology. For instance, large leading-edge firms in the information technology sector deliver 21 percent of training using learning technologies and 70 percent as instructor-led courses.

The use of innovative training and human resource practices are inversely related to the amount of instructor led training but highly correlated with learning technology delivered training. Companies that engage in more competency-based training, high performance work practices and innovative training practices are more likely to use learning technologies. Such results support the idea that innovative companies are moving towards learning technologies and away from classroom instruction.

A look at the types of presentation and delivery methods that companies use brings us back to reality. Overall, companies continue to rely most heavily on conventional instruction methods. More than 90 percent of all respondents to the HPPS reported that they are using new interactive digital technologies—such as videodiscs, Intranets, the Internet and Electronic Performance Support System (EPSS). Although more than 35 percent of the corporate training industry as a whole is not using any learning technologies, the leading-edge firms use learning technologies such as computer-based training (CBT), CD-ROM and web based delivery more often than the rest of the industry.

Distance Learning Framework

The principal characteristic of any form of distance learning is that the student does not have to be present in a classroom in order to participate in the instruction. Broadly defined, distance learning is *any* approach to education that delivery replaces the same time, same place face-to-face environment of a traditional classroom. A framework for various potential student markets with time and space dimensionalities that has been adapted from DeSanctis and Gallupe's (1987) matrix for group decision support systems and proposed by Lu and Johnson (1998) as education learning/delivery alternatives is illustrated in Tables 2 and 3. These frameworks can be used for long-range planning by the education/training provider. The new educational paradigm represented by these education learning alternatives and education delivery technologies shifts the old definition of productivity as cost per hour of instruction per student to a new definition of productivity as cost per unit of learning per student (Ives and Jarvenpaa, 1996; Baer, 1998).

Distributed Learning Framework[1]

Distributed learning is a type of distance learning in which technology-enabled, learning team-focused education is facilitated by a content expert, and delivered anytime anywhere. A framework for distributed learning which integrates learning objectives, instructional models and enabling technologies is illustrated in Figure 1.

The traditional teaching methods of lecturing, which is labeled by the term Instructor Centered, is most often used when the learning objective is the transfer of information and knowledge. This approach is based on many underlying pedagogical assumptions regarding both learning and teaching. In terms of learning, the purpose of receiving information is to acquire and memorize it rather than to interpret or change it (Jonassen, 1993; http://www.lotus.com/products/learningsp.html [June 9, 1998]). From the teaching point of view, the Instructor Centered approach assumes that the expert controls the material and the pace of learning while transmitting knowledge to the student. Most face-to-face classes, correspondence courses and textbook learning follows the Instructor Centered Approach.

The underlying pedagogical assumption of the Learner Centered approach is that each person must interpret information, not merely receive it, in order to create new knowledge. The mind is not only a tool for reproducing factual knowledge, but also a mechanism for internalizing knowledge through observation and experience. In this approach, students learn through discovery while also setting the pace of their learning. To facilitate learning, instructors coach students and design individual experiences through which students develop new skills. Many computer simulations, internships, and term projects use the learner-centered approach.

The Learning Team Centered approach creates an environment in which

Table 2: Education Learning Alternative

Time			
		Asynchronous	Synchronous
	Asynchronous	Distance Education (Correspondence Courses, Internship, Independent Studies)	Distance Education (Regular Courses, Theory Seminars, Tutorials, Workshops)
Space	Synchronous	Programming Learning Waiver Exams, Tutorials, Workshops, Prior Learning Assessment	Regular Courses Theory Seminars, Tutorials, Workshops, Prior Learning Assessment

Table 3: Education Delivery Technologies

Time		Asynchronous	Synchronous
Space	Asynchronous	Video cassette Internet Computer Assisted Instruction	Interactive Television Video Conferencing Broadcast TV
	Synchronous	Computer Assisted Instruction Multimedia Lab	Traditional Face-to-Face Teaching Multimedia Classroom Audio and Video

Figure 1: A ²framework for Distributed Learning

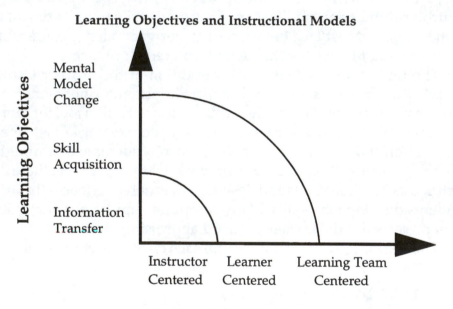

Learning Objectives and Instructional Models

Instructional Models

Source: Lotus Institute's White Paper, 1998. "Distributed Learning: Approaches, Technologies and Solutions [Online]," Available: http://www.lotus.com/products/learningsp.html [June9].

knowledge emerges and is shared though the collaboration of individuals within learning teams. An assumption of this model is that changes in the mental models and behaviors occur most successfully through a Learning Team Centered approach. In a learning team, expertise and prior knowledge are explicitly incorporated into the knowledge transfer process with the creation of new knowledge as the result. The Learning Team Centered approach is most effective in problem solving or research oriented contexts where the articulated learning objective is to create new knowledge or to synthesize existing knowledge and apply it creatively to resolve new challenges. This approach has also been used extensively in learning intended to bring about not only challenges. This approach has also been used extensively in learning intended to bring about not only individual change, but also changes in-group behavior (e.g. changing the culture of an organization).

The instructor's role in the Learning Team Centered approach is to facilitate maximum sharing of information and knowledge among learners rather than control the delivery and pace of the content. The instructor, therefore, provides direct feedback to students while also creating an environment to generate peer feedback. The Learning Team Centered approach is increasingly being adopted even when the learning objective is not specifically the creation of new knowledge. Some studies have demonstrated that this approach is also superior when the learning objective is 'information transfer' or 'skill acquisition.' (Flynn, 1992; http://www.lotus.com/products/learningsp.html [June 9]). Students actively learning in cooperative groups have demonstrated an ability to generate higher-level reasoning strategies, greater diversity of ideas, more critical thinking, and increased creative responses compared to learning individually or competitively (Schlechter, 1990). The Learning Team Centered model emphasizes the "second-level" social effects of technology discussed by Sproull and Kiesler (1995) by promoting effective teamwork and communication. It also helps debunk the myth that in the absence of face-to-face interaction, relations automatically become more distant and impersonal (http://www.lotus.com/products/ learningsp.html [June 9]).

Enabling Technologies[2]
It is pertinent that technology tools developed for distributed learning must support collaboration and facilitate group interaction while allowing flexible delivery. These technologies need to support all three modes of instruction, allowing an instructor to mix modes of instruction in an extended learning experience. These technologies must be adaptable both to augment and to in many cases replace traditional face-to-face classroom instruction.

The learning objectives and instructional models described above serve as a valuable framework against which Figure 2 maps technology classifications that enable distributed learning.

Distribution Technologies most often support the Instructor Centered approach along with the Information Transfer learning objective. These technologies include broadcast TV, audiotape, and videotape; in other words,

Figure 2: Technology Classifications that enable Distributed Learning

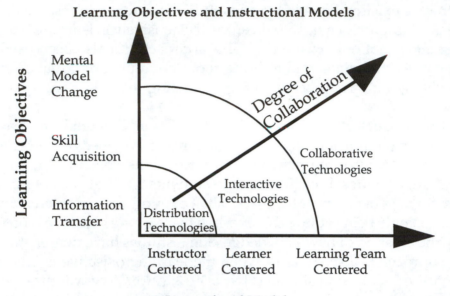

Source: Lotus Institute's White Paper, 1998. "Distributed Learning: Approaches, Technologies and Solutions [Online]," Available: http:// www.lotus.com/products/learningsp.html [June9].

they support one-to-many communication. The single most popular form of distribution technology for distance education is TV broadcast. In the United States PBS has 350,000 subscribers to its open university, and there are currently 75 accredited business schools that offer degree granting programs primarily through the use of broadcast. The National Technical University in Colorado now serves thousands of students providing courses primarily in engineering and computer science. Broadcast types of distribution technologies require that the student receive the instruction at a specific time although they do allow geographic flexibility. These technologies are similar to the traditional face-to-face lecture method in that the student is a passive learner.

Computer-based training (CBT), CD-ROMs and simulations provide anytime, anyplace access and are most frequently used to support the Skill Acquisition learning objective along with the Learner Centered approach. We classify these technologies as Interactive Technologies. CBT allows the student to progress at his or her own pace through required exercises and self-assessments. CBT is limited in that it does not provide for interaction with other students or an instructor; the student interacts with only the technology. In many Fortune 500 companies CBT has been embraced as an acceptable for   object based training. Although CBT has many elements attractive to many Adult Learning Theorists, it does not adequately replace the effects of a true collaborative learning environment.

Collaborative Technologies support the learning objective of Mental Model and Behavior Change in conjunction with Learning Team Centered education. Collaborative technologies offer a rich, shared, virtual workspace in which interactions occur not between an individual and technology, but as many-to-many, interpersonal communication, among people who share a common goal. These interactions can be facilitated by an instructor or monitored by an expert.

Collaborative technologies include the use of chat groups and bulletin boards, although these technologies are real-time and require students and instructors to be consistently connected and in constant attendance. Multipoint videoconferences can be used to create a virtual classroom that spans geographical distance. On the other hand, videoconferences also require same-time interaction and are not supportive of teams needing to collaborate. These examples of collaborative technologies do not enable an instructor to support the most effective, Learning Team Centered approach. The trend in corporate America has moved away from the Learning Team Centered approach primarily due to cost factors. Collaborative technology platforms such as Digital Think (www.digitalthink.com), Lotus Notes (www.lotus.com), Learn Linc (www.ilinc.com), and Symposium (www.symposium.com) best support collaborative learning with anytime, anywhere delivery. They provide a shared, virtual space, which can be either accessed in a connected fashion or in an asynchronous, disconnected manner.

Why is interactive multimedia so effective?

The five primary advantages of interactive multimedia are:

1. Increased consistency (standardization of content and delivery): Multimedia learning ensures that the content presented to every student will be the same since it is not subject to trainer variability in experience, skill, or presentation style.
2. Learner flexibility: Computer-based training allows each student to progress at their own pace, exercising individual control over the amount of time they need to learn the content.
3. Course compression: Reducing time-in-training is probably the most consistent research finding across studies, regardless of the subject matter or diversity in the target audience. One researcher analyzed over 30 evaluations of multimedia programs and found the average reduction in training time to be 50%.

4. Cost savings: While the initial cost of equipment and development of multimedia training may appear high when life-cycle cost-effectiveness factors are included in the equation, the actual cost-per-instructional hour is significantly less than with traditional classroom instruction.

5. Increased student achievement: Learners' understanding and retention of the content increase by as much as 56% over classroom versions of the same courseware.

Interactive multimedia seems to produce significantly better learning than traditional classroom instruction, because the multi-sensory capabilities (text, graphics, colors, audio, video) of this medium create a much stronger, lasting impression than single or even dual-sensory input. Another reason for such dramatic results is that this training is interactive. Any instruction that incorporates "active responding" will produce greater learning gains. Traditional classroom instruction allows learners passivity — a disinterested or shy student can choose to observe rather than become an involved participant. With interactive multimedia instruction, active responding is required from each and every learner.

Table 4: Comparison of different learning models

	Advantages	Disadvantages
INSTRUCTOR LED	- Skill Based Learning - Mentoring - Network of Learners - Hands On/Real Time	- Class Limited to Slowest Learner - Style and Pace of Facilitator Inconsistency - Content Representation Inconsistent - Relative High cost (Opportunity Cost-Fixed Cost) - Retention Levels of Student After Attending the Class
COMPUTER-BASED TRAINING PROGRAM (CD-ROM)	- Self Paced (Anywhere, Anytime) - Objective Based Training - Cost Effective in Large Distribution Class - Adapts to many Different Learning Styles - Modular Approach Allows for Chunking of Information	- Cost on Small Scale - Keeping Content Updated - No Expert to Assist in the Learning - One-to-One Learning
WEB-BASED TRAINING	- One-to-Many Learning - Cost Effective - Collaborative Elements in Learning Environment - Instructor facilitated - Network of Learners	- Technology Barriers - Distribution and Support Demands - Minimal Multimedia Elements

Table 5: Electronic Learning Technology Statistics

Learning Technologies	% Using Technology in 1997	% Using Technology in 1998	Rank in the Year 2000
CBT: disc/hard drive	55.2	63.5	9
Video-teleconferencing	53.1	56.3	5
CBT: CD-ROM-CD-I	42.7	54.2	10
Interacitve Television (Satellite)	37.5	42.7	6
Multimedia: CDROM	29.2	37.5	7
Internet/Web	27.1	47.9	3
CBT:LAN/WAN	21.9	41.7	4
Computer Teleconferencing	14.6	22.9	8
Intranet	13.5	44.8	1
Multimedia:LAN/WAN	12.5	24.0	2
EPSS	4.2	13.5	11
Virtual Reality	1.0	2.1	12

Source: American Society for Training & Development, "Training Industry Trends", Laurie J. Bassi, Scott Cheney, and Mark Van Buren. 1998)

The disadvantages of providing Web infrastructure for information access and distance learning courses are that it requires additional cost and resources and faculty training. There is also a potential resistance to change from the faculty, staff, administrators and students. Table 4 illustrates the comparison of three different learning models (i.e., instructor-led, computer based, and web based training).

The use of electronic learning technologies is illustrated in table 5.

The next section discusses a web based synchronous learning environment and then evaluates two organizations with different corporate cultures using this solution for their corporate training needs. It is important to note that the choice of solution/companies is not reflective of any marketing/ sales agenda on the behalf of the authors. DigitalThink was chosen primarily to demonstrate the conceptual models discussed above and the companies for the case studies were chosen to validate the model.

DigitalThink: A Closer Look at a Web Based Synchronous Learning Solution

Founded in March 1996, with corporate sponsors Adobe Systems, Intel, and Texas Instruments, DigitalThink (www.digitalthink.com) already has 60,000 registered users worldwide. DigitalThink's courses focus on emerging technologies and are taken by individuals employed at companies such as Intel, Lucent Technologies, Texas Instruments, Claremont Technology Group, Johnson & Johnson Vision Products, Adobe Systems, Raytheon,

Figure 3: An example of web based synchronous learning

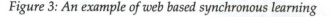
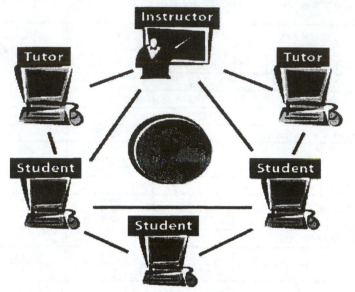

Motorola, Sun Microsystems, Informix and many others.

Numerous studies from leading experts such as Macromedia (http://www.macromedia.com) and the American Society for Training and Development (http://www.astd.org) confirm that self-paced multimedia training is a superior way for students to learn. DigitalThink delivers training to employees and customers at a fraction of the cost of traditional classroom-based training. All courses are available 24 hours a day, seven days a week at the desktop and feature no-cost access to expert tutors who provide ongoing support and feedback.

Currently, DigitalThink offers more than 80 virtual courses on computer programming, systems administration, and applications training for the engineering industry, both "off the shelf" and custom, in embedded design and programming instruction in Java, C and C++ and Perl for programmers, developers, system administrators and end users.

Training Methodology

The training methodology encompassing each course actively creates an on-line community of students, tutors, and instructors. The appeal of a CD-ROM course is apparent. Trainees learn at their own pace, at their own workstations — no travel expenses for curriculums taught in distant locales, and no downtime away from the office. But CD-ROMs require software to be installed on hundreds of not necessarily compatible computers and neither provides feedback from the teacher to answer students' questions nor actively monitor a student's progress. Figure 3 depicts the DigitalThink model of learning.

This learning environment has a great many benefits:

- Each learner is provided a personal locker page, which provides links to their courses, instructors, tutors, and classmates
- All courses include color graphics, hypertext, and audio
- All quizzes are interactive
- Course-specific discussion 'bulletin' boards are provided
- Instructors conduct live chat sessions focusing on course content
- In addition to instructor support, DigitalThink courses offer tutor assistance. Tutors answer individual e-mail messages and engage in threaded discussions and chat sessions. This assistance is *provided for six months* from the time the learner is enrolled into the course
- DigitalThink has signed exclusive agreements with best-selling authors and topic experts to create original content just for the Web. For instance, among the instructors are Sun Microsystems engineer Ken Arnold, a member of the original Java development team, and C++ expert Ira Pohl, a professor at the University of California at Santa Cruz
- DigitalThink provides online student progress reports so training administrators can see how trainees are doing. It also offers trained tutors who exchange e-mail with students whenever needed. Its service also includes online chats and threaded discussions among classmates.

Figure 4 demonstrates the different modes of learning and the cost, control, interactivity and flexibility of paper Based, CD- ROM based, web-based, broadcast based, and instructor led training (ILT) efforts.

Key Differentiators

There are three models of Web Based Learning. They are Web Based Delivery, Web Supported Learning and Web Based Learning. Web Based Delivery entails the downloading of course information to be taken from a remote client-server environment. The Internet is utilized as a delivery medium for downloadable objects, personal document files (PDF), and course information. The Web Supported Learning model is best illustrated by Ziff Davis On-Line University. This learning environment utilizes both Web Delivered courses, but also utilizes the chat functions and threaded discussion groups to support learners. This type of training/learning utilizes the web as a communicator, not the learning medium. The Web Based Learning Model utilizes the browser and the many functions of the web to build a learning environment. This method of delivering training should not require extensive software plugins, downloads or technical requirements to deliver. The Web Based Learning Model should simply require a browser, an Internet connection and a thin client computer with the technical minimums should be required to take courses online in the method of delivery.

In addition to start-ups, such as DigitalThink, several established software companies have launched divisions specializing in Web-based training. Oracle Corp. (www.oracle.com) recently launched the Oracle Leaning Architecture, and Sun Microsystems Inc. (www.sun.com) offers training through its Sun Service division. Ironically, Sun University (the training arm of Sun Microsystems) utilizes DigitalThink as a training source for JAVA. The next three sections evaluate the effectiveness of web based training in three separate organizations with three different corporate cultures.

Motorola: Organization and Human Effectiveness

Motorola's Semiconductor Sector has a very diverse workforce derived of 11,000 fabrication workers and engineers. The Motorola Organization & Human Effectiveness Group (OHE) selected Web Based Training from DigitalThink Because of DigitalThink's unique combination of integrated tutor support, high quality content and platform independence.

"With DigitalThink, Motorola can immediately deploy a technology training program across multiple computer platforms," said Doug Ferguson, Training Operations Specialist, for Motorola OHE. "Students can train at their desktops without having to go to a learning lab, on any computer that runs a standard web browser." Web Based training is the solution for companies who have to train a global workforce on fast-changing technology topics.

These questions are typical of large organizations. Unfortunately this small segment within a large organization was not faced with logistical challenges of a globally distributed workforce. Motorola OHE looked at CBT-Self-Paced Training, looked at the structure of their instructor led classroom environment at two facilities and evaluated their current technological infrastructure to deliver Intranet or Internet based training. After months of evaluating and investigating different technologies available, they chose a combination of delivery methods. While still heavily leveraged in classroom instruction, they felt the best approach was to offer the employees a variety of methods of learning.. Still available to employees were select instructor-led classes extending 1,2 and 3- day courses. Finding that this was a very poplular method of delivery, but still too costly, they decided to look at DigitalThink, Inc as a means of delivering a Hybrid Approach to collaborative learning. DigitalThink's learning model is a "hybrid" to CBT and ILT. It embraces the elements the learner desires in an instructor led class:

Texas Instruments: Digital Signal Processing

Texas Instruments (TI), one of the largest employers in the Dallas area is one of the original investors in DigitalThink. TI saw the potential of Web-based training and has invested several million dollars in this small startup company out of San Francisco. The TI Digital Signal Processing Group viewed DigitalThink as a means of developing and delivering technical training on the DSP technology to their channel partners via the Internet. Distributors and channel partners needed to learn more about the capabilities of a new product, TI's C54X digital signal processors. In the past these partners would have flown its personnel to Dallas for a short course. It instead can keep its engineers at their desks where they can view a 4-6 hour training courses on "Designing with the C54X DSKplus."

With it attendant convenience and cost savings, web-based training is taking root in a growing number of companies. "You don't have to be a rocket scientist to use web-based training. DigitalThink's model eliminates any technical issue to deploying, maintaining the course or any client technical issues." said Clark Hise, sales and marketing manager for training at TI DSP group.

For a nominal fee of $200, the four to six hour course instructs users on designing with the C54X. The courses uses the video and audio technology from DigitalThink along with chat rooms, interactive quizzes to engage the engineers as they run through the short lectures, exams and practice sessions.

TI's Organization Effectiveness Group is in charge of supplying training to the 20,000 plus TI and Raytheon employees in the Dallas area. They chose to use DigitalThink's catalog of Information Technology courses as a means of delivering training to 12 facilities in Dallas as well as distribute training to TI Europe. The Internet is an ideal medium due to its scalability, flexibility and reach.

Current Challenges

The key challenges for the successful planning, implementation and maintenance of a web enabled education/training initiative are twofold. On the one hand, are the technology issues such as compatibility of platforms, scalability of hardware/software solutions to accommodate multimedia, growing enrolments, new features/functionality and so forth. On the other hand are the people issues such as convincing faculty members that they need to develop/partner with developers of their courses using a fundamentally new approach to conveying the message and ensuring that the requisite learning takes place. Some other people issues are getting a commitment from the top management for the distance learning initiatives and the necessary budget/resources approved to make the project a success. With the commercialization of on-line education and universities positioned at the gateway of the knowledge economy, the key question is who has control of

Figure 4: Comparison of Different Modes of Learning

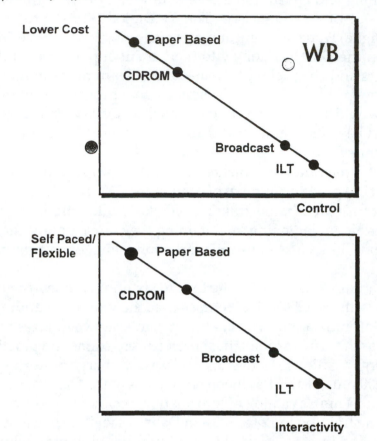

the content? Is it the professors/authors that developed that material, or is it the university/college/ administrators, that own the intellectual property rights/copyright and control the curriculum? (Woody, 1998). The radical metamorphosis in higher education by virtue of technology deployed for distance learning is an opportunity that could be worth $3 million to $4 million a year by conservative estimates in the next three to four years to the institutions of higher learning. Will that make full-time tenured faculty/ classroom teachers expendable? Can the professors/content developers defend their tradition of intellectual independence from the exigencies of the distance learning marketplace? Finally, how do we value a university professor's/teacher's/subject expert's productive labor as a knowledge worker in this new web-enabled technology environment? These issues will continue to grow in importance as we approach and enter the new millennium.

Implications for Management

The critical issues involved with managing web-enabled technologies for education and training which can be viewed as opportunities and challenges are as follows:

- Integrating new instructional technologies into an industry that demands excellence coupled with an intense focus on the cost-effectiveness of those technologies since the globalization of the economy necessitates technologies to be applicable across multicultural, international training environments.
- Forming strategic alliances with other organizations to collaborate on design and delivery of the material used for education and/or training.
- Striving to deliver high-tech and high-touch solutions with a focus on global customer service, while simultaneously keeping abreast of the rapid changes in the technological, legal, and business environment.
- Being aware that one solution does not fit all. There are pros and cons to web-based technology for education and training that affect each individual differently. Psychological profiles of the student/learner may be necessary to determine cognitive fit of the task and technology variables.

Conclusion

This chapter proposes a framework for potential students of higher education and highlights a case on a distance learning provider and three case studies of web-based training. John Dewey once said, "Education is not preparation for life; education is life itself. " These online universities teach knowledge beyond the books since its peer-to-peer knowledge sharing provides value enhancement in this collaborative discussion and team projects model. This is in stark contrast to the vertical /top-down knowledge delivery model in which the professor lectures or "professes" and there is lack of flexibility to accommodate demanding and/or erratic work schedules/personal responsibilities. As Dr. Eli M. Noam at the Graduate School of Business, Columbia University points out, "In the past, people came to information, which was stored in the university. In the future, the information will come to the people, wherever they are."

Appendix A:
Economic Issues Of Web-enabled Education And Training[3]

ROI as a tool for assessing the value of a business function

In the 1960s and 1970s, when corporate America was experiencing consistent profitability, the value of training to the organization was seldom questioned. Although training may not have been the highest priority of corporate decision makers, it was still viewed as a necessary cost center. Most corporate decision makers simply believed that training was beneficial. If asked why, they would probably have echoed the statement of Harvard's past President Dr. Derek Bok: "If you think education is expensive, try ignorance." To not train, or to deliver substandard training, can be expensive indeed. But in those days, the training function in many organizations enjoyed a privileged ride on the coattails of corporate success, and the value of any knowledge transfer was rarely, if ever, measured and quantified to the bottom line.

The past decade has witnessed a dramatic reversal of the profitability of many sectors of corporate America. The result is that all departments and functions are being assessed as to their value to the business. A general belief in the inherent value of something is no longer a sufficient rationale for its continued existence. Newly proposed methodologies vie with existing programs for corporate funds, and all must meet a company's internal test of business value to begin or continue their existence. ROI is not, as some have suggested, a devious strategy to justify cuts in training budgets and departments. Neither is it esoteric from the world of accounting. ROI is a straightforward financial calculation that provides an excellent opportunity to establish a realistic measure of the business value of one's endeavors.

Calculating and using ROI

There are two different formulae for calculating how much an investment returns to a company's bottom line. These two are typically called the benefits-to-cost ratio (BCR) and the ROI:

BCR = (Program benefits / program costs)

ROI (%) = (net program benefits / program costs)

The BCR uses the total benefits and costs, whereas the ROI uses only the net benefits (total benefits less costs). For example, if a certain program provides benefits of $ 800,000 at a cost of $ 200,000, the BCR is:

BCR= ($800,000 / $ 200,000) = 4, or 4 to 1

That is, for every $1 invested, $4 in benefits are returned. This is often called a 4-to-1 investment.

The net benefits in this example would be $600,000 ($600,000 - $ 200,000) x 100 = 300%. The ROI means that for each $1 invested, there is a $3 return in net benefits. Benefits and costs are usually calculated on an annual basis. Typical ROI values for training and interactive multimedia programs are in the 100 to 400 percent ranges.

Both the BCR and the ROI can be used to assess the value of investing in a certain training program versus investing those same dollars in some entirely different endeavor, such as building a new office building. This type of analysis — evaluating which option offers the best return — is known as cost-benefit analysis. A cost effectiveness analysis usually centers on comparison of only one pair of objectives such as, should we fund a multimedia project or stay with the existing training program? Moreover, either or both of these can be used to evaluate a program at different stages of the implementation.

Benefits of ROI analysis

More than 30 years ago, D. L. Kirkpatrick proposed a scheme of evaluation levels that focus on the issue of training effectiveness. Although most companies collect end-of-class feedback, a "reaction" or Level 1 evaluation in Kirkpatrick's parlance, few use valid Level IV measures ñ measures of results (Kirkpatrick, 1998). Organizations have failed to evaluate Level IV variables primarily because business-results evaluation in much more difficult and time-consuming than evaluating student reactions. ROI, however, can help us steer forward valid Level IV evaluation.

Seeking to compute the ROI for any project or program makes us accountable for real change and real contribution, so it is imperative to understand how it is computed and how the training efforts correlate with the bottom line. After all, that is just good management and good corporate stewardship.

In accumulating data for an ROI calculation, you:
- are forced to try to identify all component costs and quantifiable benefits of your project, not just those that are obvious;
- create or find valid measurement techniques/ instruments that bear "justification" fruit over the life of the project, not just at the beginning
- develop a realistic appraisal of how your efforts affect the corporate bottom line.

Two caveats with respect to measuring ROI are as follows:
1. Beware of positing causal relationships between your research variables and the training event. Strong correlation is all that is necessary, and that will translate into a much more believable (and defensible) position.
2. Be realistic: Select only one or two variables that you believe your training event will affect and track those in detail. Ancillary change may occur in other areas, but don't dilute your results by trying to focus on too many variables at the same time.

The good news is that good training, particularly good interactive multimedia can show positive results and a significant ROI. The dilemma is that, as we desire to be held accountable for realistic measures of our efforts, the data required for those measures are sometimes elusive.

Notes

1 Excerpt from Lotus Institute's White Paper, 1998, "Distributed Learning: Approaches, Technologies and Solutions [Online]," Available: http://www.lotus.com/ products/ learningsp.html [June 9].

2 Excerpt from Lotus Institute's White Paper, 1998, "Distributed Learning: Approaches, Technologies and Solutions [Online]," Available: http://www.lotus.com/ products/ learningsp.html [June 9].

3 Excerpt from AMR Training and Consulting Group, 1993, "The American Airlines Training Center CAI Project," A White Paper.

References

AMR Training and Consulting Group (1993). "The American Airlines Training Center CAI Project," A White Paper.

Baer, Walter S. (1998). "Will the Internet Transform Higher Education?," *The Emerging Internet: Annual Review*, Queenstown, MD: The Aspen Institute.

Bassi , Laurie J. and Van Buren, Mark (1998). "The Current State of the Industry," American Society for Training & Development.

Bassi , Laurie J., Cheney, Scott, and Van Buren, Mark (1998). "Training Industry Trends", American Society for Training & Development.

Carnevale, Anthony (1996). "Training should be teamed with Smart HR Practices," *Corporate University Review*, March/April.

DeSanctis, G. and Gallupe, B. (1987). "A foundation for the Study of Group Decision Support Systems," *Management Science*, 33:5, pp. 589-609.

Flynn, J. L. (1992). "Cooperative Learning and Gagne's Events of Instruction: A Syncretic View," Educational Technology, October, 53-60.

Gibson, Jane W. And Herrera, Jorge M. (1999). "How to Go From Classroom Based to Online Delivery in Eighteen Months or Less: A Case Study in Online Program Development," *Technology Horizons in Education Journal*, January, 57-60.

Hall, Brandon (1997). *Web-Based Training: Market Trends, Risks, and Opportunities*

Ives, B. And Jarvenpaaa, S. (1996). "Will the Internet Revolutionize Business Education and Research?," *Sloan Management Review*, 37(3), 33-40.

Jonassen, D. H. (1993). "Thinking Technology," *Educational Technology*, January, 35-37.

Kirkpatrick, Donald, L. (1998). "Evaluating Training Programs at Four Levels," Berrett-Koehler Publishing Co.

Kroder, Stanley L., Suess, Jayne and Sachs, David (1998). "Lessons in Launching Web-based Graduate Courses," *Technology Horizons in Education Journal*, May, .66-69.

Lu, Ming-Te Lu and Johnson, Nancy, 1998."A Virtual B-School Through Information Technology: Framework and Case Study," *Journal of Computer Information Systems*, Spring,, 58-63.

Lotus Institute's White Paper, 1998, "Distributed Learning: Approaches, Technologies and Solutions [Online]," Available: http://www.lotus.com/products/ learningsp.html [June 9].

Sproull, Lee and Kiesler Sara, 1995, *Connections: New Ways of Working in the Networked Organization*, Cambridge, MA: MIT Press.

Schlechter, T. M. 1990, "The Relative Instructional Efficiency of Small Group Computer-Based Training," *Journal of Educational Computing Research*, 6:3, 329-341.

Woody, Todd, 1998.,"Higher Earning: The Fight to Control The Academy's Intellectual Capital," *The Industry Standard*, June 29, 21-22.

About the Authors

Book Editor

Mehdi Khosrowpour is currently an Associate Professor of Information Systems at Penn State Harrisburg. He is the editor-in-charge of the Information Resources Management Journal and Information Management. In addition, he also serves on the editorial review boards of six other international information systems journals.

Dr. Khosrowpour is the author/editor of 12 books and more than 30 articles published in various scholarly and professional journals, such as the Journal of Information Systems Management, Business Review, Journal of Systems Management, Journal of Applied Business Research, Computing Review, Journal of Computer Information Systems, Journal of Education Technology Systems and Journal of Microcomputer Systems Management. He is a frequent speaker at many international meetings and organizations, such as the Association of Federal Information Resources Management, Contract Management Association, Financial Women Association, National Association of States Information Resources Executives and IBM.

Contributing Authors

Paul Darbyshire is a lecturer in the Department of Information Systems at Victoria University of Technology, Melbourne Australia. He lecturers in Object Oriented systems, C and Java programming, and has research interests in the application of Java and Web technologies to the support of teaching. Paul's current research is into the use of the Web for university subject management and the use of AI techniques for the development of second generation Web based teaching support software.

Paul Hendriks (Ph.D. in social science, 1986, University of Nijmegen, The Netherlands) is an Associate Professor of Management Information Science. He has worked at the Free University of Amsterdam and the University of Nijmegen where he is currently a member of the Nijmegen Business School. His current research interests include the role of information and communication technology in knowledge management. He has published several books on research methodology, geographical information systems and computers. He has also published in such journals as The International Journal of Geographical Information Science, Information and Management, Knowledge-Based Systems, Decision Support Systems, Expert Systems With Applications and Knowledge and Process Management.

Sherif Kamel, Ph.D. is an assistant professor of management support systems at the American University in Cairo. He is also the Director of the Regional Information Technology Institute in Cairo, Egypt. His research interests include management support systems and information technology transfer to developing countries and its implications on socioeconomic development. He is a graduate of London School of Economics and Political Science and the American University in Cairo. He designed and delivered professional development programs in information systems applications for public and private sector organizations in different countries in Africa, Asia, the Far East and Eastern Europe. He is one of the founding members of the Internet Society of Egypt. He serves on the editorial and review boards of a number of information systems and management journals and has published several articles and chapters on the application of information and communication technology in developing countries.

Kihyun Kim is a graduate student majoring in Management Information Systems at the University of Nebraska – Lincoln. He is also a research fellow at the Hyundai Research Institute in South Korea. He received his M.B.A. and B.S. degrees from Korea University in South Korea. His research interests and consulting experiences include business process reengineering, management of strategic information systems, Internet technology in e-commerce, and issues in objected-oriented systems design and development.

Mathew J. Klempa is a consultant in the application of computer information systems. He has taught at the University of Southern California and the California State University. He holds a B.S. in Mathematics/Economics from Allegheny College, M.S. in Management Science, M.B.A. in International Business, and Ph.D. in Business Administration from the University of Southern California. His doctoral majors were Decision Support Systems and Corporate Policy and Strategy. He was formerly a corporate planning officer for a major bank holding company, systems analyst, and operations research analyst. His research interests include organization impacts of information technology; the interaction among information technology and organization structures, control mechanisms, culture, learning, work processes, and performance; business process change; business process reengineering; management of innovation; information technology diffusion; and cognitive and individual differences in DSS use.

Ming-te Lu is Chair Professor of Information Systems at Lingnan College in Hong Kong. His research interests include decision support systems, information systems development in emerging economies, electronic commerce, and IS educational issues. He is on the editorial review boards of *Journal of End User Computing, Journal of Global Information Management, International Journal of Management Theory and Practices, Sun Yat-Sen Management Review*, and is the Associate Editor of *Journal of Global Information Technology Management*. His articles have appeared in Decision Sciences, Information and Management, Journal of Global Information Management, Journal of End-User Computing, The Journal of Computer Information Systems, Journal of Systems and Software, Journal of Information Systems Management, Expert Systems, International Journal of Information Management, and Internet Research, among others.

Fui Hoon (Fiona) Nah is Assistant Professor of Management Information Systems at the College of Business Administration, University of Nebraska – Lincoln. She received her Ph.D. in Management Information Systems from the University of British Columbia in 1997. Her current research interests are in evaluating information systems for supporting group decision making, using information technology to overcome human cognitive biases, designing and evaluating knowledge management systems, and assessing theory building in information systems research.

Nancy L. Russo received her Ph.D. in MIS from Georgia State University. Currently she is an Associate Professor in the Operations Management & Information Systems

Department at Northern Illinois University. In addition to on-going studies of the use and customization of system development methods, her research has addressed web application development, the impact of enterprise-wide software adoption on the IS function, IT innovation, and IS research and education issues. Her work has appeared in *Information Systems Journal, Journal of Information Technology, Journal of Computer Information Systems, System Development Management, Journal of Systems and Software*, and various conference proceedings.

Arno Scharl (scharl@wu-wien.ac.at) holds a Ph.D. and M.B.A. from the Vienna University of Economics and Business Administration where he is employed as assistant professor in the MIS Department (electronic commerce research group). Additionally, he received a Ph.D. and M.Sc. from the University of Vienna, Department of Sports Physiology. Currently spending a semester as visiting research fellow at the University of California at Berkeley (Fisher Center for IT & Marketplace Transformation), his research and teaching interests focus on the various aspects of Web information systems modeling, commercial electronic transactions, adaptive hypertext, and the customization of electronic catalogs.

Dirk Vriens (Ph.D. in policy science, 1998, University of Nijmegen, The Netherlands) is an Associate Professor of Management Information Science. He is currently working at the Nijmegen Business School, University of Nijmegen. His research interests include information management, knowledge management and business intelligence. Dirk Vriens also works as a senior consultant for a consultancy firm specializing in business intelligence.

Andrew Wenn lectures in the Department of Information Systems at Victoria University of Technology. He has interests in the area of internet based education, particularly where it can be utilized to enhance the learning experience and enable students to have increased access to learning materials. Andrew's main field of research is the nexus between the social and the technical, particularly, in the area of global information systems.

Tammy Whalen is a Customer Systems Consultant at Bell Nexxia, a subsidiary of Bell Canada specializing in broadband telecommunications and internetworking. She is also a graduate student in the Master of Business Administration program at the University of Ottawa and is writing her thesis on the business case for distance learning.

David Wright is a Full Professor at the University of Ottawa. He has provided distance education using a variety of technologies and is currently sponsored by the federally funded Network of Centers of Excellence in Telelearning to investigate cost effective distance education alternatives and their economic impact. He has 25 fully refereed publications in a range of journals, plus many conference papers, and is the author of the book *Broadband: Business Services, Technologies and Strategic Impact* published by Artech House, Boston. He is coauthor of the book *Telelearning via the Internet* published by Idea Group in 1999.

W. L. Yeung completed his PhD in Computer Science in UK in 1992 and has since been teaching in universities in both UK and Hong Kong. He is currently an assistant professor at the Lingnan College in Hong Kong. His research interests are in systems development methodology and the development of business Web applications.

Index